Affirmative Action and Minority Enrollments in Medical and Law Schools

SUSAN WELCH

and

JOHN GRUHL

Ann Arbor

THE UNIVERSITY OF MICHIGAN PRESS

A CIP catalog record for this book is available from the British Library.

Library of Congress Cataloging-in-Publication Data

Welch, Susan.
    Affirmative action and minority enrollments in medical and law schools
    / Susan Welch and John Gruhl.
        p.   cm.
    Includes bibliographical references (p.) and index.
    ISBN 0-472-10850-6 (cloth : acid-free paper)
    1. Discrimination in education—Law and legislation—United
States.   2. Universities and colleges—Admission—Law and legislation—
United States.   3. Affirmative action programs—Law and legislation—
United   States.   4. Bakke, Allan Paul.   I. Gruhl, John, 1947–   .
II. Title.
KF4155.W45   1998
344.73′0798—dc21   97-33946
                                                            CIP

Contents

Preface   vii

Introduction   1

Chapter 1. Desegregation, Affirmative Action,
    and *Bakke*   7

Chapter 2. The Context of *Bakke:* Resources
    and Competition   37

Chapter 3. Perceptions of *Bakke* and Its Impact   61

Chapter 4. *Bakke* and the Applicant Pool   85

Chapter 5. *Bakke* and Admissions Decisions   107

Chapter 6. Minority Enrollment and the Courts   133

Appendixes

Appendix A. The Survey   179

Appendix B. Schools Whose Surveys Were Completed   181

*Appendix C. Statistical Information for Chapters 4
    and 5*   184

Notes   187

References   197

Subject and Author Index   213

Index of Court Opinions   223

Preface

When we began this project in the late 1980s, affirmative action and the compromises articulated in the *Bakke* decision seemed to be a settled and accepted part of public policy. To be sure, much of the white public had never accepted some of the more far-reaching affirmative action practices, but even so, there was some support for giving black Americans extra opportunities in education and employment. The Reagan administration opposed affirmative action, but the administration's attempts to dismantle programs were largely frustrated by Congress and the courts. In that setting, our objective was to determine how much of an impact on medical and law school enrollments the landmark, but confusing, *Bakke* case had actually made.

As we complete this book in 1997, the political climate for affirmative action has altered dramatically. The United States Supreme Court has shifted ground, with a stream of cases narrowing the scope of affirmative action practices. One U.S. Court of Appeals has barred the use of race in admissions decisions, a decision left standing by the Supreme Court's refusal to review the case. The Republican majority of Congress stridently opposes affirmative action. Californians voted for an amendment to their state constitution to bar race, sex, color, ethnicity, and national origin as considerations in "either discriminating against, or granting preferential treatment to, any individual or group in the operation of the State's system of public employment, public education or public contracting" (Lemann 1995, 39). The Regents of the University of California, the defendants in the *Bakke* case, have barred racial preference schemes in admission to the university, and other institutions are reviewing their practices in light of the changed legal and political climate.

Black Americans continue to favor affirmative action, but even in that community, strong voices oppose it. Supreme Court justice Clarence Thomas and University of California regent Ward Connerly, for example, are outspoken opponents of preferential treatment in admissions and scholarships. Their opposition and that of several other prominent African American public figures and scholars give legitimacy to white opposition.

In that changed context, our assessment of *Bakke*'s impact takes on a new dimension. The extent to which the *Bakke* decision affected minority enrollment in professional schools continues to be an important issue. But we will also examine the impact *Bakke* had in legitimizing the practice of affirmative action in education. And we will analyze how the principles of the decision are playing out in today's debate over affirmative action and how those principles might be interpreted to broaden the support for a new affirmative action policy.

The authors gratefully acknowledge support for this project provided by the National Science Foundation's Program on Law and Society. The foundation's support enabled us to undertake the unique survey of medical and law schools that forms a basis of our study. The conclusions reached are those of the authors and not of the foundation. The authors also are grateful for the assistance of Angella Bowman, Kidae Kim, David R. Johnson, John Hibbing, and Faye Moulton, all of the University of Nebraska, Robert F. Welch of Victoria, Minnesota, and Rick Morgan of the American Bar Association, and for wonderful colleagues at the University of Nebraska and The Pennsylvania State University, whose ideas and support contributed greatly to this work.

Introduction

In 1978 the U.S. Supreme Court announced its famous, or infamous, decision in the case of *Regents of the University of California v. Bakke* (438 U.S. 265). The ruling invalidated the admissions plan of the medical school at the University of California–Davis, which reserved 16 of 100 places in each year's entering class for racial minorities. The divided Court held that the school could not reserve a certain number of places for minorities but that it could use race as a positive factor in admissions. The ruling generally has been interpreted to mean that schools cannot use quotas but can practice affirmative action. Although "affirmative action" has come to mean different things to different people, in general the concept entails positive steps, rather than just passive nondiscrimination, to advance equality in education and employment.

Rarely has there been a case like *Bakke*. It had been followed as it climbed step-by-step through the California courts. When the U.S. Supreme Court agreed to hear it, more than one hundred organizations filed a record number of amicus curiae (friend of the court) briefs for one side or the other (Murphy and Pritchett 1979, 267, 305). Magazines had cover stories on the case, and commentators anticipated the result. It was called the most important civil rights case since *Brown v. Board of Education* (347 U.S. 483, 1954; 349 U.S. 294, 1955). It would determine not only the validity of one school's admissions plan, but also the composition of many schools' classes for years to come. Moreover, it was expected to determine the legality of affirmative action and the speed of further civil rights progress in American society.

Even years after *Bakke,* the case seemed important. In 1987 when Justice Lewis Powell, who authored the main opinion, retired, he was asked which of his opinions was the most important. "*Bakke,*" he replied without hesitation (B. Schwartz 1988, 1). Today, almost two decades after the case was decided, its principles and holdings have become a centerpiece of a broad renewed public debate over affirmative action.

In the years after *Bakke,* there were many normative and legalistic evaluations. But, despite all the attention lavished on this single case, there has been scarcely any systematic research assessing its impact. Simmons (1982) surveyed nearly five hundred managers of affirmative action and other special programs in higher education to determine their perception of *Bakke*'s impact, but the survey was done too close to the time of *Bakke* to determine the actual impact.[1] An examination of interest-group activity in the *Bakke* suit is found in O'Neill (1985), and a historical analysis of black medical enrollment trends, implying that *Bakke* had an effect, is found in Shea and Fullilove (1985). Blackwell (1987) examined black enrollment trends in a variety of professional schools but did not focus on *Bakke.* Aside from this, social scientists have devoted no systematic attention to *Bakke*'s effects.[2]

This book assesses *Bakke*'s impact on applications and admissions to medical and law schools. The real effects of *Bakke,* after all, lie not in journalistic or academic rhetoric, but in the actual impact on students and schools. We chose to examine medical and law schools specifically, even though the decision affected many other educational programs. We looked at medical schools because the case specifically involved one of these schools. If the ruling had any impact, it should be on medical school admissions. We also looked at law schools for several reasons. A previous case (*DeFunis v. Odegaard,* 416 U.S. 312 [1974]), which the Supreme Court sidestepped, involved one of these schools. Law schools are filled with faculty sensitive to law and legal decisions, so if the ruling had an impact, we should see it in law schools. Moreover, according to one survey in the year *Bakke* was decided, medical and law schools had more special programs to recruit and retain minorities than did other professional schools (Atesek and Gomberg 1978, 6–7). Thus, they should have been the most affected.

Our examination of the impact of an important Supreme Court decision owes much in its conceptualization to previous studies of judicial impact. Prompted by much obvious noncompliance with the Court's *Brown v. Board of Education* rulings in the 1950s, legal scholars have examined the impact of many of the Court's decisions (Wasby 1970; C. Johnson and Canon 1984; Rosenberg 1991). Their studies have confirmed the impression that often the impact is different than what would be expected simply from knowing the Court's decision or reading the media reports of the decision and its consequences. Cases considered significant at the time do not always have an impact other than the legal and political commentary that follows in their wake. Indeed, the most fundamental finding of judicial impact research is that rulings do not always change behavior, at least to the extent they are expected to.

Those who are supposed to comply with the ruling might not do so. Even if they do comply, the results might not be the ones intended, might be far less than anticipated, and often will vary from place to place (C. Johnson and Canon 1984, chap. 7). Studies relevant to *Bakke* have concluded that decisions that are ambiguous (Canon 1977; Neubauer 1974; Rodgers and Bullock 1972), that contradict the norms of the community or beliefs of those who are to enforce the law (Birkby 1966; Dolbeare and Hammond 1971; R. Johnson 1967; Laubauch 1969; Muir 1967), or that challenge the organizational status quo (Medalie et al. 1968; Rosenberg 1991) may be less likely to be implemented fully.

In assessing the impact of the case, we looked both at the ultimate targets of the decision, the students themselves, and at those who had to implement the decision, the admissions officers of medical and law schools. Thus, part of our assessment is based on enrollment trends over a twenty-year period before and after *Bakke*. Longitudinal data on national enrollments allow us to track the big picture of changing enrollments from year to year. Similar data on national applications illuminate trends in students' decisions to apply. Cross-sectional information for individual schools shows microlevel changes in minority enrollments across schools.

Another important part of this assessment is data from a unique survey of law and medical school admissions officers done in 1989, eleven years after the *Bakke* decision. We were able to obtain information from well over half the medical and law schools in the United States. These questionnaire responses tap admissions officials' perceptions of *Bakke*'s impact and of their admissions policies.

In addition to examining *Bakke*'s impact in the decade after the decision was reached, we also will look at its impact today. In the roiling discussion over affirmative action and the challenge to the principles and practices of affirmative action, in what ways is *Bakke* still relevant?

Our model of *Bakke*'s impact assumes that the decision affected applications, admissions, and ultimately enrollments. But the model also takes into account other factors that could exaggerate or mitigate the decision's effect. Both the "supply" of minority candidates and the "demand" for them could affect the trends in applications, admissions, and enrollments as well.

Several conditions affect the supply of minority candidates. Certainly the overall black and Hispanic population in an area at a given time is an important factor explaining supply. Other things being equal, there should be more African American applicants to a state school in a state that is 30 percent black than one in a state that is 3 percent black.[3] Supply is affected by factors such as incomes of black and Latino families and the amount of financial aid available to them. As each becomes larger, we believe that the number of minority applicants should increase. Supply of minority candidates is probably also reflective of more general patterns of applications to medical and law schools. For example, medical school applications peaked in 1975 and dropped by one-third over the next twelve years. We assume that the fads and fancies, as well as the economic factors, that influence these trends affect black and Hispanic as well as Anglo students. Thus, our model also takes into account these overall trends.

The demand for minority candidates, we speculate, is affected by the general societal interest in promoting opportunities for minorities. This is a somewhat tautological statement, and operationalizing it is a challenge. But such factors as federal policies toward civil rights and affirmative action and spending on civil rights enforcement are the kinds of concrete indicators that reflect such an interest. The demand for minority students is also indicated by the efforts that schools, individually and collectively, make to recruit and retain them.

We have explained our model of black and Hispanic applications and enrollments in quite general terms. We will offer more detail later. At this point, it is most important to note that we view the *Bakke* decision in the context of other societal conditions that may certainly have affected temporal trends in minority students' decisions to apply for professional school as well as the decisions of admissions officers whether to take more or fewer of these students.

In the first chapter we will explain the *Bakke* decision to show the potential impact it might have. We will put the decision into perspective by addressing previous and subsequent cases involving desegregation and affirmative action and by looking at the political climate in the years after *Bakke*.

Chapter 2 will consider important social and demographic changes taking place in the black and Hispanic communities, changes that could have affected the size of the pool of black and Hispanic students eligible to apply for admission to medical and law schools and their willingness to do so. We also discuss changes in financial support available to students and changes in the medical and legal educational environment that also affected admissions policies before and after *Bakke*.

In chapter 3 we turn to our survey data to find out what current admissions officials in medical and law schools think about *Bakke* and its effects. We also present some information from officials making admissions decisions at the time of *Bakke* about the ruling's immediate impact. We look at these issues in the context of the information flow from medical and law school professional associations to their members.

In chapter 4 we move to a consideration of minority applicants. Has the number and quality of applicants changed over time, and can these changes be linked to *Bakke*? In this chapter we use aggregate national data on medical school applications as well as perceptual information from our survey respondents. We not only employ descriptive data, but also begin to test some models of change before and after *Bakke*.

Applications are only the first part of a process that leads to a student's enrollment. In chapter 5 we examine acceptance of applications and first-year enrollments. We use data on aggregate national enrollment and on individual institutional enrollment. Can we link acceptances and enrollments to *Bakke*?

In the final chapter we assess these disparate strands of evidence to draw conclusions about the past, present, and future impact of *Bakke* and affirmative action. Did *Bakke* ever have an impact, and if so, how is the impact likely to be sustained in the new anti–affirmative action public climate of the 1990s?

Chapter 1

Desegregation, Affirmative Action, and *Bakke*

When the Supreme Court established the separate-but-equal doctrine in *Plessy v. Ferguson* in 1896, Justice John Harlan, a former slaveholder, was the sole dissenter: "Our Constitution is color-blind, and neither knows nor tolerates classes among citizens" (163 U.S. 537, 559). During the first decades of the civil rights movement, Harlan's statement would be quoted by proponents of equality as the embodiment of the real meaning of the Fourteenth Amendment's equal protection clause. But after the initial gains, and inherent limitations, of the movement, the use of race-conscious remedies would be urged by many proponents of equality, while Harlan's statement would be quoted by some persons who seemed to have little desire for equality among the races. The question of whether and under what circumstances could government policies not be color-blind is at the heart of the *Bakke* case.

Desegregation

The Separate-but-Equal Doctrine

Plessy upheld a Louisiana law mandating separate accommodations in trains. By establishing the separate-but-equal doctrine, the Court validated the numerous Jim Crow laws requiring segregation throughout southern society (and in some northern communities) that had been adopted by state legislatures after slavery had been abolished. Although, according to the doctrine, the facilities were supposed to be equal, they rarely were. Three years after *Plessy,* the Court upheld segregation in public schools (*Cumming v. Richmond County Board of Education,* 175

U.S. 528 [1899]). A Georgia school board changed a high school that blacks had attended into an elementary school for blacks but did not build a new high school for blacks or allow them to attend the existing high schools with whites. Yet the Court did not consider that a violation of the separate-but-equal doctrine. In practice, then, the doctrine meant separation but not equality.

The Supreme Court did strike down the "grandfather clause," which exempted persons whose ancestors could vote from the literacy test, in 1915 (*Guinn v. United States,* 238 U.S. 347) and a law prescribing residential segregation two years later (*Buchanan v. Warley,* 245 U.S. 60), but the Court showed little inclination to confront most Jim Crow laws or the separate-but-equal doctrine itself.

Overturning the Separate-but-Equal Doctrine

When the National Association for the Advancement of Colored People (NAACP) invigorated its legal defense arm in the 1930s, it began to challenge segregation in graduate schools, and the Supreme Court justices indicated some willingness to address this problem. Missouri had not allowed blacks to attend the state university law school and had not provided them with a separate law school. In 1938 the Court said the state had to do one or the other (*Missouri ex rel. Gaines v. Canada,* 305 U.S. 337). Texas had provided a black law school, but it was clearly inferior to the white law school, at the University of Texas, in size of faculty, student body, library, and opportunities for students to specialize. In 1950 the Court said the black school had to be substantially equal to the white one (*Sweatt v. Painter,* 339 U.S. 629). Oklahoma had allowed a black graduate student to attend the white graduate school at the University of Oklahoma, but it had designated a separate section of the classroom, library, and cafeteria for the student. In 1950 the Court said this arrangement deprived the student of the exchange of views with fellow students essential to education (*McLaurin v. Oklahoma State Regents,* 339 U.S. 637). In these decisions the Court did not invalidate the separate-but-equal doctrine, but it did make segregation almost impossible to maintain in graduate and professional schools.

With these successes, the NAACP moved to challenge segregation in grade schools and high schools. By 1950, seventeen states and the District of Columbia required segregation in their schools, and four others allowed it by local option. These states provided white students with better facilities and white teachers with better salaries. Overall, they spent from two to ten times more on white schools than on black ones (Kluger 1976, 134). The NAACP's legal defense team, headed by Thurgood Marshall, filed suits in two southern states, one border state, one northern state, and the District of Columbia. These suits were consolidated under the name of *Brown v. Board of Education,* the name of the suit from Topeka, Kansas, and decided in 1954 (347 U.S. 483). The Court's unanimous ruling invalidated de jure segregation in public schools. Chief Justice Earl Warren wrote that the separate-but-equal doctrine violated the equal protection clause not only because it resulted in unequal schools, but also because it produced feelings of inferiority in black children, hence it was inherently unequal.

The following year the Court announced the pace at which schools should desegregate—"with all deliberate speed" (*Brown v. Board of Education II,* 349 U.S. 294). Although this standard was a compromise between justices who wanted schools to desegregate immediately and those who wanted them to be able to do so gradually, the ambiguity of the phrase allowed schools to delay.

Many state governments and school districts resisted—from outright defiance to more subtle evasion of the ruling. The governor and some state legislators in Arkansas spoke such inflammatory rhetoric that citizens were encouraged to block desegregation of Little Rock schools, requiring President Dwight Eisenhower to send federal troops to quell the riot. The governors of Mississippi and Alabama themselves blocked the doors to prevent blacks from registering at their state universities, prompting President John Kennedy to send federal marshals. After such defiance, some states attempted to shut down their public schools and provide tuition grants for students to use at private schools, which at the time could segregate. Some states adopted "freedom of choice" plans that allowed students to choose the school they wanted to attend. Due to public pressure, few black students chose a white school. The Court struck down these and other similar schemes (*Griffin v. Prince Edward County School Board,* 377 U.S. 218 [1964]; *Green v. New Kent County School Board,* 391 U.S. 430 [1968]; *Norwood v. Harrison,* 413 U.S. 455 [1973]; and *Gilmore v. Montgomery,* 417 U.S. 556 [1974]). With such massive resistance, the justices might have begun to sense the enormity and difficulty of achieving what they had ordered.

Despite the Court's frequent and consistent rulings, progress was haltingly slow. If a school district was segregated, a group like the

NAACP had to spend time and money to bring a suit in the local federal district court. Individuals in that group were sometimes threatened with economic or physical punishment if they carried through with the suits. Judges in these lower courts reflected the views of the local or state political establishment, through which they had the ties to get appointed to the bench originally. Even if the suit were successful in the district court, then the school board had to prepare a desegregation plan. Members of the school board reflected the views of the community and felt the pressures from segregationists, who challenged plans in the district court. Plans upheld in the district court were often appealed to the federal court of appeals. Judges at this level, though from the South, sat farther from local communities—in Richmond or New Orleans—and were not as tied to the local or state political establishments. They usually ruled against segregation (Peltason 1961). But the segregationists could appeal to the Supreme Court. Thus, although they must have realized they would lose sooner or later, the segregationists were able to delay the process for many years.

As a result of these opportunities for interminable delays, by 1964, a decade after *Brown,* 98 percent of black children in the South still attended all-black schools (R. Cohen and Kaplan 1976, 622). Significant change would not come until Congress passed the Civil Rights Act of 1964, which, among other things, cut off federal aid to school districts that segregated. The federal education bill in 1965, providing the first sizable federal aid to education, raised the financial stakes for schools still resisting integration.

Where *Brown* and related cases addressed de jure segregation, northern cities and large southern cities had extensive de facto segregation based on residential patterns. Although the justices had held in 1948 that courts could not enforce restrictive covenants (*Shelley v. Kraemer,* 334 U.S. 1), and although Congress had passed the Civil Rights Act of 1968, which forbids discrimination in the sale or rental of housing and which also forbids steering, redlining, and blockbusting, de facto segregation continued for most minorities.

Civil rights groups proposed busing some black children to schools in white neighborhoods and some white children to schools in black neighborhoods. Although Earl Warren had retired and President Nixon, who opposed busing, had appointed Warren Burger as chief justice, the Court unanimously upheld busing in Charlotte, North Carolina, in 1971 (*Swann v. Charlotte-Mecklenburg Board of Education,* 402 U.S. 1). The

Court recognized that remedial measures might have to be undertaken to overcome the historical patterns of segregation. These measures included setting goals for certain percentages of black and white children in individual schools and adjusting boundary lines and using busing to reach these goals. Chief Justice Burger, emphasizing the "broad discretionary powers of school authorities," acknowledged that they "might well conclude . . . that in order to prepare students to live in a pluralistic society each school should have a prescribed ratio of Negro to white students reflecting the proportion for the district as a whole" (*Swann v. Charlotte-Mecklenburg*, 16). In subsequent years the Court upheld busing in various northern cities—Denver, Dayton, and Columbus (*Keyes v. School District 1, Denver*, 413 U.S. 921 [1973]; *Dayton Board of Education v. Brinkman*, 443 U.S. 526 [1979]; and *Columbus Board of Education v. Penick*, 443 U.S. 449 [1979]).[1]

Yet as more whites moved from the cities to the suburbs, and as others transferred from public schools to private schools, the extent of de facto segregation increased. In fact, in many cities there were not enough whites left to desegregate the schools, even with busing. Civil rights groups then proposed busing some black children from the cities to the suburbs and some white children from the suburbs to the cities. But the Court, by a 5–4 margin, rejected busing between Detroit and its suburbs in 1974 (*Milliken v. Bradley*, 418 U.S. 717). It held that there must be evidence of intentional segregation in both a city and its suburbs before busing between them could be ordered. Although there was at least some intentional segregation in many cities and their suburbs, it is difficult to prove both intentional segregation in a central city and intentional segregation in enough of this city's suburbs to establish an interdistrict busing plan to remedy the imbalance. Hence, such busing has been the exception.

Thus, the Court invalidated de jure school segregation but could not, or at least did not, overcome de facto school segregation. Aside from upholding busing and other remedial measures within cities, the Court did relatively little in these cases to compensate for the effects of past discrimination. Commentators suggest that the justices and the public were naive in expecting that the eradication of laws and practices by governments to proscribe or uphold segregation would result in desegregation. "It was assumed, naively but sincerely, that rapid minority strides toward equality would follow once discriminatory barriers were leveled" (Sindler 1983, 4).

In the lower grades, although some progress was made in desegregation throughout the 1960s and 1970s (Orfield 1978), segregation would persist primarily because of residential patterns. In higher education, the small numbers of blacks and other minorities in undergraduate and postgraduate institutions would continue largely because of inadequate educational opportunities at the lower levels and insufficient financial resources.

Affirmative Action

As the civil rights struggle moved from the South to the country as a whole, and as the movement's leaders saw that an official commitment to nondiscrimination was not producing equality, some urged efforts to compensate for the effects of past discrimination. Affirmative action, as it would be called, entailed going beyond practicing passive nondiscrimination to undertaking active measures to advance equality in education and employment. In particular, affirmative action has been used most visibly to boost the enrollment of minorities and women in higher education, to boost the employment of minorities and women in jobs in which they had been underrepresented, and to reserve a portion of government contracts for minority-owned businesses (Jones 1993, 346).

Actually affirmative action is not a contemporary innovation in public policy.[2] A Reconstruction-era statute—the Freedmen's Bureau Act of 1866, passed less than a month after Congress approved the Fourteenth Amendment—provided a variety of programs for black soldiers and freedmen. These programs offered education, land, charters for banks, charters for organizations that would support aged or indigent women and children, and a special hospital in the District of Columbia to treat freedmen. These programs were race conscious and were generally not restricted to identified victims of discrimination, although it is difficult to imagine that any African Americans of the era, even free northern blacks, had not been victimized (Jones 1993, 348).

Contemporary affirmative action developed from a series of executive orders in the 1960s. President Kennedy used the phrase in an executive order calling for more equality of opportunity. As one drafter of the order later reported, "I put the word 'affirmative' in there at that time. I was searching for something that would give a sense of positiveness to performance . . . and I was torn between the words 'positive action' and the words 'affirmative action.' I took 'affirmative action' because it was

alliterative" (Lemann 1995).[3] The Civil Rights Act of 1964, which pro-
hibits discrimination in employment, did not use the phrase but did
authorize bureaucratic agencies to make rules to help end discrimination
in the workplace. President Johnson also issued an executive order and in
a speech at Howard University justified affirmative action as a remedial
measure to compensate for past discrimination. "You do not take a
person who, for years, has been hobbled by chains and liberate him,
bring him up to the starting line of a race and then say, 'You are free to
compete with all the others,' and still justly believe that you have been
fair." Johnson said it was time to go beyond "equality as a right and a
theory" to "equality as a fact and equality as a result" (L. Johnson 1971,
166). The strongest thrust came when President Nixon's Labor Department made rules to implement affirmative action. The department's Philadelphia Plan required certain federal contractors to make a good-faith
effort to reach goals of minorities, based on the composition of the local
labor force and the availability of qualified minorities. Then the department's expanded rules applied to all federal contractors (and subcontrac-
tors) and required detailed plans stipulating goals and timetables to reach
them in hiring, training, and promoting minorities. Later the Equal Employment Opportunity Commission (EEOC) called for affirmative action
by governments, and the Office of Education called for it by colleges.

   Considerable confusion and controversy arose over the definition
and implementation of the requirement to identify "goals." Were they
actually quotas? On paper they were not. The goals were targets to shoot
for; they did not necessarily have to be met. An employer who fell short
might be investigated but could satisfy officials by demonstrating a good-
faith effort to reach them. The employer would not have to meet actual
quotas unless the investigation found deliberate and systematic discrimination. In practice, however, sometimes enforcement agencies sent signals blurring the distinction (Sindler 1983, 7). Agencies could monitor
the results easier than the process. Agencies might assume that inadequate results reflected an inadequate process. And some employers, in
turn, interpreted the goals as quotas.

   The wording of the Labor Department's order reinforced the perception that goals might be treated as quotas. The order specified that
the objective was "equal employment opportunity" but the procedures
were "result-oriented." The department, like President Johnson before,
viewed equality of results as the logical extension of equality of opportunity. In consequence, although distinct on paper, the concepts of equal-

ity of results and equality of opportunity would not be distinct in practice. Critics believed that even if equality of opportunity would lead to equality of results in the long run, it would not necessarily do so in the short run, due to the legacy of discrimination. They feared that if affirmative action programs were very extensive, they could threaten the quality of the schools or workplaces. For whatever motives, critics considered equality of results a perversion of equality of opportunity, because an emphasis on results diminished any emphasis on performance.

The competing interpretations of the distinction between equality of opportunity and equality of results and the competing interpretations of the distinction between goals and quotas would continue to plague the debate over affirmative action. These clashes also foreshadowed the debate between the two sides in the *Bakke* case.

Bakke

Cases Before *Bakke*

Bakke was not the first affirmative action case, nor even the first to reach the Supreme Court. Five years before, the Court granted certiorari to hear the case of *DeFunis v. Odegaard* (414 U.S. 1038 [1973]). Marco DeFunis, a white man of Spanish-Portuguese ancestry, applied to the University of Washington Law School two consecutive years but was rejected both times. (The first year he was accepted by four other schools but decided not to attend them because they were not in his home state of Washington.) A few years earlier DeFunis probably would have been accepted. But the baby boom reached graduate schools in the late 1960s, and by 1970, when DeFunis applied, about seventy thousand students applied for about thirty-five thousand law school seats. Schools became much more selective, with requirements escalating for high Law School Admission Test scores (LSATs) and grade-point averages (GPAs) (Sindler 1978, 29–31). At the same time, the University of Washington, like other law schools, established a minority admissions program which called for a "reasonable representation" of minorities, which the faculty defined as 15 to 20 percent of the entering class. The school insisted that this was not a quota, because the percentage was flexible and, regardless, would be met only if there were enough qualified minorities (90). On a measure combining the LSAT and GPA used to predict success at the school, DeFunis had a higher score than did thirty-six members of racial minorities who were accepted. Yet some other whites who also were rejected had higher scores than DeFunis, so it is not certain that DeFunis would have been admitted even without a minority program (39). Nevertheless, DeFunis sued, claiming reverse discrimination.

The state trial court ruled for DeFunis and ordered his admission. The Washington Supreme Court ruled for the university, prompting DeFunis, now a law student at the University of Washington, to appeal to the United States Supreme Court. In anticipation of an important decision, interest groups filed twenty-six amicus curiae (friend of the court) briefs. Yet by the time the Court heard oral arguments, DeFunis was in his last year of law school, so the Court pronounced the case moot a year after it had granted certiorari (*DeFunis v. Odegaard*, 416 U.S. 312 [1974]). Justices Brennan, Douglas, and Marshall dissented from this decision. "Few constitutional questions in recent history have stirred as much debate," Brennan wrote, "and they will not disappear. They must inevitably return to the federal courts and ultimately again to this Court" (*DeFunis v. Odegaard*, 416 U.S. 312, 350). Douglas wrote separately to indicate his likely views on the merits of the issue. Although perhaps the most liberal member of the Court, Douglas criticized the university's program and signaled that he would vote against such race-conscious remedies.

Douglas's dissent should have forecast the difficulty that schools would have in getting the Court to allow such remedies, though at least one observer noticed no "widespread change" in admissions policies between the *DeFunis* and *Bakke* cases (Sindler 1978, 210).

In the early and mid-1970s, other courts were hearing related cases. A federal district court struck down a quota used in hiring and promoting school administrators in San Francisco. The court concluded that the quota left whites little opportunity to hold these positions and, given the absence of past discrimination by the school system, was not justified (*Anderson v. San Francisco Unified School District*, 357 F.Supp. 248 [N.D. Cal. 1972]). Another federal district court struck down a program to provide financial aid to disadvantaged students by Georgetown College. Although the program was part of an effort to recruit more minorities, it disbursed aid to disadvantaged whites as well. Yet because 60 percent of the money went to disadvantaged minorities while 40 percent went to disadvantaged whites, the court concluded that it was more difficult for whites to get the money. Thus, this program, analogous to a quota or a set-aside, was considered discriminatory (*Flanagan v. Georgetown College*, 417 F.Supp. 377 [D.D.C. 1976]).

However, more courts upheld minority programs, especially ones focusing on admissions. A court ruled for the Downstate Medical Center in New York City, although the school admitted it gave preference to minority applicants from Brooklyn ghettos. The court said such preference was permissible in "proper circumstances." But the plaintiff's case was weakened by the fact that even without the minority program he would not have been admitted (*Alevy v. Downstate Medical Center,* 39 N.Y.2d 326, 348 N.E.2d 537 [1976]). Other courts ruled for New York University and the University of Arkansas because the plaintiffs could not show that without the minority programs they would have been admitted. Yet other courts, in North Carolina and Ohio, ruled more squarely that schools were not restricted to consideration only of academic standards. They could take into account minority and poverty status as well (Tollett 1978, 25–26).

Meanwhile, similar suits were pending against schools in Colorado and New York for preferential treatment of Mexican Americans and Puerto Ricans (Blackwell 1987, 193). The proliferation of all these suits made it clear, as Justice Brennan observed in *DeFunis,* that the issue would not go away.

The Supreme Court itself was called upon to address the issue of color blindness versus race consciousness in different contexts. In 1974 it held that the San Francisco school system must provide special instruction to Chinese students who do not speak English (*Lau v. Nichols,* 414 U.S. 563). The Court said that the system must either teach them English or teach them their subjects in Chinese. Thus, officials were required "to be cognizant of their actions" on these minorities and to adopt special programs to address the needs of these students (*Regents of the University of California v. Bakke,* 438 U.S. 265, 351 [1978]). It was not sufficient to teach them the same way the system taught non-Chinese students.

In 1978 the Court accepted race consciousness more explicitly. The United States Department of Justice, pursuant to the Voting Rights Act of 1965, evidently pressured the state of New York to draw the boundary lines for four districts of the state legislature in such a way that 65 percent of the voting population would be nonwhite and presumably would be able to elect representatives who were nonwhite. For one district the result split a community of thirty thousand Hasidic Jews who under the previous plan had been together. In *United Jewish Organizations v. Carey,* the Court upheld the boundary lines but fragmented over the breadth of the ruling (430 U.S. 144 [1977]). All seven justices in the majority accepted the need to take race into account in reapportioning under the Voting Rights Act. The plurality of four and a partially over-lapping group of three agreed that states can create or preserve districts with nonwhite majorities as long as they give whites representation that approximates their proportion of the county. In these circumstances quotas are valid. (These justices might have bent over backwards in deference to the act or to Congress. Chief Justice Burger, the lone dis-senter, cited evidence that the Department of Justice pressured the state to use the 65 percent figure. If so, the issue was not whether the states in our federal system can configure their districts in this manner, but whether the federal government can pressure them to do so. But with the majority adopting the former, rather than the latter, as the issue, even Justice Rehnquist joined the majority.)

Justice Brennan wanted to go further than the others in the majority, insisting that even without a voting rights act, states "plausibly could" draw boundary lines this way to overcome the disadvantages nonwhites face in registration or turnout (*United Jewish Organizations v. Carey*, 170). Here Brennan foreshadowed his opinion in *Bakke* one year later.

The Court's decision in *United Jewish Organizations* and similar decisions in other cases (e.g., *Richmond v. United States*, 422 U.S. 358 [1975]; *Beer v. United States*, 425 U.S. 130 [1976]) led to criticism like that leveled at affirmative action policies: "The most common objection to the recent evolution in voting rights is that it bestows special represen-tational advantages upon some racial and ethnic groups but not others and pulls the United States back away from its much cherished ideal of a color-blind society" (Cain 1990, 1).

The *Bakke* Case

One person who was following these cases, especially the one brought by Marco DeFunis, was Allan Bakke. Bakke, a white, was an engineer with a National Aeronautics and Space Administration (NASA) lab in Califor-nia. After working with physicians studying the effects of radiation and outer space on animals and people, he decided to become a doctor. He took premed courses and volunteered in the emergency room of a local hospital while working full time (O'Neill 1985, 21). When he applied to the medical school at the University of California–Davis in 1973, Bakke was one of nearly twenty-five hundred applicants vying for one of one hundred places in the class. That year he also applied to ten other schools. He had a good record, scoring above the ninetieth percentile in three of four categories (science, math, and verbal, but not general knowledge) on the Medical College Admission Test (MCAT). These scores were higher than those of the average student accepted by Davis (Dreyfuss and Lawrence 1979, 16). However, he completed his applications late in the academic year, and at age thirty-three he was older than medical schools preferred. The latter factor, according to Davis records, was his "main hardship" (O'Neill 1985, 22). So he was rejected by Davis and also by the ten other schools.

The next year he applied to Davis again, but he received a low score on his interview by the chair of the admissions committee, apparently because of his criticism of the special admissions program (O'Neill 1985, 24–25). The chair wrote that Bakke was "a rather rigidly oriented young man who has a tendency to arrive at conclusions based more upon his personal impressions than upon thoughtful processes using available sources of information." So he was rejected again.

In both years applicants who had lower benchmark scores—an amalgam of the MCAT score, GPA, GPA in science courses, interview score, extracurricular activities, and letters of recommendation—than Bakke were admitted through the special admissions program. Yet some whites who had a lower benchmark score than Bakke also were admitted through the regular admissions program (Dreyfuss and Lawrence 1979, 19).[4]

When the medical school at Davis opened its doors in 1968, it had no black or Hispanic students. The next year it had just two blacks and one Hispanic. At the time, the University of California system had no policy on affirmative action; each UC campus could set its own. Because of the small number of minority applicants, in 1970 the Davis faculty, like many other institutions' faculties, voted to establish a special admissions program for "economically or educationally disadvantaged" students. When the school doubled its entering class to one hundred in 1971, it reserved sixteen of these places for disadvantaged students. (It is not clear why the faculty adopted the number sixteen. The state's minority population was about 22 percent [*Regents v. Bakke,* 438 U.S. 374, n. 57]).

Although the program was open to "disadvantaged" students of all races, it was directed primarily to racial minorities, especially blacks and Hispanics. Few Native Americans applied; numerous Asians applied, but most were evaluated through the regular admissions procedures. Quite a few whites (272 from 1971 to 1974) applied, but none was accepted through the special admissions program (B. Schwartz 1988, 4). The program's administrators assumed that minorities would be disadvantaged while whites would not be. The dean of admissions later acknowledged that the program was not tailored to take into account applications from lower-class whites or middle-class minorities (Dreyfuss and Lawrence 1979, 42).[5]

Because he had been passed over in favor of minority applicants with lower scores, Bakke considered suing either Davis or Stanford, which stated that it set aside twelve places for minorities. But Bakke might have felt miffed by Davis's denial of his request to be put on standby or be allowed to audit a class. Or Bakke might have been swayed by his correspondence and meetings with an assistant to the dean at Davis. The assistant, apparently bending over backwards to be sympathetic to Bakke's questions and complaints, essentially encouraged him to sue the school (Dreyfuss and Lawrence 1979, 12–27). So Bakke sued Davis. He used the Fourteenth Amendment's equal protection clause and claimed reverse discrimination. There were whites with higher scores than his who also were rejected (thirty-two in 1974). And there were whites with lower scores than his who were accepted, but there was no legal basis for challenging the school for admitting these applicants. Moreover, Bakke seemed angered by the special admissions program. Consequently, the case would be based on race.

When Bakke filed suit, the university counsel's office seemed relatively unconcerned about the outcome. The university's attorneys did not try to delay or to keep the focus of the suit narrow, and during depositions they were not aggressive. According to Bakke's attorney, "They were not taking the view of hard-nosed litigators" (Dreyfuss and Lawrence 1979, 58). When Bakke's attorney tried to negotiate a settlement just weeks before the beginning of a new school year—"There's a law of the universe that there's always room for one more, so why don't you find another cadaver for Mr. Bakke up there at Davis?" (48)—they refused, even though a settlement would buy time and allow the university to fine-tune the admissions program at Davis and at other campuses before another disgruntled applicant brought suit.[6] Some observers concluded that the university was simply seeking guidance from the judiciary. The chief counsel himself seemed ambivalent about the case. When asked if he had any minorities on his staff of eighteen attorneys, he pointed to just one Hispanic member and remarked, "It wouldn't be fair to bring in someone who couldn't cut it" (53–54). Other observers concluded that the university was very confident about the outcome (O'Neill 1985, 40). Even the West Coast office of the NAACP was relatively unconcerned. Invited to participate, it declined. The case was not the cause célèbre it would become. For various reasons, then, a relatively detached university would carry the ball for affirmative action, while the minority groups most affected would sit on the sidelines. One black law professor later would call this "litigation without representation" (Bell 1978, 19).

The trial judge, who was retired but was called up for this day, expecting the usual cases, rejected the university's overarching argument that it could take race into account in admissions. Yet the judge also rejected Bakke's demand for admission, because the plaintiff could not prove that he would have been admitted without the existence of the special program. The judge emphasized that admission "is so peculiarly a discretionary function of the school that the court feels that it should not be interfered with by a court, absent a showing of fraud, unfairness, bad faith, arbitrariness or capriciousness, none of which has been shown" (O'Neill 1985, 40).

Both sides appealed to the California Supreme Court. With only one of the seven justices dissenting, that court also denied the university's assertion that it could take race into account in admissions (*Regents of the University of California v. Bakke* 18 Cal.3d 34, 553 P.2d 1152 [1976]). The court held it to be a violation of the equal protection clause. The majority, emphasizing that it would accept flexibility in admissions, said the university could use a program for disadvantaged students if the program was available for all races.

The key, according to one pivotal justice, was that the medical school at Davis, so new, had no record of past discrimination (O'Neill 1985, 42). Yet other schools or campuses of the university might have been guilty of some past discrimination, but neither Bakke nor the university had any incentive to investigate and introduce such evidence. It would have weakened Bakke's case, and it would have opened the university to other suits. Some cities in the state had been found guilty of operating segregated schools unconstitutionally by this very court (*Regents v. Bakke*, 438 U.S. 372). This discrimination conceivably could justify remedial action such as special admissions programs at the university level, but the court chose not to consider this relevant. As long as there was no evidence of discrimination by the university itself, there was insufficient justification to use race in admissions, in the opinion of the majority.

The court, rather than ask Bakke to prove that he would have been admitted without the special program, shifted the burden of proof and asked the university to prove that Bakke would not have been admitted without the special program. The university said it could not prove this, so the court ordered the school to admit him.[7] Initially the university was uncertain whether to appeal to the United States Supreme Court. Perhaps this uncertainty reflected its ambivalence over the issue, or perhaps it reflected the competition between factions inside and outside the university. Some officials wanted to appeal to overturn the ruling, while some conservatives on the Board of Regents wanted to appeal to cement the ruling by a like-minded Supreme Court. Civil rights leaders also were split. When eventually the Board of Regents voted to appeal, sixteen organizations, including the Mexican American Legal Defense and Educational Fund (MALDEF), petitioned the Court to deny certiorari (O'Neill 1985, 46–48).

But when the U.S. Supreme Court granted certiorari, the battle was joined. One hundred seventeen organizations filed fifty-one amicus curiae briefs (O'Neill 1985, 3), a record number at the time. The Carter administration filed one of them. After the infighting, the brief asserted that "rigid quotas" are exclusionary and therefore unconstitutional, whereas "flexible affirmative action programs using goals" are acceptable.[8]

The media, which had paid very little attention to affirmative action before, took notice now. The number of magazine articles and television news stories on affirmative action shot up in anticipation of the case (Lynch 1985). The *New York Times* quoted legal experts who predicted that it could be a landmark case (Fosburgh 1975). Some predicted that it would be as important as *Brown* or at least the most important since *Brown*. The coverage was so extensive that one law professor concluded, "No lawsuit has ever been more widely watched or more thoroughly debated in the national press before the Court's decision" (Dworkin 1977, 11).

Officials in academic institutions were not oblivious to the case and its buildup. The decision of the California Supreme Court and the preliminary skirmishes among interest groups when the U.S. Supreme Court prepared to decide the case had been given coverage in higher-education publications such as the *Chronicle of Higher Education*. Conferences concerning *Bakke*'s potential implications had been held even before the Court issued its ruling (*Bakke and Beyond* 1978).

Despite the anticipation, some justices were dissatisfied with the factual record of the case and were inclined to hold it over until the following term, when more information could be obtained. Yet, concerned that they would appear to be ducking the highly contested issue, they decided to tackle it without a postponement (O'Neill 1985, 56–57).

In June 1978, the U.S. Supreme Court issued its decision. Justice Powell, announcing the decision, did not exaggerate when he said, "We speak today with a notable lack of unanimity." There was no majority opinion. In six separate opinions the justices split on the two key issues. One bloc of four apparently concluded that both the quota and any use of race as a positive factor in admissions were invalid, while another bloc of four concluded that both were valid. Powell was the swing justice, basically maintaining that the quota was unconstitutional but the use of race as a positive factor in admissions was not. Thus, Powell provided the fifth vote for one issue for each side, and his opinion became the controlling opinion.[9]

Justice Stevens, writing for Chief Justice Burger and Justices Rehnquist and Stewart, said the denial of admission to Bakke violated Title VI of the Civil Rights Act of 1964. This provision stipulates, "No person in the United States shall, on the ground of race, color, or national origin, be excluded from participation in, be denied the benefits of, or be subjected to discrimination under any program or activity receiving federal financial assistance." The university admitted that it was receiving federal financial assistance. With little examination of the applicability of the terms of Title VI to the special admissions program, Stevens concluded that Bakke was excluded from the medical school on the basis of his race.

Stevens also criticized the opinions of the remaining five justices for addressing the issue of race as a positive factor in admissions. Stevens considered these statements dicta. Yet Stevens himself seemed to address this issue implicitly. It is hard to imagine that Stevens and the rest of his bloc could reach any conclusion other than that race could not be used at all, at least in university admissions, given their interpretation of Title VI.

The remaining five justices held that Title VI did not erect any barriers that the equal protection clause already did not establish. That is, Title VI did not provide any independent basis for deciding cases such as Bakke. Instead, these justices addressed the scope of the equal protection clause.

Justice Brennan, writing for Justices Blackmun, Marshall, and White, said the university's special admissions program and its rejection of Bakke did not violate the equal protection clause. A state government may adopt race-conscious programs if the goal is "to remove the disparate racial impact its actions might otherwise have and if there is reason to believe that the disparate impact is itself the product of past discrimination, whether its own or that of society at large" (*Regents v. Bakke*, 438 U.S. 369). The key, then, is the existence of a disparate racial impact. Presumably the existence of such an impact would be due to past discrimination, at least by society at large if not by the government in question. Why else would there be any disparate impact? Brennan considered this idea so obvious that he made clear that a government can proceed without an initial judicial finding of discrimination (*Regents v. Bakke*, 438 U.S. 368–73). Thus, the second of these two conditions is not very restrictive. Brennan also said that race-conscious programs must be reasonable and must not stigmatize discrete groups or individuals.

These conditions were fulfilled in this case by facts demonstrating the underrepresentation of minorities in medicine and the history of discrimination against minorities in education; by the school's conclusion that the underrepresentation of minorities in medicine would continue without some special admissions programs and the school's operation of its particular special admissions program; and by the absence of any stigma against whites or Bakke himself. "Unlike discrimination against racial minorities," Brennan wrote, "the use of racial preferences for remedial purposes does not inflict a pervasive injury upon individual whites in the sense that wherever they go or whatever they do there is a significant likelihood that they will be treated as second-class citizens because of their color" (*Regents v. Bakke*, 438 U.S. 375). Thus, the situation is not analogous to the segregation of black children in *Brown*.

Brennan rejected Bakke's charge of reverse discrimination. If the low number of minorities who qualified for admission under the school's regular procedures is due to past discrimination, then there is "a reasonable likelihood" that Bakke would not have been admitted if there were no past discrimination or present special admissions program (*Regents v. Bakke*, 468 U.S. 365–66). That is, without the past discrimination, more minorities would have scored high enough that they would have passed Bakke, so he still would have been below the cutoff line. Brennan's statement apparently is the closest any justice has come to articulating this crucial refutation of the reverse discrimination charge and at the same time providing a theoretical justification of affirmative action programs (Fiscus 1992, 39).

The other justices in the Brennan bloc also wrote separate, shorter opinions. Marshall underscored the irony that for most of the country's history, the Supreme Court interpreted the Constitution to allow many forms of discrimination against blacks, but now when a state acts to remedy the effects of this history, a majority of the Court interprets the Constitution to disallow the effort. Marshall asserted that a group-based program is legitimate for the group-based discrimination that preceded it. Blackmun voiced this same point: "In order to get beyond racism, we must first take account of race" (*Regents v. Bakke*, 438 U.S. 407). Marshall and Blackmun cited precedents to support the race-conscious program by Davis—the school busing cases, the *Lau* and *United Jewish Organizations* cases, and various American Indian programs.

Justice Powell, according to a biographer, knew as soon as he read the briefs what the Court should not do: "It should neither condemn affirmative action categorically nor approve it unreservedly. Faced with two intellectually coherent, morally defensible and diametrically opposed positions, Powell chose neither" (Jeffries 1994, 469). At the oral conference, Powell expressed his ambivalence on this issue. He came out against the Davis program but commented favorably about the Harvard plan that did take race into consideration (B. Schwartz 1988, 93–98). Ultimately Powell's opinion would reflect these initial feelings.

Powell said that because race is a "suspect classification" the Court should exercise "strict scrutiny" of any law or policy, such as Davis's program, that classifies according to race. (The Brennan bloc urged scrutiny that was less stringent for remedial efforts to overcome past discrimination.) As a result, the Court required the university to show that Davis's program served "a compelling governmental interest" rather than merely "important governmental objectives."[10]

The university asserted four justifications for the program: to reduce the underrepresentation of minorities in medicine, to increase the number of doctors in minority communities that were underserved, to counter the effects of discrimination in society, and to provide educational benefits for an ethnically diverse student body. Powell concluded that the first was invalid on its face and the second was invalid because there was no proof that admitting more minorities would produce more doctors for minority communities. (Studies in subsequent years have found that black doctors typically serve black patients to a greater extent than white doctors do, while Hispanic doctors typically serve Hispanic patients [Guernsey 1996].) Powell concluded that the third justification might be valid, but courts, legislatures, or administrative agencies operating under authority of legislatures would be the proper bodies to establish such a program—not universities. Powell concluded that the fourth was valid, but it was not necessary to set aside a certain number of seats to accomplish this goal.

The university had insisted that setting aside sixteen places for minorities was a "goal," not a "quota," because this number would not be filled if there were not sixteen qualified minority candidates who applied through the special program, and it could be exceeded if some were admitted through the regular procedures. Yet the California courts had characterized it as a quota because whites could not compete for the sixteen places. Powell dismissed the argument as a "semantic distinction" that was "beside the point" (*Regents v. Bakke*, 438 U.S. 289). Rather, the point was that the program classified according to race and allowed minorities to compete for one hundred seats while it allowed whites to compete for eighty-four seats. Thus, the school violated both the equal protection clause and Title VI of the Civil Rights Act of 1964.

Where Brennan justified such an outcome by suggesting that without the legacy of past discrimination against minorities, Bakke and other whites near the cutoff would not gain admission because more minorities would score higher, Powell responded, "The breadth of this hypothesis is unprecedented in our constitutional system. . . . [It] involves a speculative leap. . . . Not one word in the record supports this conclusion . . . " Actually, the very proximity of Bakke to the cutoff suggests this conclusion. But, of course, adopting Brennan's assumption would be a major step, if not a leap, for the Court to take, and Powell was not ready for the Court to take it.

Powell's dismissal of the distinction between goals and quotas was sufficient for his opinion, but it did little to clarify the underlying confusion between these two concepts.[11] This confusion would emerge as a significant factor in the impact of the case and in the continuing discussion of affirmative action.

Muddying the factual record of admissions to Davis were the exceptions made for veterans; applicants with "unusual" records; and "special friends" of the university, as chosen by the dean of the medical school. As many as five places were allotted to, or at least used by, the dean. Some students admitted by the dean had been rejected by the admissions committee for falling short of the basic standards. Thus, admissions were not always based strictly on merit anyway. (This information, which was not made public at the time of the trial, was made available, courtesy of a medical student, before the Supreme Court decided the case [O'Neill 1985, 27].)

Although Powell essentially rejected a set-aside or quota, regardless of which term he would use to characterize it, he accepted the use of race as a means to attain a more diverse student body, which would contribute to a well-rounded education. He approvingly cited the Harvard and Princeton programs in this context. In an appendix he added an explanation of the Harvard program, from an amicus curiae brief by the universities of Harvard, Columbia, Pennsylvania, and Stanford, and in his opinion he quoted extensively from it:

> In recent years Harvard College has expanded the concept of diversity to include students from disadvantaged economic, racial, and ethnic groups. Harvard College now recruits not only Californians or Louisianans but also blacks and Chicanos and other minority students.
>
> In practice, this new definition of diversity has meant that race has been a factor in some admission decisions. When the Committee on Admissions reviews the large middle group of applicants who are "admissible" and deemed capable of doing good work in their courses, the race of an applicant may tip the balance in his favor just as geographic origin or a life spent on a farm may tip the balance in other candidates' cases. A farm boy from Idaho can bring something to Harvard College that a Bostonian cannot offer. Similarly, a black student can usually bring something that a white person cannot offer.
>
> In Harvard College admissions the Committee has not set target-quotas for the number of blacks, or of musicians, football players, physicists or Californians to be admitted in a given year. . . . It means only that in choosing among thousands of applicants who are not only "admissible" academically but have other strong qualities, the Committee, with a number of criteria in mind, pays some attention to distribution among many types and categories of students. (*Regents v. Bakke*, 438 U.S. 321–24)

Powell found the Harvard plan acceptable because it considers race a plus but "does not insulate the individual from comparison with all other candidates." Thus, an African American's race might not be decisive over an Italian American's ethnicity if the latter applicant has other exceptional qualities that also contribute to diversity. In short, Powell calls for an admissions program "flexible enough to consider all pertinent elements of diversity" (*Regents v. Bakke*, 438 U.S. 317).

Powell's paean to diversity, however appropriate in a multicultural society, does have the effect of diminishing the relevance of the African American experience for affirmative action purposes. Where Marshall had noted, "The experience of Negroes in America has been different in kind, not just in degree, from that of other ethnic groups" (*Regents v. Bakke*, 438 U.S. 400), Powell wrote, "During the dormancy of the equal protection clause, the United States had become a nation of minorities. Each had to struggle—and to some extent struggles still—to overcome the prejudices not of a monolithic majority, but of a 'majority' composed of various minority groups . . . " (*Regents v. Bakke*, 438 U.S. 292). Thus, in this view, the African American experience of slavery, segregation, and discrimination is just one among many immigrant experiences, all of which deserve (equal?) consideration in selecting a student body.

Ironically, Powell's emphasis on diversity establishes the foundation for an affirmative action that would continue indefinitely. The justification that affirmative action is intended to compensate for past discrimination and disadvantage theoretically at least allows for an end to these programs—whenever the compensation is deemed sufficient. But the justification that affirmative action is intended to provide diversity does not foresee any end to these programs. Even after the recipients might be compensated sufficiently, schools and work places (and other arenas in society?) would still need to maintain or better achieve diversity. And groups besides those who suffered the worst discrimination and disadvantage would be included in this diversity. In these ways Powell's justification unwittingly lengthens and broadens affirmative action. So years later his home town of Richmond, Virginia, would adopt affirmative action policies that, on paper, include Aleuts.

Aside from this justification for his opinion, another question about Powell's opinion remains: Is it workable? Is there a clear distinction between what schools can and cannot do? Between taking race into account as a positive factor and using a set-aside or quota? Between the flexibility of the former and the lesser flexibility of the latter?

Brennan maintained that there is "no difference" constitutionally between the two approaches. The only difference is that the Harvard plan "proceeds in a manner that is not immediately apparent to the public," whereas the Davis program is relatively open (*Regents v. Bakke*,

438 U.S. 379). Blackmun echoed these views, saying the line is "thin and indistinct" (*Regents v. Bakke,* 438 U.S. 406). Powell replied that the difference is the "facial intent to discriminate." Further, quoting Justice Frankfurter, he said, "'A boundary line is none the worse for being narrow'" (*McLeod v. Dilworth,* 322 U.S. 327, 329 [1944]). Even so, he seemed to realize just how narrow that line is, observing that a plan that uses race as a plus could be "simply a subtle and more sophisticated— but no less effective—means of according racial preference than the Davis program" (*Regents v. Bakke,* 438 U.S. 319–20).

School officials responsible for complying with this ruling have had to predict how courts would characterize their plan—as one that used race as a "positive factor" or perhaps one that used a "flexible goal," or, on the other hand, one that used a less flexible "set-aside" or "quota." Note that Harvard acknowledged that it considered "numbers" and implied that it set a goal, albeit not a fixed goal. However, in a passage that seems directed toward school officials, Powell assured that "a court would not assume that a university, professing to employ a facially non-discriminatory admissions policy, would operate it as a cover for the functional equivalent of a quota system. In short, good faith would be presumed . . . " (*Regents v. Bakke,* 438 U.S. 318–19).

When the justices announced the decision and summarized their opinions from the bench, Brennan tried to portray the ruling in the best light possible. (Today we would say he tried to put a favorable spin on it.) With an eye toward media coverage of the ruling, Brennan announced that "the central meaning of today's opinion is this: Government may take race into account when it acts not to demean or insult any racial group, but to remedy disadvantages cast on minorities by past racial prejudice . . . " Powell did not agree that this was the central meaning of his opinion, but he did not disagree publicly (B. Schwartz 1988, 146–47).

So observers might be excused if they felt confused. One analyst concluded that the Court "did little to resolve the issues, and even less to clarify them" (Livingston 1979, 16). One law professor remarked, "This is a landmark case, but we don't know what it marks" ("Landmark Bakke Ruling," 1978, 31). Another commented, "It was a landmark occasion, but the Court failed to produce a landmark decision" ("Bakke Wins," 1978, 16). Perhaps the closest the Court came to achieving landmark status was the assertion and justification by four justices—the Brennan bloc—of the legitimacy of preferences and even quotas for minorities (Sindler 1978, 301). But people should not have been surprised.

Bakke was the justices' first step in the area of affirmative action, and usually the Court's first step in any area is tentative.

Instead, historians may well conclude that Powell's opinion, however open to criticism on constitutional or moral grounds, was politically astute, even Solomonic. It gave both sides something. The opinion probably appeased whites who dreaded quotas. If so, it probably slowed the backlash against civil rights that was building and that would become more prominent in the 1980s and 1990s. At the same time, the opinion allowed institutions to continue practicing affirmative action while fine-tuning their programs. Of course, the opinion did not pressure institutions to begin or continue practicing affirmative action if they were not already inclined to do so.

Whether Powell intentionally straddled the issue for political purposes is not known. Nor do we know whether he consciously reflected the administration's brief as he formulated his own opinion. But the result, though by the slimmest margin, certainly reflects McCloskey's classic conclusion that the Court is a political institution and behaves like one (1960, 225).

Aftermath of *Bakke*

The *Bakke* decision was covered extensively by the media (Lynch 1985). Commentators were divided about the likely effect (Dreyfuss and Lawrence 1979, 225–27), probably reflecting the split ruling. The *New York Times* concluded that "No one lost," and the *Wall Street Journal* declared that "Everyone won" (B. Schwartz 1988, 148–49). A political cartoon, frequently reprinted, showed two boxers—a white one labeled "Bakke" and a black one labeled "affirmative action." The referee proclaimed, "The Winner!" and raised one arm of each in victory.

One study of editorial reaction by nineteen daily newspapers spanning the ideological spectrum found an emphasis upon the balanced outcome of the decision (Haltom 1994?). There was relatively little criticism, even though more than half of the papers previously had opposed the Carter administration's amicus curiae brief, which the Powell opinion essentially embodied. Perhaps the compromise of the result, and possibly the ambiguity of the ruling, neutralized potential opponents in the press. Most editorialists seemed relieved that their "side" had not lost completely and uncertain what the effect of the ruling would be.

Civil rights activists, perhaps taking their cue from Marshall's pessimistic opinion or perhaps sensing less support from the Court than

they had been accustomed to since the 1950s, foresaw negative consequences for minorities and disapproved of the ruling (Dreyfuss and
Lawrence 1979, 225–27). The NAACP called the ruling "a major disap-
pointment" (NAACP 1979). A black newspaper, the *Amsterdam News,*
headlined the story, "*Bakke:* We Lose!" ("The Age of Less," 1978, 19).
Kenneth Clark, a black psychologist whose research had been cited in the
Brown opinion, wrote, "The effect of the *Bakke* decision psychologically,
legally, socially and morally is devastating" (1978, 38). Jesse Jackson
likened the decision to the withdrawal of federal troops from the South
after Reconstruction and argued, "Black people will again be un-
protected . . . we must not greet this decision with a conspiracy of silence
. . . we must rebel" (Cheryl Fields 1978, 12). And Stephen Carter, in his
1991 essay on affirmative action, recalls that African American student
protesters at Yale wore buttons reading "Fight Racism, Overturn *Bakke*"
(Carter 1991, 25).

The Congressional Black Caucus, however, emphasized that the
Court had upheld the use of race, and the caucus urged that this point be
publicized to shore up support for affirmative action policies (Sindler
1978, 317). The representative for the Mexican American Legal Defense
and Educational Fund also put a positive face on the decision. He noted
that while Bakke had prevailed and thus won a symbolic victory, most
affirmative action systems would be legal by the standards of this case
(Cheryl Fields 1978, 12).

Some opponents of affirmative action seemed to read the ruling the
same way civil rights activists did, but they, of course, generally ap-
plauded the decision as a step in the right direction. The *National Review*
concluded its story by commenting that universities have a "powerful
legal base from which to resist the doctrinaire levelling of Eleanor
Holmes Norton and her associates, who [believe] there is a positive duty
to integrate color-consciously, even when no discrimination is proved"
("Bakke: Enduring Question" 1978, 879). (Norton was then head of the
EEOC; she later was elected to the House of Representatives from the
District of Columbia.) The Anti-Defamation League representative stated
that the decision was a "significant victory in the effort to halt the use
of quotas and their equivalents in admission to colleges and graduate
schools" (Cheryl Fields 1978, 1).

Both sides realized that schools still could use race as a plus and
thereby admit about as many minority applicants as before, but they
doubted that most schools would. Referring to the "chilling effect" of

Bakke (Farrell 1983, 11), they said that the ruling would take pressure off schools to increase the number of minority students and also would discourage potential minority applicants by suggesting that it would be harder for them to get admitted.

One observer, though, predicted that the impact would vary according to the type of school. Selective schools could implement plans like Harvard's, but most schools could not because their minority applicants would not be nearly as qualified as the selective schools' minority applicants. Thus, most schools could not simply use race as a plus and still admit as many minorities as before. For these schools, "considerable reassessment and revamping of existing practices were likely to occur" (Sindler 1978, 319). The assumption was that a qualifications gap between white and minority applicants existed and that it was greater for the less selective schools.

Yet other commentators expected little change. They predicted that Powell's ruling would drive quota programs "underground" (Glazer 1978, 41), that universities would purport to adopt the Harvard plan but would continue to use de facto quota programs. Thus, Powell's opinion would "produce much the same result" as before but with "an encouragement of duplicity" (Bennett and Eastland 1978, 34).

Much of the public probably was confused by these interpretations or by media coverage itself. People who relied on television for their news probably were most confused. A study of network news broadcasts found that although they presented numerous stories of substantial length, many focused on Allan Bakke himself rather than his legal claim (Slotnick 1991). And although they addressed Powell's opinion, only one clearly explained that this opinion allowed affirmative action in admissions decisions. Instead, they emphasized the reaction to the ruling by various groups. Thus, adhering to their usual practices, the networks sacrificed explanation of substantive matters to coverage of conflict and human interest.

Reports of the reaction to the ruling by various groups, especially by civil rights organizations, perhaps cued the public. Whites were more favorable toward the decision than blacks were. The poll that focused most specifically on Bakke found 77 percent of the white respondents favoring the decision, with only 29 percent of the black respondents doing so. Eleven percent of the whites and 23 percent of the blacks were uncertain (Sigelman and Welch 1991, 144; Jacobson 1983, 301). However, the question posed in this Harris poll was 171 words long. This outcome contrasts with that of a Harris poll earlier in the same year that found that 68 percent of whites and 91 percent of blacks said they approved of "affirmative action progress in higher education for blacks, providing there are no rigid quotas" (Sigelman and Welch 1991, 131). And just a year before, a CBS–*New York Times* poll found that minorities of both whites (32 percent) and blacks (46 percent) approved "a school reserving a certain number of places for qualified minority applicants even if some qualified white applicants wouldn't be admitted." These items, then, showed more consensus between the races than the question specifically on *Bakke* did, but these items, of course, were not affected by the reaction of various groups to the *Bakke* ruling.

In fact, opinion on affirmative action is extremely difficult to measure and probably very changeable (see Sniderman and Piazza 1993). Varying the wording—adding or deleting words like *quotas, reverse discrimination,* or *qualified* in the questions—leads to large differences in the responses. Apparently in hearing the 171-word question specifically on Bakke, whites must have paid more attention to the news about quotas, while blacks may have paid more attention to the characterization that Bakke was a victim of reverse discrimination. Some respondents of both races also may have taken their cues from the negative statements by civil rights leaders or the positive statements by some conservative commentators.

Racial Preference Cases in the Decade after *Bakke*

Although *Bakke* was the only case involving school admissions decided by the Supreme Court until the 1990s, the Court did decide other affirmative action cases in the decade after *Bakke,* mostly involving employment. Because these cases entailed the same underlying issue of racial preference, they conceivably could have affected the impact of *Bakke.*

We will describe these cases here as important background to understanding the potential impact of *Bakke.* In Chapter 6, we will examine more recent court decisions that are retreating from the *Bakke* precedent.

One year after *Bakke,* the Court permitted a quota in a craft training program at a Kaiser Aluminum and Chemical plant in Louisiana in *United Steelworkers v. Weber* (443 U.S. 193, 1979). Fifty percent of the openings in the program were reserved for blacks until they constituted the same percentage of craft workers in the plant as in the local labor force. Previously the openings were filled according to seniority in the company. Brian Weber, a white worker with more seniority who was passed over in favor of several black workers, sued. By a 5–2 vote (dissenters were Burger and Rehnquist; Powell did not participate), the Court upheld the quota because it had been voluntarily adopted as part of a collective bargaining agreement between the company and the union. Yet two other Kaiser plants in the state had histories of past discrimination, and the company risked losing federal contracts. Further, the craft training program apparently had operated in such a way that craft workers could indicate a preference for particular other employees to receive the craft training. Thus, white craft workers essentially established a pipeline of white employees to join them in these more desirable jobs (Ezorsky 1991, 35). Consequently, Kaiser's agreement undoubtedly was not as voluntary as it appeared. In this way the case differed from *Bakke,* because there was no record that the Davis medical school or even the Davis campus of the University of California had discriminated.

The next year the Court permitted a set-aside of federal contract funds for minority businesses in *Fullilove v. Klutznick* (448 U.S. 448, 1980). Ten percent of funds for local public works projects were set aside, or reserved like a quota, for minority contractors. The six-justice majority, noting Congress's broad remedial powers under the Fourteenth Amendment, said such legislation was permissible because of the history of widespread discrimination in the construction industry.

If any cases affected the impact of *Bakke, Weber* and *Fullilove* probably were the ones. They came soon after *Bakke,* and they upheld affirmative action. Indeed, they upheld quotas. Although both presumably were decided at least in part because of past discrimination (and *Fullilove* at least in part because of the congressional statute), they reaffirmed the legitimacy of race-conscious policies. As a result, *Bakke, Weber,* and *Fullilove* often were lumped together and cited as evidence that the Supreme Court sanctioned affirmative action.

The next case came four years later, when the Court rejected a layoff plan that incorporated affirmative action for firefighters in Memphis (*Firefighters Local Union v. Stotts,* 467 U.S. 561 [1984]). When layoffs were necessary in the past, the city had done so according to seniority— "last hired, first fired"—as is customary for employers who have collective bargaining agreements with unions. But the city had a relatively recent affirmative action plan to increase the number of minorities in the fire department, so layoffs according to seniority would have disproportionately hurt minority workers, who were hired later, and hindered the city's goals. Instead the city favored affirmative action; it essentially gave retroactive seniority to those hired under the plan. But a six-justice majority seemed to believe that favoring minorities in firing decisions was more discriminatory against whites than was favoring minorities in hiring decisions. In a similar case involving teachers in Jackson, Michigan, two years later, the majority ruled similarly and articulated its distinction between hiring, on one hand, and firing or laying off, on the other (*Wygant v. Jackson Board of Education*, 476 U.S. 267 [1986]). Not getting a job because of affirmative action happens to numerous individuals, Powell reasoned, but being laid off from a job because of affirmative action happens to relatively few, particular individuals, and it imposes "the entire burden of achieving racial equality" upon them, and in the process seriously disrupts their lives (*Wygant v. Jackson Board of Education*, 282–83).

Despite some simplistic media coverage suggesting that the Court was retreating from its support of affirmative action, these cases could be fairly clearly distinguished from the previous ones. Importantly, these rulings reaffirmed, indirectly and directly, the validity of race-conscious hiring programs. Thus, it is unlikely that these cases would have had a significant effect on the impressions or practices of admissions officials.

The pattern initially did not change under the Rehnquist Court. In a series of three cases in 1986 and 1987, the Court upheld quotas in hiring and promoting (*Sheet Metal Workers' International Association v. EEOC*, 478 U.S. 421 [1986]; *International Association of Firefighters v. Cleveland*, 478 U.S. 501 [1986]; *U.S. v. Paradise*, 480 U.S. 149 [1987]). The Sheet Metal Workers' union in New York City, the fire department in Cleveland, and the state troopers in Alabama all had histories of discrimination.

Then the Court extended its affirmative action doctrine to cover women as well as racial minorities in 1987 (*Johnson v. Transportation Agency*, 480 U.S. 616). The Transportation Agency of Santa Clara County, California, promoted a woman over a man who was considered marginally better qualified according to the personnel measures used by the agency. The agency did not use quotas, and the Court, comparing the agency's promotion decision to the Harvard admission plan in *Bakke*, upheld it.

Thus, at least through 1987, the Court sanctioned affirmative action. It upheld race-conscious remedies, even quotas, if there was evidence of prior discrimination. It invalidated affirmative action only when white employees with more seniority were laid off instead of minority employees with less seniority. Overall, if these rulings had any effect on the impact of *Bakke,* they should have reinforced the use of race as a positive factor.

Administration Affirmative Action Policies in the Decade after *Bakke*

Individuals, whether school officials or potential applicants, may look for cues not only from the courts, but also from executive agencies that implement government policies. And while the Supreme Court was generally supporting affirmative action during the decade following *Bakke,* the Reagan administration was trying to dismantle such policies.

It was apparent early that the administration was abandoning the federal government's leadership, stretching from the Johnson administration through successive Republican and Democratic administrations, in promoting affirmative action in general and goals and timetables in employment in particular. A series of Reagan appointees to key civil rights positions in the government, including the head of the Civil Rights Division in the Justice Department, head of the Civil Rights Commission, and chair of the Equal Employment Opportunity Commission, publicly criticized affirmative action. The administration, in fact, urged local governments to revoke or weaken their programs, encouraged individuals to file lawsuits against the programs, and sent its lawyers to court to argue against the programs. In addition, enforcement of antidiscrimination laws, not just affirmative action policies, seemed to decline (Wood 1990). The administration showed little interest in class action suits that could bring broad relief to large groups of people at once. In short, the administration created the perception that civil rights was low on its list of priorities and the related perception that affirmative action, especially, was not being enforced and was even being challenged. The Bush administration made early statements similar to those from the Reagan administration, and it too joined suits against affirmative action.

Throughout this period, however, public opinion on affirmative action appears to have changed very little. Post-1980 surveys asked few questions about affirmative action in education. Rather, attention shifted to employment. In one of the few questions repeated with the same wording, 73 percent of whites in 1988 favored "affirmative action progress in employment for blacks provided there are no rigid quotas," compared with 67 percent of whites a decade earlier. Seventy-eight percent of blacks expressed support, compared with 89 percent a decade earlier. (It is likely that the increase in white support and decrease in black support reflect sampling error.)[12]

Other than this one piece of evidence, our knowledge of opinion on affirmative action during this period is very limited. This opinion is extremely difficult to measure and very sensitive to slight changes in wording. Depending on the wording, white support for affirmative action in the 1970s and 1980s ranged from 9 percent to 76 percent in favor, black support from 23 percent to 96 percent. Despite these wild fluctuations, however, both whites and blacks opposed quotas (whites more than blacks), but both usually accepted giving special attention to minority status in hiring and admissions (Sigelman and Welch 1991, 126–39).

Conclusion

The ruling in the *Bakke* case satisfied almost no one, but for at least a decade after the decision, it had the aura of settled law. The U.S. Supreme Court turned its attention to other matters, including affirmative action in employment. The Reagan administration was an opponent of affirmative action, but it had limited success in overturning pro–affirmative action policies in the courts or Congress. Public opinion was mixed, with clear opposition to quotas but some acceptance of making extra efforts to give minorities a chance.

The impact of *Bakke* in the decade following the decision, then, occurred in this largely supportive legal setting, but in a political and public opinion setting where support for affirmative action was mixed. In this context, then, students decided whether to apply and admissions officers decided whether to admit.

CHAPTER 2

The Context of *Bakke:* Resources and Competition

Minority enrollment in professional schools is shaped by many factors. The desire of African Americans and Hispanics to attend medical or law school is only part of the picture. Enrollment is affected by the numbers of black and Latino students graduating from college, which in turn are shaped by the resources of the minority population, the resources the larger society is willing to invest in supporting undergraduate education, especially of minority students, and the perceptions potential enrollees have about different occupational choices. This enrollment is also affected by the overall levels of competition for places in professional schools and the efforts the schools make to recruit, admit, and retain minority students. The impact of any government policy is shaped by the actions of hundreds or thousands of private individuals and private and public institutions, and the *Bakke* decision is no exception.

In this chapter, therefore, we will set the stage for the examination of the impact of *Bakke* by first exploring changes in the income and educational resources of the black and Hispanic communities during the 1960s through the 1980s. We then describe changes in federal aid to students as an indicator of support available to low-income students. And we will look at the medical and law schools themselves to see how increased competition for admission changed the nature of the admission process in the early 1960s and how efforts by the schools in the late 1960s to increase the number of minority students admitted changed the process yet again.

We start our examination of African Americans in 1960, because it allows us a longitudinal perspective, and because it is the period when we begin to see significant numbers of black youths enrolling in college. Beginning in 1960 also permits us to examine the impact of civil rights legislation on black status. Our exploration of the status of Hispanics must be more tentative until about 1970, when the U.S. Census Bureau began collecting and publishing systematic data on Hispanics. While our post-*Bakke* focus is on changes in socioeconomic conditions during the 1980s, we will also examine, where available, data from the 1990s in order to provide a background for the current minority enrollment situation.

Changes in Black and Hispanic Well-Being

Today, about one of five Americans is either black or Hispanic (or both in some cases). Both groups have historically faced substantial discrimination in the United States, but the current problems of the two groups are not identical. Blacks now make up about 12 percent of the population, and this proportion has grown by only 2 percent since 1960. Although the resources of black families and communities are much greater today than thirty years ago, and a large proportion of blacks can be classified as middle class, the condition of the black underclass is a national crisis. Moreover, as we shall see, gains in economic status among African Americans slowed nearly to a standstill in the 1980s and went backward for many.

Hispanics, about 9 percent of the nation's population, tend to be far below the average non-Hispanic white American in income and educational resources, and behind African Americans in educational status, but yet they have also assimilated faster and face less persistent discrimination than African Americans do.[1] With steadily increasing numbers due to both high birth rates and continuing immigration, the Hispanic population has increased by 45 percent since 1980 (U.S. Department of Commerce 1994, table 11). The number of young Latinos in the youngest age groups now nearly totals the number of young blacks.

Income

Income is a resource that is crucial to an individual's chances to obtain a college education. Thus, the income of black and Hispanic populations is essential to consider in understanding the patterns of their college enrollments.

Both the media and the academic press focus so heavily on the difficulties of the black population that it seems almost disloyal to the cause of racial equality to point out that in many ways the situation of

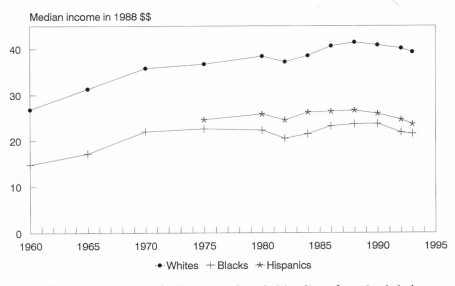

Fig. 2.1. **Changes in family income by ethnicity. (Data from *Statistical Abstract* 1990, Table 727; 1995, Table 732.)**

black Americans during the 1980s was better than before. The average African American was considerably better off financially by the end of the 1980s than in 1960 (U.S. Department of Commerce 1989, table 721). In 1988, the average black family income was 50 percent more than it was, in constant dollars, in 1960 (see fig. 2.1), and twice what it was in 1950. Since the size of the black family had shrunk (by 13 percent between 1970 and the mid-1980s), the average black family was more than twice as well off financially by the end of the 1980s as in 1950 (Sigelman and Welch 1991). Consistent with these figures, J. Smith and Welch (1987) classify fully 59 percent of black families as middle class and another 11 percent as affluent, compared to only 26 percent and 3 percent, respectively, in 1940. And opinion polls report that about 50 percent of all blacks *perceive* themselves as middle (or upper middle) class, too.

Though this trend suggests an increasing ability of black families to send their children to college and for postgraduate education, a closer look at the data yields more pessimistic conclusions. Black income is far below that of whites; indeed, it is less than 55 percent of white income. And the ratio of black-to-white income actually decreased between 1970 and 1990. Of course, people spend real dollars, not relative ones, but to the extent that the costs of a college education are premised on a certain resource level of the majority of families, black families are substantially disadvantaged.

Recent trends in black family income present another disturbing feature. Black income rose throughout the 1960s and early 1970s. After a high point in 1978, it fell dramatically, dropping 15 percent by 1982. Though it did increase a little since then, it has been largely stagnant. White income also fell in the early 1980s, but it fully recovered its peak 1970s levels by 1986–87. Thus, black income did not experience the growth that white income did throughout the 1980s. To the extent that family income is an important determinant of the ability to send the younger generation to college, black families were worse off in the late 1980s than they were in the 1970s. They were worse off absolutely—in real dollar income—and worse off relative to whites and relative to the costs of attending college, since these costs had increased substantially (Moulton 1988; U.S. Department of Commerce 1995, table 727).

Hispanic income has also diminished slightly since 1980. Though average Hispanic family income is higher than that of African Americans (U.S. Department of Commerce 1995, 727), it is significantly below white family income. Like African Americans, Hispanics are not catching up to non-Hispanic whites in income resources.

Many reasons can be found for the stagnant black and Latino family income beginning in the late 1970s. A dramatic leap in black unemployment—which reached nearly 20 percent in 1982—slowed black income gains (U.S. Bureau of Labor Statistics, *Employment and Earnings,* monthly). Hispanic unemployment is lower than that of African Americans, but its increase during the early 1980s blighted the economic advancement of tens of thousands of families.

Changing family composition in the black community also contributed to declining family income, though it was less a factor among Hispanics. Figure 2.2 reveals that female-headed households were 22 percent of all black households in 1960, but 48 percent in 1994 (U.S. Department of Commerce 1995, table 70). The proportion of white female-headed families increased greatly during the same period but still reached only 13 percent in 1994. About 25 percent of all Hispanic families are female headed. (A female-headed household is assumed to be one in which the woman is the sole parent living there.)

Whatever their ethnicity, compared to two-parent families, female-headed families are much more likely to fall below the poverty line and much less likely to be affluent (see also Farley and Allen 1987). For

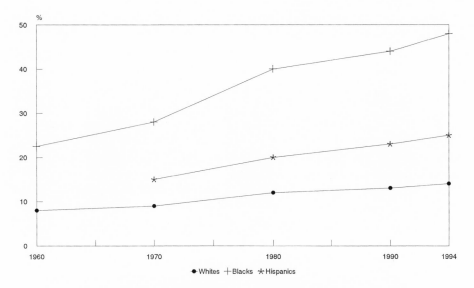

Fig. 2.2.   Female-headed families as a proportion of all families. (Data from *Statistical Abstract* 1990, Table 57; 1995, Table 70.)

example, one estimate is that 17 percent of two-parent black families are affluent, while only 3 percent of female-headed black families are (J. Smith and Welch 1987). Over half of black female-headed families and more than a third of white female-headed families receive cash public assistance (U.S. Bureau of the Census 1986). Figure 2.3 shows the striking income disparity between two-parent and female-headed families in the three groups. In each, the typical married couple has an income that would be considered by most to be middle class, relatively comfortably so among whites. But the typical black and Hispanic female-headed family is below the poverty line ($12,000 for a family of four).[2]

About half of all black families are female headed, and over 60 percent of all black children live in such families (U.S. Census 1995, table 70). Thus, the economic deprivation that afflicts many such families is disproportionately shared by children. This economic deprivation, of course, affects their chances of obtaining a good education and aspiring to attend college and, later, professional schools. By contrast, about two-thirds of Hispanic children have both parents at home; only 28 percent live in families headed by women.

A third reason for declining black and Hispanic family income is the overall state of the American economy. After gains throughout the post–

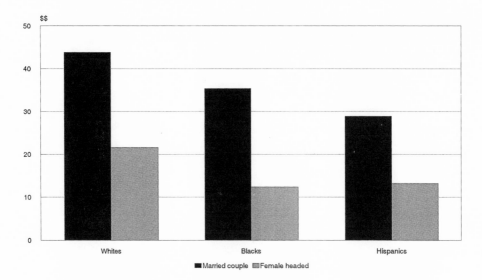

Fig. 2.3. Average family income by family type and ethnicity. (Data from *Statistical Abstract* 1995, Table 727, [1993 income].)

World War II era, in 1973, when oil prices skyrocketed, the economy slumped badly. Real incomes dropped. A brief recovery in the late 1970s came to a standstill in 1980, and real incomes dropped further in the recession of the early 1980s.

The slumping and erratic economy, coupled with tax policies of the Reagan era, hit Americans in the lower half of the income distribution hardest. Over the period from 1978 to 1987, family incomes of those in the top half of the income distribution increased, and among the top 10 percent they increased substantially (by over 20 percent). Family incomes of those in the bottom half of the income distribution decreased, and at the bottom 10 percent decreased substantially, by almost 11 percent. Put another way, the gap between the richer and poorer grew significantly during this decade (see Levy 1988; Harrison and Bluestone 1988; Rich 1987).

During this decade of stagnant family incomes and diminishing family income for poor people, the proportion of students from poor families who attended college actually dropped by 4 percent (Vobejda 1989). By the end of the decade, 68 percent of high school graduates from families in the top one-fourth of the income distribution went to college, while 29 percent of those in the bottom one-fourth did.

These general trends have obvious implications for black and Hispanic families, with their smaller average incomes. Already behind white, non-Hispanic families in the income resources necessary to provide a college education for their children, typical African American and Hispanic families were hit harder than the typical white, non-Hispanic family during the 1980s. This finding suggests that, in the decade after *Bakke,* the income resources of minority families actually shrank, making college attendance more difficult.

Wealth

The relative disadvantage of minority families in sending their children to college is reflected not only in annual income, but in total wealth. Though black net wealth has increased since 1967, the gain was far overshadowed by the increasing wealth of whites. In 1984, the average white household with an income in the $7,500-to-$15,000 range had a greater net worth than the average black household with an income of $45,000 to $60,000 (Oliver and Shapiro 1989).

The most recent data on net worth indicate that in 1988, median black family net worth was only one-tenth of that of white families, $4,170 to $43,280 (Rich 1991). Hispanic net worth was only slightly higher than that of blacks ($5,520). The net worth discrepancy, in proportional terms, is least among married-couple families, where whites exceed blacks and Hispanics by about four to one (whites having somewhat over $60,000 net worth and blacks and Hispanics $15,000 and $17,000, respectively), and is greatest in female-headed families, where whites have about thirty times the net worth of black families. Indeed, black female-headed families have a net worth of only $760, about the same as Hispanic female-headed families.

These calculations of net worth include bank accounts, stocks, bonds, and homes and other real estate. The large racial difference indicates that the financial disadvantage reflected in the income differential of minority and white families is exacerbated when one assesses the total financial resources a family can draw upon in sending a child to college.[3] As Benjamin Hooks, former executive director of the NAACP, commented on the small net worth of black and Hispanic families reflected in the 1988 statistics, "It means that you have grinding poverty, the absence of amenities, books, newspapers, magazines, encyclopedias, health care, college funds, the kind of things that build the environment that move people toward upward mobility" (Rich 1991).

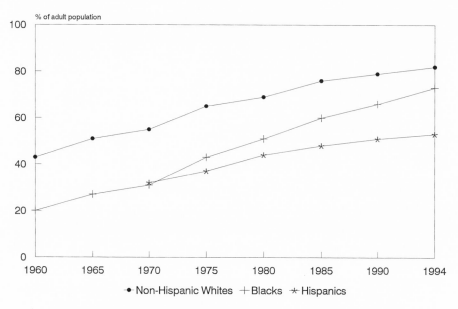

Fig. 2.4.   High school graduates, by ethnicity. (Data from *Statistical Abstract* 1995, Table 239.)

Education

Primary and secondary education is another resource essential to college education. Before students can attend college, they need to complete high school. Here blacks are making steady gains (fig. 2.4). Whereas in 1960 only 20 percent of all black adults had graduated from high school, by 1994, 65 percent had. Unlike income gains, which stagnated in the late 1970s and early 1980s, education gains continued, so that even between 1980 and 1990 the proportion of black adults graduating from high school increased by 15 percent. Moreover, the proportion of young black adults, those age twenty-five to thirty-four, with high school educations increased to 80 percent, only 7 percent less than for whites the same age.

This substantial increase was not accompanied by a similar increase in college attendance, which rose throughout the 1960s but leveled off in the 1970s and early 1980s before increasing again since then (fig. 2.5). The slump in college attendance by black students was not as sharp as the decline in real income, and the increase in enrollment in the late 1980s and through the 1990s outpaced gains in black family income.

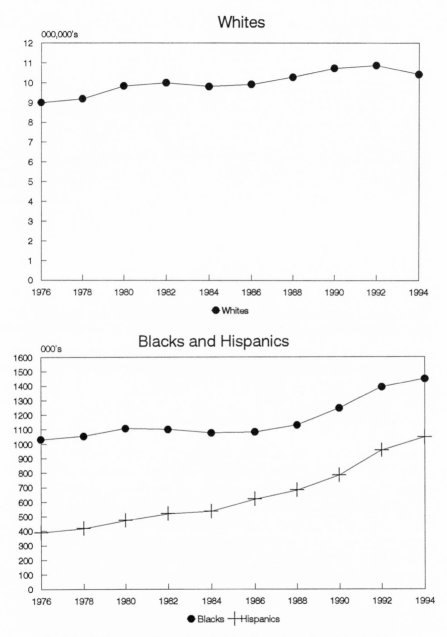

Fig. 2.5.   College enrollment by ethnicity. (Data from *Chronicle of Higher Education,* April 28, 1995, A22; May 24, 1996, A32.)

However, decreasing income in the late 1980s appeared to have affected college choices among those who could attend. In the 1980s, increasing proportions of blacks chose two-year colleges over degree-granting four-year colleges, and an increasing number noted that they chose a college to attend on the basis of its low cost (Astin 1990).

The proportion of black adults with college degrees has risen steadily since 1970, but the gap between the proportion of blacks and whites with college degrees has actually widened. In 1960, there was a 5 percent gap; today there is a 10 percent one. Over 21 percent of the white adult population are now college graduates compared with 11 percent of blacks.

The educational levels of Hispanics are lower by most measures than those of blacks. Although the proportion of Hispanics with a high school education increased from around 32 percent in 1970 to about 50 percent in 1988 (U.S. Department of Commerce 1990, tables 217, 218), the proportion of Hispanics finishing high school is substantially less than the proportion of blacks who do so (fig. 2.4). However, among high school graduates, a higher proportion of Hispanics than blacks enroll in college (U.S. Department of Commerce 1990, table 252).[4] The number of Hispanics enrolled in college increased by over 70 percent between 1976 and 1988 and continued to increase through the 1990s (table 2.1). In contrast, both black and white enrollment declined somewhat in the mid-1980s before resuming its growth in the early 1990s.

During the 1970s and 1980s, the mean educational level of Hispanics increased even though the increase in the Hispanic population included tens of thousands of immigrants from Mexico and Central America. With the exception of Cubans, new Hispanic immigrants tend to be poorly educated, are unlikely to speak English, and have few skills. Although researchers differ in their interpretations of whether Hispanics are moving up the socioeconomic ladder in ways similar to European

TABLE 2.1. **Grants, Loans, and Work as a Percentage of Total Aid (in constant 1982 dollars)**

	1976–77	1981–82	1986–87	1989–90
Grants	43	25	27	26
Loans	46	70	68	70
Work	11	6	5	4

Source: Moulton 1988, 45. Data for 1989–90 from "The Nation" 1996.

immigrants (see Chapa 1990), it is clear that, at least for Mexican Americans, second-generation immigrants are better educated than first-generation ones, and third better educated than second (Chapa 1990). In part because of high rates of Hispanic immigration, a much larger proportion of Hispanic children than black or white ones drop out before finishing high school. A study of students who in 1980 were high school sophomores found that 12 percent of Hispanics later dropped out before finishing high school, compared to 7 percent of black and 5 percent of white students ("The Nation" 1996, 14).

These trends suggest that the college enrollment trends of blacks and Hispanics are quite different in some respects. The rapidly increasing college enrollments of Hispanics indicate a high degree of upward social mobility, at least among many segments of the Hispanic community. Though there is no question that some Latinos face serious discrimination, and many Hispanics face some discrimination, it is not as pervasive as that faced by blacks.

Nonetheless, the limited educational background of many Hispanics is a barrier to enrollment in postgraduate programs. The trends in Hispanic enrollment in medical and law school must be viewed against their still relatively small numbers graduating from colleges and universities.

Financial Aid

Many students, including blacks and Hispanics, need financial aid to continue their education beyond high school. There are several kinds of financial aid, but federal aid is a large part of what is available to students on the basis of need. The rise and fall of minority enrollment in undergraduate institutions and thus the pool of potential professional school applicants may thus be linked to the increase and decrease in federal aid. In the mid-1980s, 44 percent of undergraduate students received federal aid (U.S. Department of Commerce 1990, table 265). The availability of federal aid is also directly linked to the decision to go on to postgraduate work. In the mid-1980s, 65 percent of students in professional schools, for example, received federal aid (U.S. Department of Commerce 1990, Table 266).[5]

Federal aid rose dramatically in the early 1970s, then began a downward spiral, in real dollars, that continued for more than a decade. For example, the average federal grant (Pell Grant) was worth nearly $2,400 in 1975 but tumbled to less than $1,800 in 1987. The average direct loan was nearly $1,400 in 1970 but only $900 in 1987 (Moulton 1988). The drop in the real value of student aid halted in 1985, but only the general student loan (GSL) program has shown an increase. Even so, the amount of federal aid available to students in the decade after *Bakke* was far below that available in the one before.

Moreover, the nature of the aid changed. A smaller proportion was available through outright grants, and a larger proportion came in loans (see table 2.1). Grants comprised over 40 percent of the total aid package in 1976 but only 27 percent in 1987.[6] Most of this change occurred immediately before and after *Bakke*. Thus, both in benefit size and in the claim that the benefit makes on the student, federal aid to students became progressively more limited in the decade after *Bakke*.

The declining federal aid and the increased reliance on loan rather than grant aid presents a sharp contrast to the increasing cost of attendance. Between 1980 and 1987, the cost of attending a private university increased almost 41 percent, and a public university almost 26 percent. The amount of available grant money increased less than 1 percent, and available work-study opportunities actually decreased by 22 percent. Only the amount of federal loans available increased, and its increase of almost 11 percent was far less than the increased costs of attending college (Moulton 1988, 46). Thus, during the 1980s, low-income students could have been expected to be increasingly discouraged about their ability to finance a college education.

This rather intuitive impression is confirmed by what evidence exists on the relationship between financial aid and access to higher education. Generally, financial aid is important for low-income students who desire a college education (Fife 1975; Sewell and Shah 1968; Tillery and Kildegard 1973; Crawford 1966). In a study of three thousand prospective students, Charles Fields and Morris LeMay (1973) found, for example, that recipients of need-based financial aid were more likely to enroll than others with no such offers. Low-income students were the most responsive to such offers. Indeed, students from lower-income families are more likely than those from higher-income families to respond to price changes in higher education (Jackson and Weathersby 1975).

Shrinking federal student aid hits minority students disproportionately hard. Most analysts believe that financial aid is important in increasing minority access to higher education (Spearman 1981, 293; Astin 1982; Lane 1971). The most comprehensive study is that of Moulton (1988). Examining aggregate black enrollment data and a variety of measures of federal aid from 1973 to 1986, she shows that black enrollment in higher education is strongly positively correlated with the total federal financial aid available. Enrollment is strongly negatively correlated with the percentage of that aid that is offered as a loan rather than a grant or work-study opportunity.

A 1989 survey of college freshmen documents on an individual level the importance of aid to minority students (Astin 1990). For example, proportionally twice as many black (41 percent) as white (20 percent) students obtained a Pell Grant, given on the basis of need, and three times as many blacks (15 percent) as whites (5 percent) had Pell Grants of over $1,500. About a quarter of each group had obtained loans, a figure that had risen from 10 percent of freshmen in a similar 1978 study. Moreover, 27 percent of all black students and 21 percent of white ones reported that they chose their college because of its low tuition, and only 53 percent of blacks, compared to 73 percent of whites, said they were attending their first-choice school. Over 21 percent of black freshmen and 25 percent of Hispanic freshmen declared that concern about college financing was "a major worry," compared to only 12 percent of whites (National Science Foundation 1990, table 36).

These data support the conclusion that minority students, both black and Hispanic, are much more likely than white non-Hispanic students to be poor or of modest incomes. A 1987 study, again of freshmen, provides more concrete evidence. In that study, 18 percent of blacks and 15 percent of Hispanics but only 3 percent of whites declared their family income less than $10,000. Similar ethnic differences existed in the proportions with incomes under $20,000 (37 percent, 32 percent, and 11 percent, respectively; National Science Foundation 1990, table 36). Given their financial circumstances, black and Hispanic students are much more likely to need federal grants to make higher education, at least higher education away from home, a possibility. For example, only 33 percent of black freshmen, compared to 58 percent of their white counterparts, received at least $1,500 from their parents for college. Only 3 percent of the black students had savings equal to $1,500, compared to 15 percent of all white students (Astin 1990).

Not only do black and Latino students have fewer resources to draw upon from their families and their work, they are far less likely than white students to have the kinds of family resources necessary to consider taking out a huge loan to finance an education. For middle-class students, borrowing money for a college education is not much of a risk. The expectations that the student will complete college and settle into a middle-income job (or better) are likely to be met. If the student fails to complete college or settles for a low-paying job, family resources provide a fallback if the debt comes due. For a student from a poor family, the situation is different. Aside from the fact that the experience of applying for a loan would present more of a challenge for a poor student, the loan itself might represent many times the total resources that the family possesses. As we have seen, the assets of blacks and Hispanics are far smaller than those of non-Hispanic whites. The potential burden of paying off the loan is therefore larger.

Moreover, the chance of a poverty-stricken student completing college is less than that of a middle-class student. Financial status is related to performance once in college. Generally, low socioeconomic status contributes to poor academic performance (Thomas 1981a). Black students who worked more than twenty-one hours per week, who had heavy debts, or who needed loans dropped out more than other black students (P. Cross and Astin 1981). Financial exigencies, poor prior academic preparation, and lower expectations on the part of family and peers conspire to make it more difficult for students from poor families to complete an education.[7] Given all that, accepting a loan is a riskier proposition.

A study of medical school students in the early 1990s documents that the problems of poor income follow many students into professional school. In the class of 1992, for example, 16 percent of the black and Hispanic students came from families of income less than $15,000 a year, compared with only 4 percent of the white students. About one-third of black and Hispanic students were from families earning $50,000 a year or more, compared with about two-thirds of the white students (AAMC 1993, table 8).[8] It is not surprising that an analysis of the indebtedness of medical school graduates shows that, while most students (90 percent of minorities and 80 percent of others) had debts when they graduated, minority students had larger debts. In 1989, for example, 46 percent of underrepresented minorities had debts over $50,000, compared with 31 percent of other students (AAMC 1993, table 18a).[9] Levels of indebtedness increased substantially for both groups during the 1980s.

Thus, the picture we have outlined indicates that, at the time of *Bakke,* African Americans and Hispanics were behind in the socioeconomic resources necessary to undertake professional education. In particular, their lower income status and financial resources were a barrier. Moreover, even though blacks were catching up to whites in their probabilities of having a high school education, far fewer black and Hispanic families than white families included a college graduate. The increasing proportions of single-parent families also limited the opportunities of many black students, depriving them of both income and parental resources necessary to sustain a prolonged and stressful period of education.

These disadvantages did not diminish during the decade following *Bakke*. The early and mid-1980s were not a time of increased chances for educational and economic advancement for America's minorities. The recession of the early 1980s and the growing income inequalities closed the door to higher education for many. The decline in federal student aid closed the door for many more. Typical Hispanic and black families found that the costs of sending their children to college continued to increase while their real incomes and chances for a decent-sized federal aid stipend decreased. Of course, these same pressures affected low-income white families, too, but their plight is less visible because white families, disproportionately located in the top half of the income distribution, were more likely than minority families to experience prosperity during this decade.

Given these trends, it is hardly surprising that black college enrollment actually declined during the first part of the 1980s, though it rebounded later in the decade. Trends in Hispanic enrollment were somewhat different. Though the continuous immigration flow depressed the average educational and income levels of Hispanic families, at the same time the growth of the Hispanic population provided more potential college students. Thus, the 1980s saw a sharp increase in the number, if not the proportion, of Hispanics attending college.

Those students who successfully completed their undergraduate education found themselves faced with more barriers as they contemplated professional school. If they were from an average family, their family income resources were declining as was the prospect of federal grants. Moreover, they faced a situation of increasing competition for places in medical and law schools.

The Changing Nature of Law and Medical School Admissions Processes

The Civil Rights Act, which opened the doors of many institutions of higher education to black Americans, and a growing black middle class increased the opportunities and demand for higher education by blacks in the mid-1960s. The dreadful irony is that this increased demand came exactly at a time when the admission to law and medical school had just become much more difficult. Though stemming from causes unrelated to race, the increasing demand for medical and law school meant that blacks, as well as others, would have a diminished chance of being admitted.

Increasing Competition

Until the late 1950s and early 1960s, admission to even the most desirable law and medical schools was relatively easy (cf. Dreyfuss and Lawrence 1979). Until the 1950s, not all law schools even required college attendance, let alone a college degree, as a prerequisite for law school. In 1955, for example, a survey showed that only 78 percent of practicing lawyers had even attended college, and only 49 percent had degrees (Abel 1989).

Even when requirements for law school had tightened considerably, until the early 1960s, getting admitted was not very difficult. For example, as late as 1961, a college graduate with a B average was automatically admitted to the prestigious University of California Law School, Boalt Hall. Prospective applicants needed to take the Law School Aptitude Test (LSAT) exams only if their grade point average (GPA) was less than 3.0 (on a 4.0 scale). In 1960, 517 of 708 applicants to Boalt Hall were accepted (Dreyfuss and Lawrence 1979, 128).

Within six years, the baby boom had arrived; the number of applicants skyrocketed. Consequently, admission became much more competitive. In 1966, for example, fifteen hundred students applied to Boalt Hall, and by 1972 five thousand sent their applications. Instead of a B average, successful applicants now needed a 3.66 GPA and high LSAT scores. The admission process was redirected from a procedure to select those who had a good chance of succeeding in law school to a process to select the "brightest and best" on the basis of grades and test scores from among many who could succeed. High grades and LSAT scores became crucial. As the law dean's brief to the U.S. Supreme Court in the *Bakke* case stated, "The level of . . . achievement required to gain admission to Boalt Hall is far in excess of the level which would be required if the sole criterion were a record sufficient to justify a confident prediction that the applicant could successfully complete the program and become a competent member of the bar" (quoted in Dreyfuss and Lawrence 1979, 128).

The increasing competition for places in medical school followed a similar pattern. In the 1950s and early 1960s, some schools could not fill all their places. The Medical College Aptitude Test (MCAT) was introduced in the 1950s, not to provide a yardstick against which to weed out from among a surfeit of extremely qualified applicants, but rather to help reduce the attrition rate caused by admitting too many applicants who were not qualified. Many medical schools essentially had open admissions policies. As with law schools, however, in the mid and late 1960s, competition for medical school slots had vastly increased, and high grades and test scores became essential. The Association of American Medical Colleges reported that "medical schools have raised their admissions standards well beyond the minimum level necessary to ensure completion of the course of study leading to the M.D. degree" (Dreyfuss and Lawrence 1979, 128).

Accompanying this dramatic increase in competitiveness in admissions were changes in the curriculum, especially in medical schools. The curriculum grew much tougher and considerably more oriented toward scientific research. Undergraduate training in sciences became much more important to getting into medical school and to success once students were admitted (Speich 1978).

Thus, just at the time when changes in law and public opinion seemed to be opening the doors of professional schools to black and Hispanic students, changes in the nature of the admissions process for these schools had made that process much more rigorous and competitive. And, at least in the case of medical education, blacks began to enter medical school at a time when the curriculum had become much tougher, especially for those without good training in science. In both medical and law school, much more weight was given to standardized admission tests rather than just the student's undergraduate GPA. If the civil rights revolution had occurred a decade or two earlier, minority students (like white ones) seeking admission to, and success in, medical and law schools would have had a much easier time.

Early Efforts to Increase Opportunities for African Americans and Other Minorities

The controversy over *Bakke* grew out of efforts in many professional schools to give increased opportunities to black, and later Hispanic and American Indian, students. These opportunities were crucial in light of the increased competitiveness of medical and law school admission and the dearth of black students who had attended any but the two historically black medical schools.

Medical Schools

Before the Civil Rights Act of 1964, professional schools in the United States were white enclaves. Though the first blacks were admitted to an American medical school in 1851, and by 1910, seven medical colleges for blacks were operating, reforms in medical education after 1910 resulted in five of those colleges being closed (Meier 1985, 183). These reforms, designed both to improve the quality of medical practice and to limit competition within the medical field, contained an overtly racist bias. Indeed, the 1910 Flexner report, a set of recommendations for improving the quality of medical training, stated that "an essentially untrained negro wearing an MD degree is dangerous" and that the practice of black doctors should be "limited to [their] own race" (quoted in Meier 1985, 183). Of course, the closing of most black medical schools after the report did not result in opening of doors in predominantly white schools, many of which refused to admit blacks.

Before 1964, only 3 percent of the entering students in medical school were black. And most of these black students were enrolled in two predominantly black schools, Howard University (in Washington, D.C.) and Meharry Medical College (in Nashville, Tennessee). For example, in 1951, 197 black students entered the first-year classes of medical schools across the nation; of these, 141 were enrolled in the two predominantly black colleges. The other 56 comprised less than 1 percent of the entering classes at white-dominated medical schools (S. Shea and Fullilove 1985).

The Civil Rights Act, and the realization after its passage that eliminating legal segregation would not automatically move blacks to a position of equality within society, stimulated calls for "affirmative action." In one of the first efforts of this kind directed at recruiting minorities to medical school, a white middle-aged couple, funded by a small philanthropic foundation, set out in 1966 to identify black students in the South who might gain admission to a medical school in the North (Speich 1978). Eleven were selected and eight eventually entered medical schools. These efforts quickly became more institutionalized.

The Association of American Medical Colleges (AAMC) in 1968 endorsed the idea of increasing minority representation, urging that medical schools "admit increased numbers of students from geographical areas, economic backgrounds and ethnic groups that are now inadequately represented." An AAMC committee just one year later went further, urging that by the 1975–76 academic year, 12 percent of all first-year medical students be black (Dreyfuss and Lawrence 1979, 19). The committee essentially proposed quotas, and in 1970 it began to assist medical schools in their activities designed to recruit more minorities.

By 1974, of the ninety schools responding to a survey concerning minority opportunities, every school reported having a program to increase the number of minority students (Wellington and Montero 1978). Three-fourths reported that their admission *criteria* had been altered to increase minority enrollment, with two-thirds changing their admission *procedures* (such as by making sure minorities served on the admission committees). According to another report, more than one hundred schools adopted quota systems (Dreyfuss and Lawrence 1979, 79). Stanford medical school, for example, acknowledged reserving twelve seats for minorities (Dreyfuss and Lawrence 1979, 25). Other West Coast schools reportedly reserved 20 to 25 percent of the seats in their first-year classes for minorities. These included the medical schools of the University of California at Irvine, Los Angeles, San Diego, and San Francisco; and the law schools of the University of California at Berkeley and at Los Angeles and the University of Washington (Speich 1978). Also, the medical school of the University of Southern California added twenty-eight seats to its first-year class and reserved them for minorities. Presumably the additional seats would insulate the school from charges of reverse discrimination.

The impact of these plans, along with the demise of legal segregation, caused a dramatic increase in the numbers of entering black medical students, as figure 2.6 shows. Beginning in about 1966, the number of first-year black medical students increased sixfold in an eight-year period. Of course, even at its peak in 1974, black enrollment was far from proportional to black population proportions. In that year, slightly over 7 percent of the entering students were black. Nonetheless, the increase represented an impressive change since 1965.

Though the initial focus of minority recruitment programs was on black students, by 1974, most schools had broadened their focus to include nonblack minority groups. Whereas a study of medical schools in 1968 showed that 62 percent targeted their special admissions and support programs exclusively on blacks, by 1974, only 6 percent did

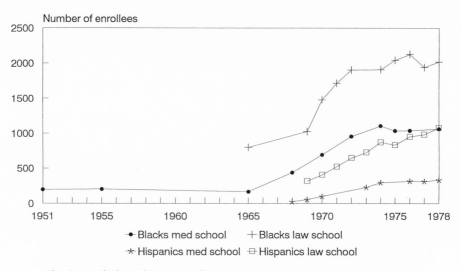

Fig. 2.6. Black and Hispanic first year enrollment before *Bakke*. (Data from Shea and Fullilove 1985; *Lawyer's Almanac* 1986; medical school admission requirements, selected years.)

(Jarecky 1969; Wellington and Montero 1978). The proportion of programs including American Indians increased from 9 to 93 percent; Mexican Americans, from 16 to 89 percent; and Puerto Ricans, from 8 to 76 percent. All but one program included blacks, and about one-third included Asians. Thus, the increased scope of affirmative action programs occurred early; programs began to be directed not just at African Americans to compensate for generations of slavery, but rather to a variety of racial and ethnic minorities.

The growing emphasis on Hispanics is reflected in increasing Hispanic enrollments between 1968 and 1974 (fig. 2.6). The rate of increase was not as steep as for blacks and the numbers were smaller, but clearly more and more Hispanic students were enrolling in medical school. (We do not have information on Hispanic enrollments before 1968.)

By 1978, just before *Bakke*, the director of the AAMC's minority education programs commented on the successes in diversifying the student body at a time when demand for admissions had "increased the pressure on admission committees, which had to reject at least two out of every three well qualified applicants" (Prieto 1978, 695). He pointed out that admissions committees had begun to shift their selection focus from choosing a homogeneous group of students to choosing a student body that incorporated more women and minorities, groups that had not been represented in medical education in significant numbers before. He urged medical schools to increase the number of "students from geographic areas, economic backgrounds, and ethnic groups that are now inadequately represented" (694).

Law Schools

Before the mid-1960s, minority law students were as rare as their medical counterparts. In 1964, less than 1 percent of the students in the predominantly white law schools were black. In 1965 and 1966, some law schools, including Harvard, began special programs to attract black applicants to law study. UCLA, for example, organized a special program designed to increase its black and Hispanic enrollment from 1 percent in 1965 to 23 percent in 1970 (Seligman 1978, 27). After several official groups involved in legal education (including the Association of American Law Schools, the American Bar Association, the National Bar Association, and the Law School Admissions Test Council) organized in 1968 to form a Council on Legal Educational Opportunity to expand opportunities for law study for "members of disadvantaged groups," many more law schools began programs of minority recruitment. Prelaw summer-school institutes were organized around the country, and between 1968 and 1975, nearly two thousand minority students attended them. Law schools also began to give special financial aid packages to minority students and to institute admissions practices that would increase the number of minorities. In some cases this was done through quotas; in other cases admissions officials began to give greater weight to factors other than LSAT scores and GPAs.

These efforts yielded some success, as the proportion of minority students in law school increased to 7 percent by 1973 (Seligman 1978, 27). A 1986 American Bar Association study shows that first-year minority enrollment (African Americans, Hispanics, Asians, and American Indians together) increased from 1,552 in 1969 to 3,571 in 1978, well over a 100 percent increase (Law School Admission Council 1986). By 1978, all minorities together were about 9 percent of law school enrollment (Speich 1978).

Our data, again shown in figure 2.6, reveal a slow increase in black law students between 1965 (the first year data are available) and 1969, and then a very steep increase between 1969 and 1972. A slower upward trend continued until 1976, at which time there was a small decline. Hispanic law school enrollment climbed at a steady pace between 1969 (the first year data are available) and 1974, and it continued to climb between 1975 and 1978.

Defining the Issues

The efforts of schools to increase their minority enrollments, along with the elimination of legal barriers and the increased numbers of minority students receiving college educations, did result in observable increases in minority enrollment in professional schools. And, whether through quotas and goals, many schools clearly gave at least some weight to race. The new awareness of the need for racial and ethnic diversity led to a number of changes designed to identify potential minority applicants and encourage them to apply, new financial aid packages targeted to these students, and special efforts to help them stay in school. None of these innovations was especially controversial at the time (though minority-targeted scholarships later became controversial). What was controversial was the reconsideration of the reliance on grade point averages and, especially, standardized test scores.

To underscore the impact of standardized scores, a study for the Law School Admissions Council (Evans 1977) found that only 18 percent of the black students in first-year classes of law schools across the country in the 1976–77 academic year would have been admitted if the schools had used race-blind procedures on their standard admissions requirements, test scores, and GPAs. Only 27 percent of the Hispanics, 39 percent of the Native Americans, and 60 percent of the Asians would have been admitted as well. Only 39 black applicants taking the LSAT in fall 1976 scored 600 or above (out of a possible 800) and also had a GPA of 3.5 or better, while 13,151 whites did (Klitgaard 1985, 175).

Data from the 1980s show a continuing differential between black and white LSAT scores and undergraduate GPAs (Wightman and Muller 1990). Even more recent data show racial disparities in the MCAT scores, too (AAMC 1993, tables 7a and 7b; Garfield 1996). Contemporary differences probably understate differences likely to have occurred in the 1970s, because test scores of African American students have increased. Data show that black students accepted to medical school have verbal reasoning, physical science, and biological science scores significantly below those of whites. Asians score higher than whites except on verbal reasoning, while Mexican Americans' and Puerto Ricans' scores are between those of whites and blacks. Differences in GPAs are similar, though the average African American admitted to medical school, like the average white, has a GPA greater than 3.0.

The average MCAT scores and GPAs of whites rejected for medical school are slightly higher than those of blacks who are accepted. This is the condition that framed the *Bakke* case and the condition that inflames opponents of affirmative action today. Of course, all these data are averages only, meaning that there are many whites who fall below the score of the average black and many blacks who stand above the score of the average white.

As we have seen, the importance of these criteria of standardized tests and grades had existed for only fifteen years before *Bakke* but, given the demand for places in law and medical schools, had been thoroughly institutionalized. Whether institutions could back away from what appeared to be a system of meritocracy, based on grades and test scores, to give weight to other factors in order to meet a target or fulfill a quota, became the issue. This controversy came to a climax in the *Bakke* case.

CHAPTER 3

Perceptions of *Bakke* and Its Impact

We begin our analyses of the impact of the *Bakke* case by examining briefly the extent to which the news of *Bakke* was disseminated to general and professional audiences. We then look at how law and medical school admissions officers viewed the impact of this decision. The unique source for this analysis is the result of a survey questionnaire sent to every accredited law and medical school in existence in 1976. Questionnaires, mailed in March 1989, were sent to the admissions officer at 164 law schools and 118 medical schools.[1] We followed up the initial mailing with two additional mailings during the fall and summer. Each contained a new questionnaire. Finally, we telephoned the nonrespondents to ask for their cooperation. A response rate of 56 percent ($N = 158$) reflected a return by fifty-four percent of all law admissions offices ($N = 89$) and 59 percent of all medical school admissions offices ($N = 69$). The appendixes contain a list of schools completing the questionnaires, a copy of the questionnaire itself, and details on the representativeness of the responding schools.[2]

Media and Professional Organizational Coverage of the Decision

As a headline story, the *Bakke* decision was reported widely in the media over several years. For example, in 1978, the year of the decision, the *New York Times* had fifty-two stories on the *Bakke* case. The *Times* had even more *Bakke* stories the previous year, when the index showed fifty-nine entries. That year, an alert *Times* reader could have read one *Bakke* story every six days. Even a not-so-alert reader would have been hard pressed to avoid the story. Though the follow-up coverage of the story was much less frequent after 1978 (only a handful of stories appeared in 1979), analysts of higher education continued to talk about the decision.

The awareness of the decision by higher education faculty and administrators was surely reinforced by the attention given to *Bakke* in the *Chronicle of Higher Education,* the weekly newspaper devoted to higher education. The *Chronicle* first took notice of *Bakke* in September 1976 with a full-page story on the California Supreme Court's decision in the case (26 September 1976, 3). From that time until the Supreme Court's decision, there were twenty-four more articles following the case as it became a focus of advocacy groups and legal opinions. On July 3, 1978, the first issue after the Supreme Court's decision, the *Chronicle* featured the story, entitling its page one coverage "In *Bakke*'s Victory No Death Knell for Affirmative Action." The complete texts of the Powell, Brennan, and Stevens opinions were printed in that issue, and the remainder of the opinions appeared in the next issue. Both issues also featured extensive commentary and reactions from both legal analysts and advocacy groups.

By July 10, the *Chronicle* reported that conferences, committees, and reports within the higher education community were forming to develop implementation plans for the decision. After July 10, the attention to the decision declined, but during the remainder of 1978 and through 1979, *Bakke* remained the subject of occasional reporting in the *Chronicle.*

Thus, in addition to the general publicity throughout the country, *Bakke* attracted focused attention in the higher education community. There were debates and demonstrations at many schools. There were also more specific notices, through academic conferences and specialized publications, directed toward school officials. For example, the American Council on Education and the Association of American Law Schools distributed a report (McCormack 1978), and the College Board sponsored a series of seminars for admissions officials (Holloway 1978).

The numerous lawyers writing the reports or participating in the seminars were in substantial agreement. The "basic conclusion" of the report was that "the Supreme Court has recognized the authority of institutions of higher education to continue under certain circumstances their affirmative action programs" (McCormack 1978, v). The lawyers emphasized Powell's endorsement of the Harvard plan, although one concluded, "The difference between the Harvard and Davis models may be easier to state than to apply" (McCormack 1978, 35), and another suggested that the difference is "nothing more than a smirk and a wink" (Fitt 1978, 6). Nevertheless, the lawyers cautioned that schools should emulate features of the Harvard plan: They should not have quotas or set-asides. They should not have separate committees or procedures to evaluate minority and nonminority candidates, as Davis had. And they should articulate their policies, including their goal of diversity. Yet they were cautioned not to adopt more explicit policies than necessary because these might open them "more readily to unwelcome external monitoring . . . than is at first discernible" (McCormack 1978, 25).

The question of numbers, of course, arose. "It is difficult to see how an admissions officer or committee," the report noted, "can exercise any degree of preference in a race-conscious program without some notion of how many minority applicants are desired in the final mix of the student body" (McCormack 1978, 33). The lawyers advised that a "numerically stated range of expected minority admittees" or a "fluid goal" might be acceptable (17–18, 33). Even quotas might be acceptable if the school received authority from the legislature, based on findings of past discrimination, or perhaps if the school were in a state that had a segregated educational system (28–29).

When participants at the seminars stated that a genuine, broad consideration of diversity, as envisioned in the Harvard plan, might be too time-consuming for many schools, a team of admissions officials from seven schools, including a medical college, generated ideas for these schools to use instead (Holloway 1978, 30–31). The dean of one law school urged that officials be "creative," and other panelists advised them to be "flexible and innovative" in their efforts to admit minorities without employing quotas (16, 19).

Schools could follow such advice, the lawyers said, because the Court would allow them "extremely broad discretion" in adopting and implementing their policies (McCormack 1978, 21). Although institutions generally receive less discretion for decisions based on race, "The courts have a long history of deferring to the judgments of an administrative officer so long as the officer's decision is within the range of discretion vested in his or her office" (McCormack 1978, 22). The dean of one law school went so far as to say that the Court probably was imprecise on purpose in order to allow institutions discretion (Holloway 1978, 11).

While Brennan's opinion was referred to, though not as often as Powell's, Stevens's opinion was barely mentioned. Schools were advised to read it narrowly because the use of race as a positive factor was not explicitly addressed. "Not one justice," the report pointed out, "stated that race may never be taken into account in the admissions process" (McCormack 1978, 10, 17).

A newspaper reporter who attended one of the seminars summarized the prevailing attitude by observing that "what was obvious and encouraging was how hard the admissions officers, the lawyers, and the university officials seemed to be working toward the end of increasing minority representation in colleges, despite the confusion over means" (Holloway 1978, 36).

In addition to these specialized reports and seminars, schools received detailed information about the *Bakke* ruling through the annual meetings of the Association of American Law Schools (AALS) and the Association of American Medical Colleges (AAMC). The annual meetings served as forums for plenary sessions, with individuals giving speeches; panel sessions, with individuals presenting papers or offering comments; and committee sessions, with members preparing reports directed to the rest of the association.

Reactions by the Legal Education Community

From 1974 through 1981, the AALS scheduled one or two plenary or panel sessions every year, except 1975. In 1974, there was a panel on the *DeFunis* case and its implications. There was also a workshop examining minority students' performance on the LSAT and schools' special programs to admit these students. In 1974, participants could attend a panel focusing on both *DeFunis* and *Bakke,* and in 1977 another panel just on *Bakke.*[3] That case was the focus of two plenary sessions in 1979, one on a "constitutional analysis" and the other on an "operational analysis" of the ruling. The latter apparently addressed ways to comply with the restrictions imposed on schools. In 1980 and 1981 there were additional panels on minority admission and retention.

During these years there were also reports by various committees of the association. In 1974, the Special Committee on Admission Standards, reflecting on *DeFunis,* expressed concern that minority admissions programs might be eliminated or diminished to avoid attack in court. The report offered advice for the schools that chose to maintain their programs. The Section on Minority Groups also addressed the *DeFunis* case and paraphrased the director of admissions at Harvard, noting that although people assume that admissions are determined purely by grades and test scores, "there is not a law school admissions committee in American [*sic*] that has ever adhered to this principle (AALS 1974, pt. 1, 118). In 1976, the Section on Minority Groups mentioned *Bakke* and noted the apparent "retrenchment" in minority admissions programs (AALS 1976, pt. 1, 87).

In short, during these years there was a great deal of discussion and concern about the courts' rulings and the schools' programs.[4] The speakers at the plenary or panel sessions and the members of the committees that addressed these matters represented over twenty different law schools.[5] We can certainly assume that the audience and readership of the reports contained faculty from many more schools. Thus, law school faculty were well informed, and continually reminded, about *Bakke* during these formative years for special admissions programs.

Reactions by the Medical Education Community

Medical faculty too were kept abreast of developments in special admissions programs. Though not as extensive as the AALS (after all, the AAMC's focus was medicine, not law), participants at national meetings and contributors to the national journals offered considerable information on *Bakke* and on minorities in medicine more generally.

As we have seen, AAMC's involvement began in 1968 at its annual meeting, and attention at its annual meeting continued. The 1977 AAMC annual meeting program included a "Minority Affairs Program," featuring a keynote address on "Minorities in Medicine: From Receptive Passivity to Positive Action 1966–1976" (AAMC 1978b). The keynoter was introduced by the president of the AAMC, suggesting the importance of the talk.

The *Journal of Medical Education* published a special symposium in August 1978 (published after the *Bakke* decision but written before it), featuring articles on the equal opportunity programs in American medical schools (Wellington and Montero 1978), a survey of graduates of Howard University's College of Medicine (Lloyd, Johnson, and Mann 1978), recruitment and retention programs for minority and disadvantaged students (Beck et al. 1978), and other related topics. The issue also featured an editorial on minorities in medical school (Prieto 1978). The editorial noted that prior to 1968, predominantly white medical schools made no effort to train African Americans, Native Americans, Mexican Americans, and other minority groups. Noting the growth in the previous decade of special-opportunity programs, Prieto commented, "It could well be that the pivotal point between the continuation or retrenchment of affirmative action programs will depend on the decision of the U.S. Supreme Court in *Bakke v. the Regents of the University of California*" (1978, 694).

An AAMC news release on the *Bakke* decision, issued immediately after the decision, contained a lengthy statement by John A. D. Cooper, M.D., the president of the group. In a sophisticated analysis, also appearing in the September issue of the *Journal of Medical Education,* Cooper (1978, 776–77) reported that the Supreme Court had "put its imprimatur on affirmative action programs." Now, he declared, medical school admissions committees must find an appropriate weight for race among the many other criteria they use in admitting students. Each school will find a different weight, he noted, and these might even change from year to year to meet changing needs of society and medicine.

Cooper went on to say that "since most of the medical schools are using admissions procedures which we feel fall within the views of the court, we see little effect of the court's ruling on the schools' affirmative action programs. As a matter of fact, the court's decision that race may be used as a factor in admissions removes some past uncertainties and should stimulate efforts to increase the admission of underrepresented minorities" (1978, 776). In the remainder of the article, Cooper explained the complex set of conflicting opinions offered by the Court.

Besides the press release, the AAMC sent a lengthy memo (1978, 78–41) to its members a few days after the decision. In addition to the same analysis just described, and a statement that the decision, by removing a cloud of uncertainty, should help schools "continue or expand their efforts" to increase the number of underrepresented minorities in their classes, the memo contained a set of fourteen questions and answers to help admissions officers interpret the rules. For example:

> *Question:* Can medical schools give preference to minorities in deciding who to admit to medical school?
>
> *Answer:* Yes. To achieve a diverse student body, race can be used as one factor in the decision process.
>
> *Question:* Can a school still decide how many minority students will be admitted?
>
> *Answer:* Not by establishing a numerical quota which sets aside a specific number of places for which others cannot compete.

Question: Can a school have a specific goal for how many minority students will be admitted?

Answer: A goal, in a limited sense, may be permissible if it does not preclude the evaluation of each applicant on an individual basis, and allows competition for all places by all applicants.

Later that year, *JAMA* (the *Journal of the American Medical Association*) also reported the *Bakke* case to its readers. The author, C. H. Ruhe, the AMA's senior vice president for scientific activities, summarized the case by noting that quota systems are not acceptable, but race or ethnic origin could be used as one criterion in the selection process, thereby giving some preference to minorities in that way. He concluded by indicating that most schools believed that their admissions programs would not be impaired and reporting that the AMA expressed the hope that medical schools would "continue to use those selective admission programs designed to increase the number of minority students" (Ruhe 1978, 2811).

The various councils of the AAMC also discussed the *Bakke* case in their 1978 meetings and reported those discussions in 1979 in the *Journal of Medical Education* (AAMC 1979b). The minutes of the Executive Council reported that the *Bakke* decision upheld affirmative action programs, but not quotas, and that the AAMC had written an amicus curiae brief in the case, urging that special minority admissions programs be declared constitutional. A report from the Committee on National Policy indicated that the AAMC, "along with the education community in general, anxiously awaited the Supreme Court decision [*Bakke*]." Reporting that the Court was "sharply divided," the minutes stated that while the Court approved the use of race as one factor, it also indicated that "any factors used in the selection process must be applied to all applicants and that all applicants must be considered for all places in a class" (AAMC 1979b, 171).

Awareness of the Decision

It is fair to say that professors, deans, and admissions officers at both law and medical schools had ample information about the *Bakke* decision at the time it was handed down and immediately afterward. Given that amount of attention in professional as well as popular media, it is not surprising that eleven years after the decision, fully 97 percent of the medical admissions officers and 99 percent of their law school counter-

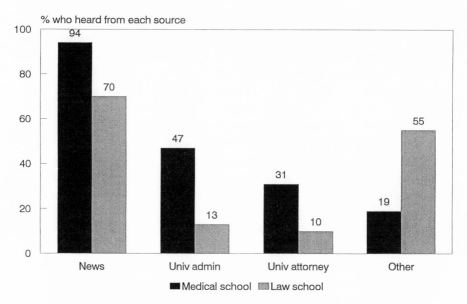

Fig. 3.1.   Source of news about *Bakke*. For medical schools, *N* = 62; for law schools, *N* = 67. (Data from survey questionnaires.)

parts had heard of the decision. (It is probably more surprising that there were a handful who *had not* heard of it!)

Most of the respondents received their initial news of the decision in the same way most people did, through the media (fig. 3.1). Substantial proportions of medical school officials also reported hearing about it from the university administration (47 percent) or the university attorney (31 percent). Law admissions officers were much less likely to report hearing from these official sources (13 percent and 10 percent, respectively). It is possible that university administrators were most alert to *Bakke*'s impact on medical schools since that was the immediate focus of the case. Indeed, one medical school official noted, "It was everywhere: Every meeting I went to, every publication I read, every administrative group that I interacted with." While 19 percent of medical school officials said they heard about it from other sources, considerably more of the law respondents (55 percent) reported hearing about it from other sources. Many law school respondents reported reading the case themselves or reading about it in various American Bar Association or Law School Admission Council publications. As one put it, "This is a law school. We tend to fixate on anything the Supreme Court does."

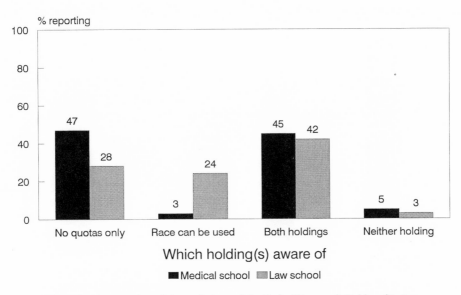

Fig. 3.2. Respondents' knowledge of both holdings of *Bakke*. (Data from survey questionnaires.)

Awareness of the decision does not, however, translate into a precise understanding of its holdings. Indeed, though only 5 percent of the medical officers and 3 percent of the law officers could not give at least a partially accurate summary of the decision, only a minority of each group gave a fully accurate account. We defined a "fully accurate" explanation to include general mention of both the invalidation of quotas and the validation of taking race into account. We defined "partially accurate" to include only one of these two holdings. As figure 3.2 indicates, most respondents reported accurately one or the other of these holdings, but only 42 percent to 45 percent of the two groups named both important parts of the decision. This partial understanding of the decision is undoubtedly due to its ambiguity and to the multiple opinions written. The multiple and seemingly contradictory opinions confused these professionals directly affected by *Bakke* just as they confused the public. Among those perceiving only one of the two elements, medical school officials were much more likely to be aware of the ban on quotas than to be aware that race could be considered a positive factor in admissions decisions. Law school officials, however, were about as likely to perceive the latter as the former.

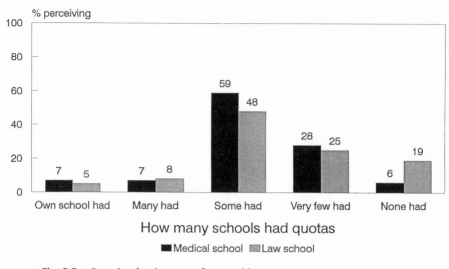

Fig. 3.3. **Perceived existence of pre-*Bakke* quotas. For medical schools, *N* = 61; for law schools, *N* = 65. (Data from survey questionnaires, those who responded to pre-*Bakke* questionnaire.)**

Admissions Policies before *Bakke*

Before we can assess the impact of *Bakke*, it would be useful to know what admissions policies were before that decision. Were quotas for minorities very common? If so, the decision in *Bakke* could have had a far greater impact than if quotas were relatively rare.

To try to estimate the prevalence of quotas, we asked our respondents whether their own school had them and whether they perceived that other schools did. In figure 3.3 we see that the consensus is that some, but not many, schools did have quota systems before *Bakke*.[6] Only a small proportion of the admissions officers reported having a quota in their own school before the *Bakke* decision. Most of our respondents did believe that at least a few schools had quotas. A small proportion of the sample believed that there were "many" schools that had quotas. Over half of the medical officers and nearly half of the law school officers believed that "some" schools had such quotas, while another quarter of each sample thought that "very few" did. The estimate of "very few" would certainly correspond with the 7 percent and 5 percent, respectively, of the medical and law admissions officers who declared that their schools did. If these figures are accurate indicators, then rumors of quotas were a bit more widespread, leading to the modal response of "some" schools having quotas.

The view that relatively few schools had quotas at the time of the decision is consistent with Cooper's (1978) belief that *Bakke* would legitimize existing admissions practices in medical schools rather than force many to drop criteria involving quotas. Cooper apparently believed that not one medical school currently had a quota system for admissions (Middleton 1978, 8). The belief that few institutions had pre-*Bakke* quotas is also consistent with the assessment made by one reporter a week after the *Bakke* decision. He noted that in the years between the time that Bakke filed his suit and the time the Supreme Court ruled on the case, "quotas have all but disappeared" (Middleton 1978, 8). He estimated that "not more than a dozen" institutions still used a system of setting aside a certain number or proportion of places for minorities.

The open-ended comments reflected varied estimates of the presence of quotas and indicate the difficulty of pinpointing what a quota is. One law school respondent said, "The admission officer at a large midwestern state university told me in 1973 that his school took the best 20 black students [who] appl[ied]. I think this policy was typical at the time." Another remarked that "the goal was to have [a student body] proportional to the population of the state . . . for groups that had known serious underrepresentation in the legal profession." But another law respondent declared, "Before *Bakke* was decided most lawyers in the law school admissions process that I know believed a quota was not defendable," and another remarked that they were "rarely able to fill their quotas with qualified students."

Though most officials denied having a quota, many noted that they had goals for minority admissions. And some implied that the line between a "quota" and a "goal" was not always easily visible. As one law admissions officer commented, " 'Quota' would be a bit too strong—perhaps '*de facto* quota.'" Another asked, "Is 'expectancy' a quota?" And a third remarked that they had a "flexible goal." In fact, 35 percent of the medical schools and 23 percent of the law schools surveyed had "goals" in addition to the 7 percent and 5 percent, respectively, that had quotas. Because these questions might be viewed by officials as asking them to admit to an illegal action, we offered the option of checking "It would be inappropriate for me to say" as an alternative to "yes" or "no." Only 2 percent of the medical and law officials checked that category, however.

These data are certainly to be viewed as suggestive, but they are supported by other observations. We believe that these officials would have indicated that past quotas were present if they were. While it is true that officials may not have wanted to admit to practices now viewed as unconstitutional, nor would some want to be in the position of tattling on their own predecessors or on other schools, before the *Bakke* decision quotas were not illegal. And, as we saw in chapter 1, the Association of American Medical Colleges essentially proposed quotas in 1968, and several schools, including the University of California at Davis, publicly admitted having them.

Quotas clearly existed at some time on the part of some schools. They might have been more prevalent on the West Coast than elsewhere. For example, the medical school of the University of Missouri–Kansas City (Calkins and Willoughby 1981) and the law school of New York University (B. Schwartz 1988, 155) apparently gave weight to race without using quotas. And quotas clearly were more prevalent a few years before *Bakke* than at the time of the decision. They may have been instituted on a trial basis as a first way to increase minority enrollments, then later modified or phased out as a reaction to the initial trial in the *Bakke* case (November 1974), to the Supreme Court's refusal to hear the *DeFunis* case (also in 1974), to the growing number of similar legal challenges at the same time, or to the difficulty of administering them.

In sum, though discussion of quotas was rife at the time of *Bakke,* the best estimate that we can make from our survey is that less than 10 percent of these professional schools still had such quotas, though a substantial minority had "goals" at least. These goals may or may not have operated as quotas in practice.

An Evaluation of the *Bakke* Decision

Probably because the ruling appeared to legitimize existing practices rather than force change on most respondents' institutions, most believed the decision was correct (table 3.1). The medical officials (63 percent) were more supportive than the law school ones (51 percent). Of course, some respondents were evaluating the decision on the basis of an incomplete, presumably erroneous, understanding of the decision. Among those who did know both holdings of the decision, the approval rate is somewhat higher, registering almost three-quarters agreement among medical officials (73 percent) and a clear majority among law school officials (60 percent). Some respondents supporting the Supreme Court made positive comments on the quota aspect of the decision: "fixed quotas deny the individual strengths of applicants" and "explicit quotas for minority groups, with separate criteria, are offensive and unconstitutional." Many comments also supported the Court's holding that race can be used as a positive factor in admissions decisions: "Race should be a factor for admission. And each person should be evaluated by a whole range of criteria to provide a diverse group"; "Race or ethnicity, by itself, should not be a sole factor. But diversity in student body, including ethnic diversity, is an important consideration." One defender of the decision remarked, "Before *Bakke* the law was unclear and considerations of race might have been illegal. *Bakke* held decisively that race could be considered."

One critic explained his or her negative reaction by noting that a "confusing array of opinions is not helpful to the public," and another declared that "*Bakke* is a problematical decision in part because of the division of the nine Justices who participated in it." However, most of the negative reactions were to the holding that quotas are unconstitutional. All of the 5 percent of medical school officials who said the decision was not right listed only the quota holding when asked to describe *Bakke*. Among the 6 percent of law school officials who disagreed with the decision, half listed only the quota holding while the other half listed both aspects. Several negative comments indicated unhappiness with outlawing quotas: "In some instances quotas are appropriate remedial devices"; "To remedy the effects of past discrimination may require action which may have an adverse impact on [the] so-called 'majority.'" Another respondent, while recognizing that the Court ruled favorably on the idea that race could be considered, believed that "the decision dampened the enthusiasm for or brought about the demise of some programs

TABLE 3.1. Agreement with the *Bakke* Decision (in percentages)

	Medical	Law
Decision was right	63	51
Decision was partially right	22	31
Unsure if decision was right	11	12
Decision was not right	5	6
Total	101[a]	100

[a]Total exceeds 100 percent due to rounding.

making good faith efforts to expand the range of opportunities for disadvantaged applicants from a variety of backgrounds."

Despite the initial controversy about the decision, it appears that in the decade after it, most officials came to support it, or at least be neutral about it. Without a comparable survey immediately after the decision, we cannot say whether the 1989 opinions represent a change. Since most officials were positive, or at minimum undecided, about the decision, it seems safe to assume that it did not generate lingering negative feelings among these school officials toward the U.S. Supreme Court or toward minorities.

It is certainly possible that those who were initially negative have become more positive, perhaps because they have seen little change from what they were doing in 1978. Most of these officials appeared to perceive that *Bakke* has had minimal impact on admissions policies. Evidence for this perception is found in several items. Officials were asked whether the decision changed their admissions policies at the time and whether it affects their policies today. Almost no one reported a "significant" change in their policies as a result of the decision, though 11 percent of the medical school officials and 17 percent of the law school officials reported that it changed their policies "somewhat" (fig. 3.4). Examples given by respondents of such small changes include one who noted that they are more conscious of what they are doing and another who said their policies are slightly more flexible. One medical official said they ceased using "two lists," one for majority and one for minority applicants, and another said that the *Bakke* decision protected what they were already doing and "thereby encouraged us to do more of it." Yet another said that before the decision, they gave special consideration to disadvantaged students, no matter what their race. After the decision, they became more race oriented: "Racial minorities now have an advantage, whether poor or rich; white majority applicants with disadvantaged backgrounds get no special treatment." Two others, however, indicated their schools made just the opposite change; before *Bakke* they recruited black students, while now they recruit from among all disadvantaged students.

Seventy-seven percent of the medical school officials and 63 percent of the law officials claimed that *Bakke* affected policies "not at all." One said that "we have always upheld affirmative action." (Clearly this respondent had a rather restrictive definition of "always"!) Another reported an affirmative action policy essentially unchanged since 1968.

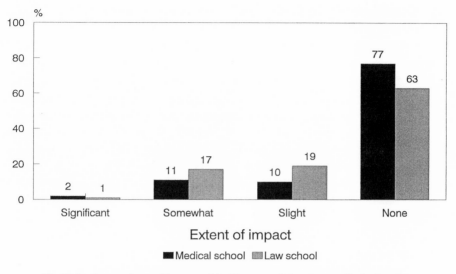

Fig. 3.4.   **Perceptions of impact of *Bakke* on policies. For medical schools, *N* = 63; for law schools, *N* = 84. (Data from survey questionnaires.)**

Thus, only a minority of schools reported that *Bakke* changed rather than reaffirmed their admissions policies.

Just as only a minority of respondents believed that *Bakke* changed their policies when the decision was handed down, so too did only a minority believe that the decision had an impact in 1989, when the survey was done. One fear of those who opposed the decision was that public attention and professional school actions would focus on the Supreme Court's decision outlawing quotas rather than its decision affirming the use of race as a positive factor. If this emphasis were to occur, these detractors believed, eventually efforts to recruit minorities would cease and opportunities for minorities diminish. However, most officials did not believe that that had happened. As shown in figure 3.5, of those who believed that *Bakke* has had a continuing impact, more believed it has worked to increase the admissions of minority students than to limit admissions. This trend is particularly strong among law school respondents; twice as many believed the decision has opened the doors wider than believed it has closed them tighter. Among medical respondents, only slightly more believed that *Bakke* has improved access for minorities than believed it has limited it. Despite these differences, the major message of our data is that most admissions officials believed that *Bakke*

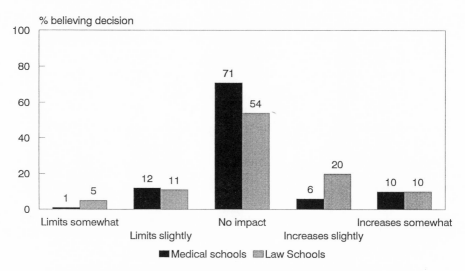

Fig. 3.5. Perceptions whether *Bakke* increases or limits admissions of minority students. For medical schools, *N* = 67; for law schools, *N* = 81. "Increases somewhat" also contains a few "increases significantly." (Data from survey questionnaires.)

legitimized existing practices rather than changed them, and where it did change practices, it improved them.

There is still more evidence that the impact of *Bakke* has been to legitimize rather than change. Respondents were asked whether they took race into account before *Bakke* and whether they "take race into account, as a positive factor, in making decisions today." Figure 3.6 shows that more schools took race into account in a positive way after the decision than before. In most cases the differences are quite small. The safest conclusion is that the decision apparently has not deterred schools from considering race as a positive factor and may even have encouraged them. The message that race could be considered a positive factor clearly has been heard. Being black, Hispanic, or Native American earns students positive credit in the admissions process at most law and medical schools. By 1989, over 95 percent of law and 90 percent of medical schools gave extra consideration to blacks. Ninety-three percent of law schools and 69 percent of medical schools did the same for Hispanics, and 89 percent of law and 77 percent of medical schools did so for Native Americans.[7]

Being an Asian American earns extra consideration at law, but not medical, schools. Most medical schools do not view that ethnic status in

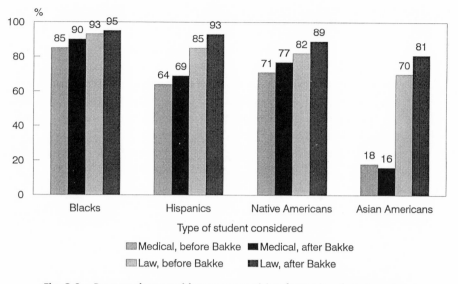

Fig. 3.6. Percent that consider race a positive factor in admissions before and after *Bakke.* For medical schools, *N* = 61 (before) and 68 (after);
for law schools, *N* = 67 (before) and 87 (after). (Data from survey questionnaires.)

the same positive light as they do other minority students. This does not
mean that they discriminate against Asian Americans, though recently
allegations have surfaced that some universities do have enrollment ceil-
ings for these students.[8] It does mean, however, that medical admissions
officers believe that they have enough Asian students to provide diversity
in this particular characteristic. However, an increasing proportion of
law school admissions officers consider Asian ancestry a positive factor
in admissions decisions. Asian applicants to law school are not as common as Asian applicants to medical school, consistent with the fact that
Asian American students outdo their fellow students in math and science
(presumably prerequisites to successful medical school candidacies) but
are about on par in verbal skills (necessary for legal training). Even for
Asian Americans, however, there is no evidence that the *Bakke* decision
lowered their status in the eyes of admissions officers.

Affirmative Action After *Bakke*

Though it outlawed racial quotas, the *Bakke* decision validated affirmative action practices that give some positive weight to the race or eth-

nicity of candidates. This validation gave legitimacy to the efforts of institutions trying to increase the numbers of minorities in higher education generally and professional schools specifically. In this final section of the chapter, we will explore the post-*Bakke* efforts of these schools to recruit minorities in the absence of quotas. And we will describe the extent to which these officials perceive that the federal and state governments and other groups exert pressure on professional schools to increase their minority admissions.

Most universities have affirmative action offices and officers with special responsibilities for diversifying their faculties and student bodies. It appears that most medical schools, but only a minority of law schools, have such offices within their own school. This generalization is based on a question asking respondents whether they had a "particular person or committee, besides the regular admissions committee, designed to identify, encourage, or in other ways have special responsibilities for qualified minorities among your applicants." Table 3.2 reports some of the findings from that question.

Reported efforts range from one person who handles minority recruiting in addition to other duties to staffs of six people whose only job is to recruit and retain minority students. Some schools have an administrative officer in charge of minority recruitment and retention, others have committees to provide advice and oversight, and still other institutions have both. The efforts appear to be on a larger scale in medical schools.

Most of those who described the duties of the minority officer or committee mentioned recruitment. Some described the recruitment efforts in some detail. One described a staff of four to six people who "personally interview minorities, generate recruitment publications [tar-

TABLE 3.2.   Minority Affairs Officers in Medical and Law Schools (in percentages)

	Medical	Law
Have such an office or officer	80	40
Activities engaged in:		
recruitment	51	39
advising minority students	12	14
working with public schools	8	0
sponsoring summer workshops for minority students	7	0
other	13	11

geted to] minorities, meet with those admitted through their special re-cruitment program, see to funding various pre-med and medical school tutorial programs, coordinate with similar efforts in other colleges and departments of the university, serve on the admissions committee and other key committees." Another reported that the special committee on minority admissions "reviews all applications from members of under-represented minority groups and recommends those to be rejected and those to be followed further. At the time of the interview, minority group persons on this committee meet informally with minority applicants. They also do follow up recruitment with accepted applicants." Other efforts are described more generally in terms that probably fit many such activities: "tracks minority applicants for recruitment;" "helps to recruit minority applicants through mailings and selected visits;" "works with admissions committee and greets minority students who are inter-viewed;" "screens all disadvantaged minorities; do[es] interviews, and makes recommendations to admissions committee."

Some medical schools work with undergraduate institutions and even high schools to try to encourage minorities in medical careers (see also Wellington and Montero 1978). Often these programs involve sum-mer workshops or short courses for minority high school or college students. This approach seems less common in law schools, perhaps because there are considerably more minority students enrolled in the social science and humanities disciplines from which law students tend to come than in the scientific disciplines commonly providing the basis for medical study.

Whatever the exact nature of these offices (and we erred by not requesting more specific information about what they do), it is clear that special recruitment and retention efforts for minorities are an institu-tionalized part of the medical school infrastructure. They are less com-mon in law schools but are still a routine feature in the organizational terrain.

The efforts made by these schools are no doubt partly a result of internal pressures to diversify the student body. But they are also un-doubtedly a function of external pressure. Yet, the political climate of the 1980s was not uniformly sympathetic to affirmative action and to im-proving the status of minorities. Certainly the Republican administration was not. In that context, just how much external pressure was there to recruit minority students?

Respondents were asked whether they felt pressure from the federal and state governments "to take race into account in making admissions decisions today." Those who responded that they felt pressure ("slight," "some," or "significant") by the federal government were then asked to check those types of pressure (listed in table 3.3) they felt. Respondents were asked if they felt pressure from any nongovernmental group, "such as, for example, national associations of medical (or law) schools, organized advocacy groups, or other sources."

The most commonly perceived pressure, as table 3.3 indicates, was not from either the federal government or the state government but from other groups. Most respondents felt that the federal government exercised little pressure. One said that "[if these actions] apply to any school, I'd like to know. In my view, the federal government has not been aggressive in pressuring schools to admit minorities." Though a few respondents reported that their university (not their professional school specifically) had been a party to a desegregation suit or was under court order to desegregate, most respondents who perceived federal pressure perceived it in a mild way: through pressure to fill out affirmative action forms and through mass mailings. Few felt pressure directed toward their

TABLE 3.3. **Perceived Pressures from Outside Agencies and Groups (in percentages)**

	Medical Schools	Law Schools
Federal government	16	15
Pressure from:		
forms to fill out	12	17
mass mailings	6	3
individualized letters	2	1
phone calls	3	1
visits	3	2
threats to withhold funds	2	3
threats of legal action	0	3
other actions	8	6
State or local government	23	15
Any group	32	46
Accreditation agencies (volunteered)	24	31

Note: The percentages for federal and state government indicate those feeling "significant" or "some" pressure. Ten percent of the medical admissions officers and 9 percent of the law officials reported "slight" pressure. The rest reported no pressure. Respondents were only asked if they had felt pressure from other groups and given a "yes" or "no" alternative. They were asked to specify which groups. The percentage listed above for accreditation agencies are those respondents who listed that in response to the "which group" question.

school individually, even through phone calls or visits from government officials. Few reported threats to withhold funds or initiate legal actions.

More respondents agree that the state or local governments are putting some pressure on schools. Several took pains to say that they did not interpret this "pressure" in a negative way, viewing it as a source of support rather than as conflict. The sources of pressure from state and local officials and agencies are quite diverse. Several respondents mentioned legislators and governors, state councils of higher education, state scholarship agencies, and the state supreme court. Some mentioned minority legislators in particular, while others mentioned the legislative committees that oversee higher education. One medical school official mentioned the Health and Hospital Oversight Board in his state. A few suggested that their university administration (including the governing board) was a source of pressure to take minority status into account.

A significant minority of officials feel pressure from nongovernmental groups. Accreditation agencies were an important source, and the official associations of medical colleges (Association of American Medical Colleges) and law schools (the Section of Legal Education and Admissions to the Bar and the Law School Admission Council) were mentioned by several. Again, many respondents noted that while professional associations such as the AAMC do remind schools about minority recruitment, their attention to this issue is welcome. Other sources of pressure (and support) named by a sprinkling of respondents included groups such as the state's black lawyers' association, the city's black community, American Indian groups, and unspecified organized advocacy groups within the university.

Overall, however, accreditation groups seem most salient as a source of pressure and support. Indeed, these organizations continue to be active in studying minority recruitment and providing information to individual schools. For example, in 1986, the Law School Admission Council prepared a comprehensive report on minority admission and success, *Law School Admission and Graduation: Minority Student Experiences and Success Rates,* for the Affirmative Action Committee of the Section of Legal Education and Admission to the Bar of the ABA (Law School Admission Council 1986). The report examined the qualifications of minorities admitted to law school and the graduation rates associated with various levels of qualifications. In their regular newsletter, the Law School Admission Council charts trends in minority enrollments. The

AAMC reports applications and acceptances by group in its annual handbook for students considering medical school.

Conclusion

Clearly the *Bakke* decision was salient to medical and law school admissions officers, even eleven years after the decision was rendered. Despite the fact that it was almost universally recognized and that at least one of its two major holdings could be articulated by all but a small minority of officials, its perceived impact was that it reinforced practices which by 1978 had become institutionalized, practices that made minority status a positive factor in admissions. As the president of the AAMC noted, "it removes . . . uncertainties" (Cooper 1978, 776).

Relatively few of these respondents believed the decision significantly changed the way their process operated either in 1978 or in 1989 when the survey was administered. Yet some officials believed that the decision did change the way things were done. While a few believed that it deterred the recruitment and admission of minorities, more believed it has had modestly improved the chances of minority applicants to enter medical and law school.

Though these generalizations apply to both law and medical officials, some differences exist between the two groups. Medical officials focus more on the holding eliminating quotas, while law officers are more knowledgeable than medical ones about the legitimization of the use of race as a positive factor in decisions. Though most law officials, like their medical counterparts, believe that the case did not change existing practices, and about the same proportions believe that the impact was negative, about twice as many law as medical respondents (30 percent compared to 16 percent) believe *Bakke*'s impact was positive. Consistent with that, law officials are more likely than medical ones to indicate that race or ethnicity are considered positive factors in admissions decisions today. The differences between medical and law officials are especially wide for Asians and fairly wide for Hispanics; being Asian is much more likely, and being Hispanic somewhat more likely, to be a positive factor at law than medical schools.

In this chapter we have examined some of the ways that the medical and legal professional organizations conveyed the news of *Bakke* to their members. We have also analyzed admission officials' perceptions of the decision and of change in minority recruitment since the decision. But these aggregated reports do not tell us much about actual trends in minority applications and admissions to law and medical school. Officials thought there has been little change or that minority chances had actually improved. But are these perceptions reflected in actual application and admissions decisions? Nor do these overall perceptions give us any insight into how, if at all, different types of schools differ in their reported experiences with *Bakke* and with minority enrollment trends. For example, were public schools more affected than private, larger more than smaller? It is to these issues we now turn. In chapter 4 we focus on minority applications, and in chapter 5 we move to minority admissions and enrollment.

CHAPTER 4

Bakke and the
Applicant Pool

In this chapter we first turn from the way the *Bakke* decision was perceived by administrative officers to how *Bakke* affected trends in applications to professional schools. Unfortunately, relatively complete temporal data exist only for medical schools, so they will be the focus of the first part of our analyses.[1] In the second part of the chapter we return to our survey data to see how both medical and law school officials assessed the changing quality of the black and Hispanic applicant pools during the 1980s.

Aggregate Trends in Medical School Enrollment

We will first examine aggregate minority applicant trends. The available information begins in 1973, five years before *Bakke,* and ends in 1987. We ended our time-series in 1987 rather than extending it into the 1990s because continuing the time-series blurs the focus on *Bakke.* In the late 1980s, the courts began to waver on the earlier affirmative action precedents; that, along with the myriad other changes in the political and economic climate, made it difficult to isolate the effect of the *Bakke* decision. However, in the final chapter we will bring the enrollment story up-to-date as we discuss how *Bakke* has shaped the contemporary debate over affirmative action.

To determine the impact of *Bakke,* we need to separate the effect of the decision from other trends. Changes in minority enrollment reflect broad economic and political conditions, as well as longer-term trends in the size of the black and Hispanic middle-class population. Beginning in the mid-1970s, improvement in the economic status of African Americans and Hispanics, as well as whites, stalled as the entire economy suffered a shock from the world oil crisis.

Plans for continuing one's education in professional schools can also be affected by changes in federal and other student aid. Such aid also began to shrink in the 1970s. Applications are influenced by the attractiveness of the profession at any given time. Law school applications dipped slightly in the early 1980s but then rose during the rest of the decade. On the other hand, the total number of applicants to medical school peaked at 42,600 in 1974 and plummeted to 28,100 in 1987 (Crowley, Etzel, and Petersen 1987; AAMC 1988). The number of applications dropped further in 1988 before rebounding strongly in the 1990s.

The substantial shift away from interest in medical school in the 1980s is difficult to explain. It may reflect decreasing interest in medicine as a career, possibly because of the changing nature of medical practice in the United States from a relatively unregulated profession to one increasingly regulated by insurers and government alike. However, these regulatory trends have accelerated in the 1990s, and medical school applications have boomed. The drop in applications during the 1980s may have been affected by the economic problems of that decade, which would have made medical school less affordable. In a decade of economic uncertainty, fewer students and their families may have been willing to undertake the kind of indebtedness that most students incur in medical school.[2]

Given this context, how did *Bakke* affect minority applications to professional schools? Simply comparing black and Hispanic applications before and after the decision would fail to take into account trends and cycles in the data that have nothing to do with *Bakke*. What is needed, therefore, is a technique that measures the effects of *Bakke,* independent of these other factors. An appropriate such technique is *interrupted time series* (ITS; cf. Lewis-Beck 1986, 1981; Lewis-Beck and Alford 1980).

The time-series methodology has been used successfully to examine the impact of policies such as the Civil Rights Act of 1964 (McCrone and Hardy 1978; Rice and Whitby 1986), Social Security (Albritton 1979), crackdowns on drunk drivers (Campbell and Ross 1968), and mining safety laws (Lewis-Beck and Alford 1980; Perry 1982), and of major political changes such as the Cuban Revolution (Lewis-Beck 1979, 1981), European integration (Caporaso and Pelowski 1971), and political party realignments (Garand and Gross 1984). These methods are well suited to an examination of the impact of *Bakke,* because they allow us to measure this impact while taking into account other factors that influence longitudinal change in black and Hispanic enrollments.

Data and Methods

We rely on data on aggregate applications published annually since 1973 by the Association of American Medical Colleges.[3] These figures include information on total applications and on those from African Americans, Puerto Ricans, Mexican Americans, other Hispanics, and American Indians. The major aggregate dependent variables we examine here are the number of black and Hispanic applicants to medical school each year from 1973 to 1987 (AAMC various years). Because of incomplete time-series data on "other" Hispanics, all the medical school data include only Mexican Americans and mainland Puerto Ricans attending mainland medical schools.[4] Because the decision was announced in April 1978, too late to affect applications and admission decisions for the class of 1978, our analysis treats the applicants of 1978 as pre-*Bakke*, those of 1979 as post-*Bakke*.

The technical details of our time-series analysis are included in appendix 2. Our analysis takes into account not only the impact of the decision, but also other important factors that we expect to influence the "supply" of minority students and the "demand" for them. We believed that the supply would be greater, thus black and Hispanic applications would be higher, when there was more financial aid available to help low-income students, since many potential black and Hispanic students would need such funds. Complete financial aid data were not available,[5] so we used the amount of federal student aid adjusted for changes in the consumer price index. We also controlled for the overall number of applicants to medical school in order to take into account the shifts in career preferences by young adults that presumably would affect minority students as well as others. Median black and Hispanic family income were initially included in the equations, but they did not improve predictions we could make from the model and caused substantial multicollinearity problems. These variables were deleted.

We conceptualized "demand" as the general societal interest in increasing the opportunities offered minorities, or at least not limiting these opportunities. We attempted to operationalize that by using budget figures for the Office of Civil Rights to assess federal resources supporting increased opportunities for minorities. When doing so proved impossible,[6] we measured demand more crudely with a dummy variable representing the Reagan administration (where the years between 1981 and

1987 were coded 1, other years were coded 0). Such coding taps the lack of enthusiasm of the Reagan administration in promoting affirmative action and in setting a climate conducive to the advancement of minorities. If these professional schools carried out minority recruitment and affirmative action policies in part because of perceived federal pressure, that pressure surely would be perceived as less in the Reagan years (Woods 1991).

In sum, we are testing our expectations that the *Bakke* decision affected longitudinal trends in minority applications to medical and professional school. But we also believe that these "supply" and "demand" measures will improve our ability to predict minority enrollments.

Findings

Figure 4.1 charts the changes in the actual and predicted numbers of black and Hispanic applicants to medical school. The predicted numbers are those derived from our time-series equations 4.1 and 4.2:

$$\text{Number of black} = 1190 + 83x_t + 145x_d - 119x_p \quad (4.1)$$
$$\text{applicants} \quad (1.42) \quad (3.25) \quad (2.17) \quad (-6.45)$$

$$+ 111^*\text{Reagan} + .005^*\text{fedaid} + 22^*\text{total} + e$$
$$(1.70) \quad (.11) \quad (2.26)$$

$R^2 = .95$; $N = 15$; DW = 1.89, corrected for first-order autocorrelation

$$\text{Number of} = -660 + 52x_t + 54x_d - 54x_p \quad (4.2)$$
$$\text{Hispanic applicants} \quad (-3.25) \quad (4.41) \quad (-1.82) \quad (-3.12)$$

$$+ 26^*\text{Reagan} + .0224^*\text{aid} + 26^*\text{total} + e$$
$$(.93) \quad (1.11) \quad (5.74)$$

$R^2 = .97$; $N = 15$; DW = 2.17, corrected for first-order autocorrelation

Figures in parentheses are t values. x_t = trend variable indicating the pre-*Bakke* slope; x_d = the pre-post dummy indicating the change in the level of the time series after *Bakke*; and x_p = the post-intervention trend

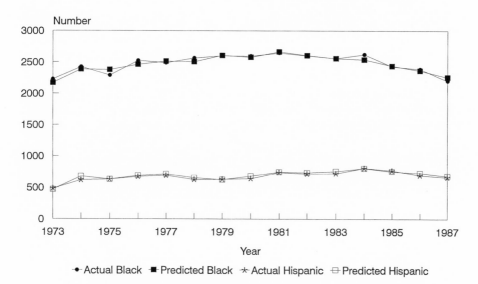

Fig. 4.1.   Black and Hispanic applications to medical school. (Data from AAMC, 1973–87.)

variable, indicating the increment or decrement to the slope of the pre-*Bakke* time-series. Aid = amount of federal student aid; total = total number of applicants to medical school.

When the predicted line approximates the actual trend, the equation is said to have a good fit with the data, which means that one or all of the variables accurately predict the trends. When the predicted values do not closely follow the actual ones, the equation is said to fit poorly. A poorly fitting equation means that the variables in that equation—in this case, the variables indicating the pre- and post-*Bakke* trend, the Reagan administration, federal financial aid, and overall applications—do not describe or predict very well the actual application trends. A poorly fitting equation, therefore, means that other variables are needed to explain the trends.

The most striking feature of the trends is how small the actual numbers and how flat the lines are. That is, the changes in numbers of black and Hispanic applicants were relatively slight during this time. In 1973 the number of black applicants was 2,227 and in 1987 was 2,203. Nonetheless, some modest patterns can be outlined. The numbers peaked in 1981 at 2,644, peaked again in 1984, and after that fell by 16 percent.

Hispanic applications rose marginally until 1977, when they reached 690, then fell in 1978. The biggest jump occurred two years after *Bakke.* Applications reached a peak of 808 in 1984 and, like black applications, have declined each year since then.

Table 4.1 summarizes these findings. The basic time-series model for blacks indicates a significant upward trend in black applicants before *Bakke* of about 83 applicants annually, a significant positive short-term effect, but a small though significant negative post-*Bakke* decline. Netting the 119 annual decline and the 83 annual increase yields a change after *Bakke* of about 36 students per year. These effects persist even though we control for the total number of medical school applicants in order to take into account the overall downward trends in medical school applications. Even though the number of total applicants was significantly related to the trend in black enrollment (each overall increase of 1,000 applicants was associated with an increase of 22 black applicants), the post-*Bakke* trend variable remained significantly negative but tiny. Neither the Reagan dummy variable nor the amount of federal aid was related significantly to black applications. Indeed, contrary to predictions, the Reagan administration variable is in the positive direction.

We also can predict the trends in Hispanic applicants extremely well (table 4.1). Like black applications, Hispanic applications rise and fall with overall applications (each gain in 1,000 total applicants increased the number of Hispanic applicants by about 26), but even so it appears that *Bakke* slowed the upward trend in Hispanic applications. However, as is the case with blacks, the actual decline in applicants began in 1985 (see fig. 4.1), undoubtedly too late to be directly affected by *Bakke.* Again, neither the federal aid nor Reagan administration variable is sig-

TABLE 4.1.   **Predicting the Number of Black and Hispanic Applicants,[a] 1973–87**

	Black	Hispanic
Increase in number of ( ) applicants per year, pre-*Bakke*	83[a]	52[a]
Short-term change in ( ) applicants	145[a]	−54
Change in number of ( ) applicants per year, after *Bakke*	−37	−2
Reagan administration increment	111	26
Increase in ( ) applicants per $1 million student aid	.005	.0224
Increase per 1,000 total applicants	22[a]	26[a]

Note: (   ) indicates black or Hispanic

[a]Coefficient significant at .05 level. This indicator is suggestive only, since this is a universe rather than a sample.

nificant, though the aid coefficient is large enough to indicate that it is probably positively related to Hispanic applications for medical school.[7]

Our models do an excellent job accounting for the ebb and flow in the number of black and Hispanic applicants to medical school. The R^2s of .95 and .97, respectively, give us confidence that our conclusions about the effect of *Bakke* are reasonable ones. Without controls for the Reagan era, student aid, and total applications, the explanatory power of the equations for both black and Hispanic applicants drops significantly, to .72 for blacks and to .44 for Hispanics. The variable indicating the total number of applicants to medical school accounts for most of this increased explanatory power. Thus, black and Hispanic applicants appear to be affected by the same forces that influence the decision of non-minority applicants to attend medical school. But other factors also influence the choices of black and Hispanic students.

These aggregate data show, then, that *Bakke* has had a very limited impact on the application of blacks and Hispanics to medical schools. In the years immediately before *Bakke,* the impetus for recruiting minorities stemming from the success of the civil rights movement, and from the attempts by medical schools in the late 1960s to recruit more African Americans, appears to have slowed, notwithstanding new affirmative action requirements put in place by the Nixon administration. Following only small and erratic increases in Hispanic and black applications throughout the 1970s and early 1980s, applications declined between 1981 and 1983, jumped in 1984, and then declined again after then. These decreases did not occur at the time of *Bakke,* but several years later. Thus, it is hard to be confident that these changes stem directly from the decision.

In the 1980s, the early stability in black and Hispanic medical school applications and their slow decline beginning in 1984 may in part reflect the very success of the civil rights movement in opening up other opportunities, including business careers, for college-educated minorities. More importantly, however, it reflected the declining college enrollments of African Americans throughout higher education ("Vital Signs" 1995). The proportion of black males enrolled in college actually fell between 1980 and 1988.[8] The decline in black undergraduate enrollments was a partial result of economic difficulties; it had a direct effect on the available pool of applicants for professional schools. The decline in applications by minorities parallels the general downward trends in applications to medical school by non-Hispanic white students and is also linked to the increasing costs of education and cutbacks in student aid (cf. Jolly, Taskel, and Beran 1987; Rich 1987).

These aggregate data give an overview of trends in minority applications. But there is considerably more to learn. These data ignore law school applications, a major focus of our attention. And the data say nothing about the quality of the applicant pool. Nor have we yet learned anything about the effectiveness of devices these schools use to attract minority applicants or the impact of external pressures.

To examine these issues, we turn back to our survey data. We focus on responses to our query about the respondents' perceptions of both the quantity and the quality of black and Hispanic men and women applicants.

Perceptions of the Black and Hispanic Applicant Pools

Medical Schools

Our national data indicate that a downward trend occurred in the mid-1980s in both Hispanic and black applications to medical schools, following several years of relative stability. In this section we see how these data square with admissions officials' perceptions of changes in the applicant pool during the decade from 1979 to 1989 (when the survey was administered). We were interested in the assessments of the admissions officers of the *quality* as well as the *quantity* of black and Hispanic applicants.[9] These assessments are mostly useful for understanding the ways in which admissions officers view the applicant pool. If the assessments conflict with the aggregate data, it does not mean that the assessments are erroneous. Applicants could have increased the average number of applications they submit, for example, thus generating more *applications* even when the number of *applicants* decreased. Or some schools could have had an increased number of applications in the face of an overall decline. We will explore differences between the types of schools experiencing rising numbers of black and Hispanic applications and those suffering declining numbers.

The first part of table 4.2 shows the perceived changes in the quantity of each of the six ethnic-gender groups. The decline in black applicants was not clearly perceived by the medical school admissions officers. Although a near majority believed that the number of black male applicants had decreased, almost one-third reported that the number had increased. And many more believed that the number of black female applicants was increasing than believed the number was decreasing.

The decline in the number of black male applicants relative to black females is consistent with trends in undergraduate enrollment, too. While the number of black women enrolled in college has exceeded the number of black men at least since 1960, this gap has been growing so that by 1987, the number of black women enrolled was over 30 percent higher than the number of black men (U.S. Department of Commerce 1989, table 245). Data on sex ratios in professional schools are less systematic, but evidence from law schools shows that in 1981, black female applicants outnumbered black male applicants for the first time and that the gap between the sexes grew between 1981 and 1986 (Law School Admission Council 1987).

The picture is somewhat different in terms of perceptions of Hispanic enrollment. By ratios of two to one and three to one, more officials believed the quantity of Hispanic male and female applications was increasing than decreasing. Though this finding seems to contradict the aggregate numbers, it could be that each Hispanic applicant applied to more schools, or that officials were comparing their current rate of Hispanic applicants with a more distant past when such applicants were extremely rare.

The most consensus exists with respect to white male applicants. Over three-quarters of the admissions officers perceived accurately the

TABLE 4.2. Perceptions of Changes in Applicants to Medical School from 1979 to 1989 (in percentages)

	Black		Hispanic		White	
	Men	Women	Men	Women	Men	Women
			Quantity			
Increased	31	55	39	45	3	47
Same	25	23	46	40	21	19
Decreased	45	22	15	15	76	34
			Quality			
Increased	51	60	41	38	16	29
Same	38	32	53	56	60	55
Decreased	12	8	7	7	24	16

Note: N's range from 61 to 65. Data based on admissions officers' response to survey question.

drop in white male applicants. This drop accounted for a large part of the overall decrease in applications to medical schools. Perceptions were mixed as to enrollment trends among white women, though more saw an increase than a decrease in applications.

In general, then, admissions officers most acutely perceived a drop in white male applications. But the officers were more likely than not to see increases in every other racial-gender group except for black men. Even for that group, however, admissions officers at some schools believed that the applicant pool had increased.

Medical school admissions officers believed the *quality* of the minority applicant pool was increasing relative to whites. Most admissions officials believed that the quality of white male applicants had stayed the same or even decreased, but most also thought that the quality of every other group had stayed the same or increased. Indeed, admissions officials were most likely to say the quality of applicants among black women and black men had increased, followed by Hispanic men and women. Admissions officials were divided in their appraisal of changes in the quality of white women who applied, but almost twice as many reported that quality had increased than had decreased.

Thus, the perceptions on the part of medical school officials about the nature of the minority applicant pool were not quite as bleak as the aggregate statistics would suggest. Most agreed that the quantity of black male applicants was lower, but officials did not perceive declines in applications from other minority groups. Moreover, the perceptions of the shrinking pool of black men was that the quality was increasing, a factor which, if accurate, could somewhat offset the declining numbers. And the quality of black women and Hispanic applicants also was perceived to be increasing. Perceptions were mixed as to whether the increasing quantity of white female applicants has been matched by increasing quality.

Law Schools

Although we do not have data showing longitudinal trends in law school applications before 1980, we do know that the number of applications dipped between 1982 and 1984 before increasing again (Prelaw Adviser 1987; Law Services Report 1994). During this same period, Hispanic applications increased steadily while those of African Americans stayed at a fairly constant level. Overall, then, law school admissions officers were not facing the same specter of shrinking applications and enrollments as their medical school colleagues.

Thus, it is not surprising that a majority of law admissions officials perceived increases in the quantity of applicants from every group, ranging from around 80 percent who believed there had been an increase in women of black, Hispanic, and non-Hispanic white background to 57 percent who believed that the number of black male applicants had increased (table 4.3). Only for perceptions of black male applicants was there a significant minority of officials (21 percent) who perceived a decrease in the quantity. Thus, the applicant pool of potential law students was becoming, in the eyes of most admissions officials, larger and more racially and ethnically heterogeneous.

Increases in quantity were accompanied by perceived increases in quality. Between 69 percent and 80 percent of these law school admissions officers perceived increased quality of women applicants of all three ethnic groups. Only a very small minority (ranging from 3 percent for Hispanic women to 6 percent for white women) perceived declining quality. A very large majority of officials (65 percent to 68 percent) also believed the male applicant pool had increased in quality. As with the quality of the pool of women candidates, almost no one (4 percent to 7 percent for the three male applicant groups) perceived that the quality of these applicants had decreased. Thus, these law school admissions offi-

TABLE 4.3.   Perceptions of Changes in Applicants to Law School from 1979 to 1989 (in percentages)

	Black		Hispanic		White	
	Men	Women	Men	Women	Men	Women
			Quantity			
Increased	57	79	79	80	61	81
Same	22	11	18	17	29	14
Decreased	21	11	4	2	11	5
			Quality			
Increased	68	80	68	69	65	73
Same	25	16	29	29	30	21
Decreased	7	4	4	3	5	6

Note: N's range from 80 to 86. Data based on admissions officers' response to survey questionnaire.

cers saw progress in achieving a high-quality pool of ethnically heterogeneous applicants.

The survey data, then, largely confirm the findings from the aggregate data from medical schools that the *Bakke* decision itself had little, if
any, negative impact on the pool of applicants from the black and Hispanic communities. Generally, admissions officials perceived black and
Hispanic applicant pools that had increased in numbers and in quality.
However, the declining number of black applicants to medical school
shown in the aggregate data was reflected in the perception on the part of
nearly half the medical school admissions officers that the quantity,
though not the quality, of applications from black men had decreased
(though it is interesting to note that over 30 percent knew or believed the
number of applications from black men to their school had increased).
The perceived decrease in the number of black male applicants is also
consistent with the more general observations that younger black women
had been moving ahead faster in obtaining educations than had younger
black men. However, the perceived decline in black male applications
was accompanied by an even more unanimous perception that white
male applications had also decreased.

Explaining Perceptions of Changing Patterns of Applications

Tables 4.2 and 4.3 indicate that there are differences among admissions
officials in their perceptions of changing application patterns for most of
the six applicant groups. Sometimes these differences were fairly small,
such as the agreement among most that there are increasing numbers of
black and Hispanic female law school applicants. Sometimes the differences are fairly striking, as when significant numbers of medical admissions officers report increases in black applicants, while others report
decreases.

Though some of these differences may simply be the way admissions
officers remembered and perceived changes, other differences may reflect
real variation in their experiences. Some schools experienced increases in
applications while others experienced decreases. In this section we will
use regression analysis to examine some of the factors that appear to be
associated with increasing applications from minorities. We are particularly interested in whether actions taken by universities to increase minority applications were related to perceived increases.

As we discussed in chapter 3, schools vary considerably in the efforts they make to recruit minorities. Here we will look at the success of these efforts. Schools that have these institutionalized mechanisms in place may be more successful in attracting minority applicants. Because we do not have detailed information, we have created one variable and coded it 1 if the respondent answered that his or her school had an officer or committee involved in minority recruitment, admission, or retention, and 0 if the school did not have such an officer or committee.

We are also interested in the impact of perceived outside pressures on minority recruitment. Do schools whose officers perceive they are under pressure from external sources recruit more successfully? As we saw in the previous chapter, significant numbers reported that they were under such pressure from either government or private groups. While such pressure might not directly affect the applicant pool, it might reflect demand for admission, and it might have encouraged schools to make more efforts to recruit applicants as well as to examine their admissions policies. On the other hand, however, negative relationships between applicant quality and quantity and external pressure might simply mean that pressure is applied most vigorously when results have been lacking.

To determine the effects on increasing applications of the university itself and of the external pressure, we need to look at changes in light of other factors that could influence minority applications, such as charac-teristics of the schools' locales. We expect schools located in areas of sizable minority populations to have increased their minority applicant pool. Most students (86 percent) attend school in their own state ("Stu-dents" 1987), and we would expect this pattern to be at least as true of minority as other students. Thus, we examine the black and Hispanic population of the state.

A second set of possible predictors includes characteristics of the medical or law school itself, such as its enrollment, whether it is public or private, and the number of black or Hispanic students attending before *Bakke*. Larger schools may have more resources to use to attract minor-ity applicants; public schools may face more pressure to do so. We cate-gorized public schools as either the major state university (such as the University of Michigan or the University of Illinois) or other state schools (such as Wayne State or Southern Illinois). We reasoned that the less prestigious public schools might have fewer resources to spend in recruit-ing minority students and providing them with financial aid. Schools that had enrolled many black or Hispanic students before *Bakke* might find it easier than others to build on that success.

We created new variables reflecting officials' perceptions of the quantity and of the quality of applicants. One is a scale aggregating perceptions of increasing numbers of black male and female applicants. Another aggregates perceptions of increasing numbers of Hispanic male and female applicants. The scales range from 0, when the respondent believed that the quantity of both black (or Hispanic) men and women applicants had decreased, to 4, when the respondent perceived that both had increased. A value of 1 indicated that the respondent believed that the quantity of one group had decreased while the other stayed the same; the midpoint value, 2, reflected either that both had stayed the same or that one increased while the other decreased; a value of 3 indicated that the quantity of one group had increased while the other stayed the same. We created similar scales with similar meanings to the values for the perceptions of quality of applicants. Overall, then, four new variables were created, two for blacks and two for Hispanics.

Medical Schools

In tables 4.4 and 4.5 we examine the combined impact of the predictor variables on perceptions of black and Hispanic applications for medical schools. Table 4.4 indicates that perceptions of the *quantity* of black applicants to medical school are only modestly related to our predictors. Only two stand out as having a positive effect. Having an officer or committee to work on minority recruitment, admissions, or retention is positively associated with perceiving more black applicants. It appears that devoting resources and organizational efforts to minority recruitment can pay off. The relationship between the presence of a minority officer and the perceived *quality* of black applicants is also positive, falling just short of the levels necessary to achieve statistical significance at the .05 level.

The second variable significantly related to an increasing quantity of black medical school applicants is pressure from private groups, such as the national association of medical schools (AAMC), organizations of black doctors, black interest groups of other sorts, civil rights groups, and the press. Those officials reporting such pressure also report an increased black applicant pool. The impact of pressure from other external agencies is mixed. The perception of pressure from the federal government is positively associated with the perception of more black applicants, though the relationship falls somewhat short of statistical signif-

TABLE 4.4. Predictors of Perceptions of Change in the Black and Hispanic Applicant Pool for Medical Schools

	Blacks				Hispanics			
	Quantity		Quality		Quantity		Quality	
	b	t	b	t	b	t	b	t
% black in state population	.03	1.32	−.02	−1.05	−.03	−2.29*	.00	.26
% Hispanic in state population	.01	.23	.06	1.78*	.05	1.84*	−.02	−.56
Total enrollment	−.00	−1.22	−.00	−.87	.00	1.05	.00	.54
Major state university	.25	.48	−1.10	−2.92*	−.88	−2.20*	.37	.84
Other state universities	.71	1.20	−.12	−.26	.20	.41	−.20	−.33
Pressure from:								
Federal government	.39	1.55	.58	2.91*	.28	1.43	.08	.33
State government	−.17	−.71	−.63	−3.23*	−.42	−2.25	.18	.78
Private groups	1.14	1.66*	.49	.91	.07	.12	.58	.85
Accreditation	−.38	−.78	−1.62	−1.63	−.57	−.50	.25	.52
Minority affairs officer	1.08	2.02*	.69	1.63	.58	1.49	.24	.49
Constant	1.14		3.40		2.66		1.35	
R^2	.24		.34		.31		.10	
Adjusted R^2	.07		.20		.15		.00	

Note: $N = 57$ (for the black analysis) and 56 (for the Hispanic analysis). Coefficients significant at the .05 level are shown in boldface.

*Indicates significance at the .05 level.

TABLE 4.5. Predictors of Perceptions of Change in the Black and Hispanic Applicant Pool for Law Schools

	Blacks				Hispanics			
	Quantity		Quality		Quantity		Quality	
	b	t	b	t	b	t	b	t
% black in state population	.00	.83	.73	.00	.62	-.00	-.60	-.00
% Hispanic in state population	-.00	-.02	.01	1.16	.00	.12	.01	.76
Total enrollment	-.00	-.03	-.00	-.02	.03	1.47	**.04**	**1.70***
Major state university	-.52	-1.25	-.05	-.18	-.39	-1.40	-.04	-.12
Other state universities	.28	.59	.04	.12	.15	.45	.29	.76
Pressure from:								
Federal government	-.15	-.49	.27	1.16	-.28	-1.37	.06	.25
State government	-.10	-.28	-.34	-1.35	.12	.48	-.10	-.36
Private groups	.33	.62	-.30	-.74	.46	1.18	.19	.43
Accreditation	-.07	-.16	.66	1.59	.26	.99	-.15	-.47
Minority affairs officer	.27	.79	**.54**	**2.11***	.06	.25	.41	1.52
Constant	2.95		2.71		3.35		2.95	
R^2	.10		.17		.16		.11	
Adjusted R^2	.00		.04		.03		.00	
N	75		75		74		74	

Note: Those coefficients that are significant are indicated in boldface.
*Indicates significance at the .05 level.

icance. Pressures from state agencies and accreditation groups are negatively related, but in a minuscule way.

Neither the percentage black in the state, the percentage Hispanic in the state, the size of the school, nor the public or private control of the university had a significant impact on perceived numbers of black applicants.

We also examined the impact of existing minority enrollments and regional location on this, and the other, dependent variables. However, multicollinearity among those variables and the proportion black or Latino in the state forced us to drop the minority enrollment and regional variables. Minority enrollment proportions are highly related to the proportions of minorities in the state: the southern region is highly related to the proportion of blacks in the state, while the Southwest variable is strongly related to the proportion of Hispanics in the state. Removing these variables hardly reduces the R^2 and does make the coefficients for the remaining variables much more interpretable.

Perceived increases in the *quality* of black applicants to medical school are somewhat more predictable than perceptions of increased *quantity*. Some of the significant relationships are in the expected direction. Perceived federal pressure is positively related (this time significantly) with perceived improvements in the quality of the black applicant pools. The presence of an officer or committee charged with minority recruitment and tracking of minority applicants is positively related, slightly short of significance, however. On the other hand, the relationship between the proportion Hispanic in the state and perceived black applicant quality is unexpectedly strong. It suggests that the quality of black applicants is growing in states of the Southwest, where the proportion of Hispanics in the state is large. The improvement in quality of black applicants is significantly less in major state universities, and a little less in other state universities, than in private schools. Thus, while the quantity of applicants appears to be increasing at state institutions, improvements in quality are seen as more rapid in private institutions.

Surprisingly, perhaps, the proportion of blacks in the state is negatively, though not significantly, related to the perceived improvement in the quality of the black applicant pool. And pressures from state agencies and institutions and accreditation agencies are negatively related (in the former case significantly so) with improvements in both quality and quantity of the applicant pool, while pressure from external groups is slightly positively related. It is possible that the negative relationships between pressure from accreditation agencies and the state to the black application pool come about because these external groups are reacting to poor performance in the past. That poor performance would be indicated by lack of improvement in the quality or quantity of the applicant pool. However, to test this idea more thoroughly, we must wait until the next chapter, when we can look at the relationship between existing proportions of black students and these external pressures. We must also remember that "state" pressures include not only formal pressure from state Equal Employment Opportunity offices, but also pressure from the legislature and its committees, black caucuses, state education agencies, and other sources.

On the whole, then, perceived improvements in the quality and quantity of the black applicant pool were most positively related to the perception of federal pressure, external group pressure, and institutional arrangements providing an officer or committee in charge of minority recruitment.[10] Private schools appeared to be experiencing a greater improvement in quality, though not quantity, of black applicants. Neither quantity nor quality, surprisingly, were significantly related to the proportion of blacks in the state.

In general, perceptions of improvements in the quantity of Hispanic applicants are more predictable than for black applicants, but the reverse is true for perceptions of improvement in the quality. The proportion of the state's population that is Hispanic is a significant predictor of improvement in the numbers of Hispanic applicants. And the proportion of the state's population that is black is an equally important predictor, but in the negative direction. In other words, Hispanic applicants are perceived to be increasing fastest in states with larger Hispanic populations and smaller black ones. Hispanic applicants are increasing fastest in state schools, but not the major state universities. In fact, the perceived increase is significantly less at major state universities than at either other state schools or private schools, the latter of which occupy a middle position.

Pressure from external groups is significantly related in only one case: state efforts to put pressure on schools is negatively related to the perceived quantity of applications, again perhaps reflecting the response of a variety of state agencies and officials to prior poor performance. Pressure from the federal government is related in a positive direction but is not significant. Pressure from groups and accreditation agencies are little related. Having an officer or committee charged with minority recruitment and other minority activities is positively related to perceived increases in Hispanic applicants, but not significantly so.

Turning from perceptions of quantity to those of quality, no predictors are significantly related, and the adjusted R^2s are around 0. None of the predictors has a t value of more than 1, indicating that even the direction of the relationship is not stable. These facts indicate that perceptions of improvement in the quality of Hispanic applicants are very much idiosyncratic and not shaped by the kinds of institutional and external factors we examined here.

For medical schools, then, it appears that having officials in charge of minority recruitment is positively related to perceived quality and quantity of black applicants and the quantity of Hispanic ones. Federal pressure is positively related, though not always significantly, to improvements in the quality and quantity of black and Hispanic applicant pools, while private pressure is significantly related to the quantity of black applications. Other sources of pressure have no consistent effect.

Law Schools

Patterns of perceptions of the applicant pool among law admissions officials are somewhat different than those of medical officials. Turning to table 4.5, we see generally that patterns appear more random, with smaller R^2 coefficients. Indeed, in two of the four equations, the adjusted R^2 is 0.

Looking first at blacks, we see that there is only one significant predictor of perceptions of increasing either quantity or quality of the applicant pool. The presence of an officer or committee charged with minority recruitment is positively related to the perception of improvement in the *quality* of the black applicant pool. As expected, the black population proportions and pressure from the federal government and from accreditation agencies are positively related to perceptions of increasing quality in the applicant pool, as indicated by t values over 1. On the other hand, pressure from the state government is negatively related, as it was for black medical applicants. No other coefficients are even that strongly related.

Turning to admissions officers' perceptions of the changes in the quantity and quality of Hispanic applicants, only the Hispanic population in the state is related significantly to improvements in the quality of the applicant pool, and it is nearly significantly related to improvements in the quantity. Perceived numerical increases are also positively associated with pressure from external groups and negatively related to being the major state university and receiving pressure from the federal government. None of these coefficients is significant, however. The presence of a minority recruitment officer or committee is positively, and nearly significantly, related to improvements in the quality of Hispanic applicants. No other variables approach significance in either equation.

Because most Hispanics live in one of only a few states, and most states have Hispanic populations of only 1 or 2 percent, we also examined perceptions of the Hispanic applicant pool in only those schools in states with at least a 5 percent Hispanic population. Unfortunately, the number of such schools is small (eighteen medical schools and twenty-six law schools). Nonetheless, replicating the analyses of tables 4.4 and 4.5 with this smaller group of schools largely confirms our earlier conclusions. Most important, federal pressure is significantly positive in its relationship with the perceived quality of the Hispanic medical school applicant pool. And, in the law school applicant pool analysis, both pressure from accreditation bodies and proportion black in the population are significantly negative in their relationship with the quality of the Hispanic pool. In each of these cases, the sign is the same as in the earlier analysis, but the relationship is stronger despite the relatively few cases.

Conclusion

We first summarize some of the major substantive findings of these analyses. Both the aggregate data and the perceptions of admissions officers support the conclusion that *Bakke* had little impact on the applicant pool. Though our regression equation indicated a significant negative coefficient for the post-*Bakke* years, this decline in applications occurred after 1984. Furthermore, admissions officers at both medical and law schools have perceived increases in the quantity and quality of minority applicants over the past decade. One partial exception is the quantity of black male applicants; a significant proportion of medical school admissions officers believed that this pool had shrunk over the past decade. This perception, however, is more likely to reflect the declining enrollment of black men in college than any tie to *Bakke*. On the whole, *Bakke* seems not to have made much of an impact on applications.

These admissions officers, however, differ in their perceptions about the applicant pools. In the concluding sections of the chapter we exam-

ined factors that predict whether different schools are experiencing declining or increasing quantities and qualities of minority applicants. We
analyzed characteristics of the state, the type of university or college,
pressure from external groups and agencies, and the presence of a minority recruitment and admissions office.

Though the proportion Hispanic in a state was weakly related to
increases in Hispanic applications, in general, the composition of the
state's population was not as important as we had expected in predicting
changes in applications. Probably the minority proportions of the state's
population are more related to absolute proportions enrolled rather than
changes in applications or enrollments, especially for blacks, whose population is rather stable. Increases in Hispanic applications may reflect
increases in Latino populations in those states, especially in the Southwest and in Florida, whose Hispanic populations were relatively large to
begin with.

The nature of the university had some effects on changing levels of
perceived applications. Major state universities did not succeed in improving either the quantity or the quality of their applications compared
with private schools, on the one hand, and other state institutions, on the
other. It is possible that these "other" state institutions tend to be located
in urban areas where more minorities, particularly African Americans,
are located. Or, it might be that the major state universities have higher
costs and higher admissions standards, particularly in terms of test
scores, that might deter some minority candidates.

Pressure from outside groups and agencies had mixed relationships
with these perceived applicant pool changes. Pressures from the federal
government are largely positively related with improved quantities and
quality of the applicant pools. This finding suggests, though certainly
does not prove, that federal oversight might have spurred institutional
efforts to recruit minorities. On the other hand, perceived pressure from
the states has mostly a negative relationship with improvements in quality and quantity of the minority applicant pools. Though an ad hoc
explanation, it is certainly possible that these state efforts are reflecting
past poor performances on the part of certain schools. Compared to the
federal government, state agencies, legislators, black caucuses, and the
like are more closely positioned to monitor the performance of these
medical and law schools and may react more vigorously when they perceive that minority recruitment efforts are not doing well. Federal pressure, on the other hand, is more institutionalized and remote.

Pressures from private groups and from accreditation agencies are largely unrelated to improvements in the pools. Though some significant relationships exist, they appear to be somewhat random.

All these findings help explain *perceptions* of change in applicant pools. But perceptions could be out of sync with reality. Perhaps our findings are more related to the state of the respondents' minds than the state of the minority applicant pools. Thus, we need to relate our measures of demography, pressure, and minority affairs officials to actual enrollments and to changes in enrollments over time. It is to the consideration of these enrollments that our next chapter turns.

Chapter 5

Bakke and Admissions Decisions

The analyses of the previous chapter suggest that the *Bakke* decision had little effect on individual minority students considering applying to law or medical school. But perhaps *Bakke* was of greater moment to medical and law school admissions officials. After all, admissions officers and university legal advisers were keenly aware of the decision, whereas some individual applicants possibly had never heard of *Bakke*. Their decisions to apply for professional school likely were much more influenced by their personal academic and financial resources than by this court decision. So we need to assess the impact of the decision on actions taken by admissions officials. To do so, we turn to a consideration of trends in minority acceptances and first-year enrollments.

We examine three different types of information. First, we use our aggregate time-series to explore nationwide trends in first-year black and Hispanic enrollments in medical and law schools.[1] For medical schools, we also compare the proportion of black and Hispanic applicants accepted with the proportion of all applicants accepted. These data can show us how, if at all, admissions committees changed their behavior over time in response to *Bakke* or to other factors. We then turn to enrollment data for individual medical schools to examine changing patterns in minority enrollments. We examine the institutions that gained and lost minority enrollment since the pre-*Bakke* years and test possible reasons for their changing rates. In our analysis of institutions, we also use information from the survey of admissions officials. Thus, this chapter relies on each of the data sources we have collected.

National Trends in Enrollments and Acceptances

Our longitudinal analyses focus on entering classes, since total minority enrollment reflects not only admissions decisions but also retention rates.

Factors affecting retention include academic performance, ability to cope with the stress of the demands made on students, and financial and other personal resources. These factors are important in understanding the dynamics of black and Hispanic success in professional schools, but they are ignored here because they are not directly germane to the admissions decisions made by the schools. Because of differences in available information, the time-series data on medical school enrollments are longer and wider in scope than those for law schools.

Our time-series data begin in the late 1960s and early 1970s (depending on the earliest available data) and stretch to 1987. We chose 1987 as the cutoff to balance our desire to have a reasonably long post-*Bakke* data series against the desire to end the time-series before the many confounding factors that occur with the passage of time made it difficult to focus on the effect of *Bakke* per se.

In this chapter we explore four aggregate variables for blacks and Hispanics:

1. The proportion of blacks and Hispanics in the entering classes of medical school each year from 1968 to 1987 (AAMC various years). Hispanics here include only Mexican Americans and mainland Puerto Ricans. Even though data are now collected on "other Hispanics," such data were not available at the beginning of our time-series. Adding them in midway would cause a serious disruption in the time-series, since "other Hispanics" in medical school are nearly as numerous as Mexican Americans. In 1987, for example, Mexican Americans were 1.8 percent of the entering class, Puerto Ricans .8 percent, and "other Hispanics" 1.6 percent. Many of these "other Hispanics" are Cubans, a relatively well-educated population, but some are other Central and South Americans.[2]
2. The proportion of blacks and Hispanics in the entering classes of law school each year from 1971 to 1987 (Lawyer's Almanac 1990; ABA 1987). These data on Hispanics include Mexican Americans, Puerto Ricans attending mainland law schools, and a category labeled "other Hispano Americans," including Cubans.
3. The proportion of black and Hispanic applicants to medical school accepted each year from 1974 to 1987 (AAMC, various years).
4. The ratios of black and Hispanic applicants accepted to medical school to the acceptance rate for all students each year from 1974 to 1987 (AAMC, various years).

Enrollments

We begin by examining the aggregate trends in black and Hispanic first-year medical school enrollment. Black enrollment increased from less than 3 percent of the entering class in 1968 to 7.5 percent in 1974. Then it fell, and by 1987 it was only at the level of 1970, about 6 percent. Black enrollment fell slightly between 1978 and 1979, before and after *Bakke,* but rebounded the next year. Hispanic enrollment rose fairly steadily from a bare 0.3 percent in 1968 to 2.7 percent in 1985, but then declined slightly in 1986 and 1987. Unlike black enrollment, Hispanic enrollment showed a small increase in 1979.

As we did in chapter 4, we examine how well these data are predicted by the *Bakke* decision trend variables, financial aid, and the Reagan administration variable (see appendix 2 for the explanation of the time-series analyses). Our basic time-series equations show only a mediocre fit to the black enrollment data, explaining only 43 percent of the variation (equation 5.1), but a good fit to the Hispanic enrollment data, explaining 98 percent of the variation (equation 5.2). Figure 5.1 shows these results. Note the sometimes large deviations from the predicted line in the black data, especially before 1975, but the close approximation of the predicted to the actual value among Hispanics.

$$\text{\% blacks in} = 3.97 + .33x_t - .48x_d - .49x_p \qquad (5.1)$$
$$\text{medical class} \quad (4.21) \quad (2.93) \quad (-.95) \quad (-1.89)$$

$$+ .38^*\text{Reagan} + .0003^*\text{aid} + e$$
$$(.69) \qquad\qquad (.09)$$

$R^2 = .43; N = 20; DW = 2.24$, corrected for second-order autocorrelation
   Figures in parentheses are t values; symbols are as explained in chapter 4, with Reagan representing a dummy variable for the years of the Reagan administration and aid representing the amount of federal student aid available (in 000's).

$$\text{\% Hispanics in} = .44 + .25x_t - .01x_d - .19x_p \qquad (5.2)$$
$$\text{medical class} \quad (6.09) \quad (13.76) \quad (.05) \quad (-7.20)$$

$$+ .43^*\text{Reagan} - .0003^*\text{aid} + e$$
$$(2.74) \qquad\qquad (-4.68)$$

$R^2 = .98; N = 20; DW = 2.00$, corrected for second-order autocorrelation

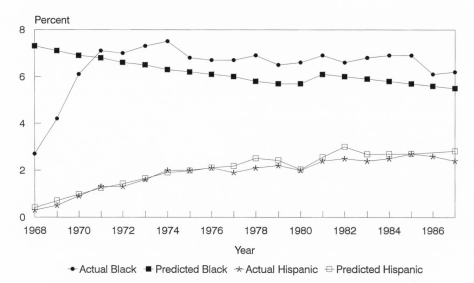

Fig. 5.1.   Black and Hispanic enrollment as percentage of first-year medical classes. (Data from AAMC, 1968–87.)

The equation for black enrollment shows a significant pre-*Bakke* increase of about .33 percent a year, but nonsignificant short-term and long-term decreases after *Bakke*. Neither the coefficients nor the visual inspection of the line in figure 5.1 seem to support the argument that *Bakke* had a significant impact on black enrollment (see table 5.1 for a summary). Black enrollment as a proportion of first-year students did not exceed its all-time high reached in 1974, four years before the decision, until 1992, much later than the period analyzed here. A small decrease in black enrollment between 1978 and 1979 could be attributable to *Bakke*. However, black enrollment from 1981 through 1985 looks very much like that from 1975 through 1978.

Before *Bakke*, Hispanic enrollment increased at about .25 percent a year (see summary, table 5.1). The short-term effect of *Bakke* was nil, but following the decision Hispanic enrollment increased, on average, at a slower rate of about .06 percent annually (.25 − .19 = .06). Interestingly, both the coefficients for the Reagan administration and federal aid are significantly positive, opposite from the expected directions. These results are somewhat puzzling. They suggest that *Bakke* did slow Hispanic enrollment, but that the Reagan era increased it.

Because the Reagan era started only three years after the *Bakke* decision, we might examine Hispanic enrollment trends during the three years between the decision and the Reagan presidency. Figure 5.1 shows that Hispanic enrollment increased between 1978 and 1979, dropped in 1980, and rebounded in 1981 to a level slightly higher than either 1979 or previous highs (all these differences are very small, however). The rest of the Reagan years showed a rather constant Hispanic proportion, with a small increase in 1985 and a decrease thereafter. Thus, the visual inspection does not suggest that *Bakke* caused a decrease in Hispanic enrollment or that the Reagan years saw an increase *unless* one attributes great significance to the 1979 decline.

Another reason for the somewhat anomalous results might be that the growing Latino population provided the basis for increasing Hispanic enrollment despite shrinking federal aid and an administration that viewed affirmative action with distaste. This argument would be even stronger if Cuban Americans were included in the Hispanic numbers, since they are much more likely to have college degrees than are Mexican Americans or Puerto Ricans. Despite their absence, it is still true that the growth in the Hispanic population beginning in the early 1970s provided a larger potential pool by the late 1970s and 1980s.

Now let us turn from black and Hispanic enrollments in medical schools to those in law schools (fig. 5.2). Between 1971 and 1987, black law school enrollment fluctuated only between 4.7 percent and 5.7 percent, with no clear temporal pattern. This enrollment stayed constant between 1978 and 1979 before increasing slightly in the early 1980s. The impact of the *Bakke* decision and of our other independent factors are shown in equation 5.3 and summarized in table 5.2.

TABLE 5.1.   Predicting Black and Hispanic Medical School Enrollment, 1968–87

	Blacks	Hispanics
Change in % of ( ) each year, pre-*Bakke*	.33*	.25*
Short-term change in % of ( )	−.48	.01
Change in % of ( ) per year, after *Bakke*	−.16	.06
Reagan administration increment	.38	.43
Change in % of ( ) per $1,000,000 student aid	.30	−.30

Note: For details see equations 5.1 and 5.2. (   ) indicates black or Hispanic. The dependent variable in this analysis is the proportion of the entering class that is black or Hispanic. The first line of the table indicates, therefore, that before *Bakke,* black enrollment was increasing at a rate of .33 of 1 percent annually and Hispanic enrollment .25 of 1 percent. $N = 20$.

*Indicates significance at the .05 level.

$$\% \text{ blacks in} = \underset{(32.76)}{5.10} - \underset{(-.12)}{.01x_t} - \underset{(-.64)}{.15x_d} + \underset{(1.61)}{.09x_p} \quad (5.3)$$
$$\text{law class}$$

$$+ \underset{(.37)}{.08^*\text{Reagan}} - \underset{(-.12)}{.00^*\text{aid}} + e$$

$$R^2 = .65; N = 17; DW = 2.30$$

The equation and summary table confirm the small longitudinal change in black law school enrollments and the limited effect of *Bakke*. Before the decision, enrollments were essentially holding steady (decreasing .01 percent per year on average); after a onetime decrease of .15 percent, they began increasing at a minimal rate (.08 percent per year). The Reagan administration variable, with a positive coefficient, and the financial aid variable, with a negative one, also had minimal effects. Given these small effects, it is not surprising that the overall R^2 for the equation is a fairly modest (by time-series standards) .65.

In contrast, the equation predicting changing Hispanic enrollment in law schools fits the actual data quite well, with an R^2 of .93 (see equation 5.4 and table 5.2). Hispanic law school enrollment increased from 1.4

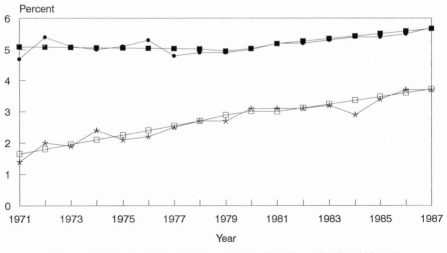

-•- Actual Black   -■- Predicted Black   -*- Actual Hispanic   -⊟- Predicted Hispanic

Fig. 5.2. Black and Hispanic enrollment as percent of first year law classes. (Data from *Lawyer's Almanac*, selected years.)

TABLE 5.2.   Predicting Black and Hispanic Law School Enrollment, 1971–87

	Blacks	Hispanics
Change in % of ( ) each year, pre-*Bakke*	−.01	.15*
Short-term change in % of ( )	−.15	−.08
Change in % of ( ) per year, after *Bakke*	.08	.11
Reagan administration increment	.08	−.11
Change in % of ( ) per $1,000 student aid	−.00	−.00

Note: For details see equations 5.3 and 5.4. (   ) indicates black or Hispanic. The dependent variable in this analysis is the proportion of the entering class that is black or Hispanic. $R^2 = .65$ for the analysis of black enrollment, .93 for the analysis of Hispanic enrollment. $N = 17$.
*Indicates significance at the .05 level.

percent in 1971 to 3.7 percent in 1987. Yet the pre- and post-*Bakke* enrollment fluctuated very little. The analysis indicates a significant but tiny annual increase in Hispanic students before *Bakke* (about .15 percent a year) and no significant change after.

$$\text{\% Hispanics in} = \underset{(8.66)}{1.50} + \underset{(2.59)}{.15x_t} + \underset{(.27)}{.08x_d} - \underset{(-.46)}{.04x_p} \quad (5.4)$$
$$\text{law class}$$

$$- \underset{(-.53)}{.11^*\text{Reagan}} - \underset{(-.05)}{.00^*\text{aid}} + e$$

$$R^2 = .93; \, N = 17; \, DW = 2.20$$

These results suggest a minimal impact of *Bakke* on black and Hispanic enrollments in medical and law schools. There is some slight indication it slowed growth in the number of blacks and Hispanics in medical school, but a closer inspection of the data casts doubt on whether the decision itself caused the decline in the early 1980s. The equations assessing the impact of *Bakke* on law school enrollments suggest no impact at all. A closer inspection of those data confirm that interpretation.

Acceptances

The size of a minority class is affected not only by applications, but by the proportion of minority applicants accepted. Unfortunately, longitudinal data on acceptances are available only for medical schools.

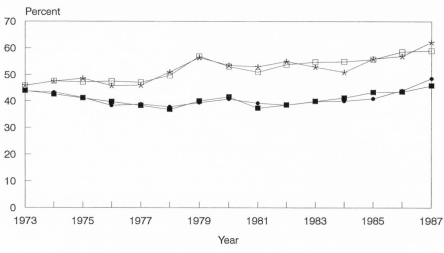

—●— Actual Black   —■— Predicted Black   —✳— Actual Hispanic   —⊟— Predicted Hispanic

Fig. 5.3.   Percentage of black and Hispanic applicants accepted to medical school. (Data from AAMC, Medical School Admission Requirements, selected years.)

Figure 5.3 illustrates the actual and predicted acceptance rates for black and Hispanic applicants. The proportion of black applicants who were accepted fell from 44 percent to 38 percent between 1973 and 1976, fluctuated in this range between 1977 and 1986, and jumped to 48 percent in 1987. Hispanic acceptance rates rose from 47 percent in 1973 to 62 percent in 1987. *Bakke*'s impact on the number of applications accepted appears positive in the short term for Hispanics and in both the shorter and longer terms for blacks (see equations 5.5 and 5.6 and table 5.3). For blacks, the decision seems to have halted a decline in the proportion of black applicants accepted. For Hispanics, the proportion accepted had been increasing before *Bakke*, but following the decision there was a jump in that proportion.

$$\begin{aligned} \% \text{ blacks accepted} = \quad & 45.2 \quad - \quad 1.46x_t \quad + \quad 1.73x_d \\ \text{to medical school} \quad & (29.52) \quad (-2.36) \quad\quad (.86) \end{aligned} \tag{5.5}$$

$$\begin{aligned} & + \; 2.79x_p \; - \; 5.55^*\text{Reagan} \; + \; .0002^*\text{aid} + e \\ & \quad (4.90) \quad\quad (-2.36) \quad\quad\quad\quad (.11) \end{aligned}$$

$R^2 = .88$; $N = 15$; DW $= 1.95$, adjusted for second-order autocorrelation

$$\text{\% Hispanics accepted} = \quad 44.2 \quad + \quad 1.70x_t + 7.36x_d \qquad (5.6)$$
$$\text{to medical school} \quad (14.42) \quad (2.11) \quad (2.67)$$

$$- \ .19x_p \ - 4.05^*\text{Reagan} - \ .00^*\text{aid} \ + e$$
$$(-.24) \qquad (-1.55) \qquad (-1.94)$$

$$R^2 = .86; N = 15; DW = 1.89$$

These equations predict the actual acceptances well. The Reagan administration coefficient is negatively related to acceptance rates for both blacks and Hispanics, significantly so in the equation predicting acceptances of blacks. In both equations, the financial aid variable has a negative relationship with acceptances, significantly so in the case of Hispanics. While we predicted a positive link between financial aid and the number of minority applicants and enrollments, it is logical to expect a negative relationship here. Other things equal, lesser financial aid should be associated with fewer applicants. Fewer applicants, other things being equal, should increase the acceptance rates.

If the impact of *Bakke* on minority enrollments in medical school is minimal, or if anything slightly negative, it is certainly not because the decision led to a higher rate of rejection of minority applications. These equations suggest that, if anything, the acceptance rates increased after the decision. The declining acceptance rate for blacks before the decision may reflect the reaction of admissions committees to evidence that blacks accepted in the early affirmative action programs had a high attrition rate relative to other students ("Undergraduate Medical Education 1975, 1339; R. Smith 1981; Fisher 1981; Speich 1978).[3] It may also reflect the diminishing numbers of schools using quotas. The increasing acceptance

TABLE 5.3. **Predicting Black and Hispanic Medical School Acceptances, 1973–87**

	Blacks	Hispanics
Change in % of ( ) accepted each year, pre-*Bakke*	−1.46*	1.70*
Short-term change in % of ( ) accepted	1.73	7.36*
Change in % of ( ) accepted per year, after *Bakke*	1.33	1.51
Reagan administration increment	−5.55*	−4.05
Change in % of ( ) accepted per $1,000 student aid	−.00	−.00

Note: For details see equations 5.5 and 5.6. (   ) indicates black or Hispanic. The dependent variable in this analysis is the proportion of black or Hispanic applicants accepted. $R^2 = .88$ for the analysis of black acceptances, .86 for the analysis of Hispanic acceptances. $N = 17$.

*Indicates significance at the .05 level.

rates in the mid-1980s reflect the shrinking applicant pool and the concommitant need to select a higher proportion of applicants to fill medical school seats.

Our final analysis compares the ratio of acceptances of black and Hispanic students to acceptances of all applicants. A value of 1.0 indicates that black or Hispanic students are accepted at the same rate as all students; a value of less than 1.0 indicates a lower rate of acceptance of blacks or Hispanics, while a value of more than 1.0 indicates a greater rate. This ratio allows us to see whether the increase in acceptance rates is a reflection of what was happening to the larger pool of applicants.

The data show that before 1977, blacks were accepted at a higher rate than whites; afterwards, they were accepted at an increasingly lower rate. The decreasing ratio, now around .80, predated *Bakke*. The acceptance ratio for Hispanics remains above 1.0, but it dropped from 1.35 in 1974 to 1.13 in 1978. In 1979, that ratio increased to 1.21, but it dropped again, falling to 1.03 by 1987. Again, the falling ratio precedes *Bakke*. Figure 5.4 illustrates these trends, along with the acceptance ratios predicted by our data.

For blacks, the pre-*Bakke* drop in the acceptance ratio was about 6 percent a year (see equation 5.7 and table 5.4). In an extremely well-fitting model that includes again a control for total applicants along with federal aid and the Reagan administration, the coefficients for the short- and long-term effects of *Bakke* indicate that it halted the drop. The post-*Bakke* coefficient is strongly positive.

$$\text{Acceptance ratio} = \underset{(3.87)}{.71} - \underset{(-6.15)}{.06x_t} - \underset{(-.66)}{.02x_d} + \underset{(10.02)}{.08x_p} \quad (5.7)$$

$$\underset{(-2.78)}{- .08*\text{Reagan}} + \underset{(.37)}{.000*\text{aid}} + \underset{(3.46)}{.01*\text{total}} + e$$

$R^2 = .99$; $N = 15$; DW = 2.07, corrected for first-order autocorrelation

The acceptance ratio for blacks also reflects the impact of two other variables in the equation. The ratio decreased during the Reagan administration. It rose with increases in the number of applicants overall, a finding that supports the conclusion that the *quality* of the black applicant pool has been increasing relative to the white (S. Shea and Fullilove 1985).

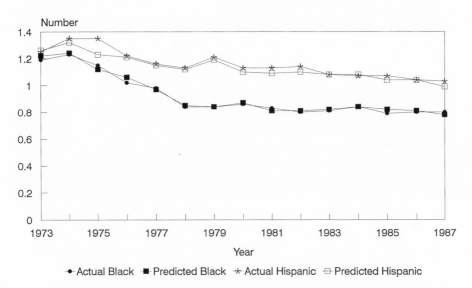

Fig. 5.4.   Acceptance ratio of black and Hispanic applicants to all medical school applicants. (Data from AAMC, 1973–87.)

The pre-*Bakke* drop in the acceptance ratio of Hispanics was about 1 percent a year (see equation 5.8 and table 5.4). The decision appears to have resulted in a short-term reversal of that trend and a nonsignificant long-term drop in the rate of decrease.

$$\begin{aligned}
\text{Acceptance ratio} &= \quad .87 \quad - \quad .01x_t \quad + \quad .10x_d \quad + \quad .01x_p \qquad (5.8)\\
\text{for Hispanics} \quad &\quad (3.18) \quad\ (-.35) \quad\ (2.08) \quad\ (.50)
\end{aligned}$$

$$- .03^*\text{Reagan} - .0001^*\text{aid} + .01^*\text{total} + e$$
$$(-.57) \qquad\qquad (-1.74) \qquad\quad (1.94)$$

$R^2 = .91; N = 15; DW = 2.11$

In sum, these results support the conclusion that *Bakke* had a minimal effect on minority enrollments. It may have had a small dampening effect on black and Hispanic applications to medical school, but, if anything, it is positively associated with acceptance rates and the relative acceptance rates of minorities and nonminorities. The slowdown in the rate of minority entrance into both medical and law school appear to have been related to other factors than *Bakke*.

Our model incorporates two of these factors explicitly. Federal student aid had little significant effect on black and Hispanic enrollment. One of the significant coefficients was in the opposite from predicted direction. It may be that the aggregate federal aid variable is too crude to accurately assess aid available to these professional school students, a tiny proportion of all potential aid recipients. Certainly overall minority enrollment is related to the amount of federal student aid (Moulton 1988). It could also be that professional school students receive a large share of their financial aid from nonfederal government sources.

The Reagan administration variable had a significant negative effect for two of the five variables assessing black applications, acceptances, and enrollment. The effects on the other three variables were insignificantly positive. The Reagan variable had no significant negative effects on Hispanic applications and enrollments. Indeed, one of the five relationships was significantly positive, which might reflect the Republican party's efforts during the 1980s to woo Hispanic voters, especially middle-class ones. The administration's anti–affirmative action signals usually involved blacks, not Latinos.

Another important factor, income resources, was included only indirectly in the model. We attempted to include black and Hispanic median income as predictors of applications and enrollments. However, it was so highly related to other variables in the model that it could not be used. This is one limitation of our methods. The beginning of the decline in black and Hispanic median incomes occurred at about the time of *Bakke*.[4] Thus, the variables assessing *Bakke* are to some extent capturing

---

TABLE 5.4.   Predicting Black and Hispanic Medical School Acceptance Ratios, 1973–87

	Blacks	Hispanics
Annual change in accept ratio of ( ), pre-*Bakke*	−.06*	−.01
Short-term change in ratio of ( ) accepted	.02	.10*
Change in ratio of ( ) accepted per year, after *Bakke*	.02	.00
Reagan administration increment	−.08*	−.03
Increase in ratio of ( ) per $1,000 student aid	.00	−.0001
Total number of applicants	.01*	.01

Note: For full details see equations 5.7 and 5.8. (   ) indicates black or Hispanic. The dependent variable in this analysis is the ratio of the proportion of black or Hispanic applicants accepted to all applicants. R^2 = .99 for the analysis of black ratios, .91 for the analysis of Hispanic ratios. $N = 15$.
   *Indicates significance at the .05 level.

the impact of the falling median incomes at the beginning of the 1980s. While we cannot disentangle this effect directly, we can notice that black and Hispanic applications and enrollments rose somewhat after black and Hispanic incomes begin to rise in the mid-1980s.

Still other factors are not considered at all. For example, how much of the fluctuation in applications and acceptances is due to the perceptions of applicants that it is no use enrolling because they will not succeed? Especially in the early 1970s, attrition rates were much higher for minorities than for nonminorities in both medical and law school. At least one analyst argues that this factor diminished the pool of potential minority students (R. Smith 1981). Perceptions of these attrition rates may have also influenced admissions officers as they examined applications from minority students with low test scores. We will discuss this possible impact on trends in minority applications and acceptances again in the final chapter.

Institutional Differences in Minority Enrollments

Institutions differ in the motivation and ability of their faculty and administrators to recruit minority students. Institutions that were most inclined to do so, and most successful at it, might have been less influenced by *Bakke* than institutions without the motivation or the record of success. An analysis of individual institutions will show which types might have been affected by *Bakke*. It will enable us to judge which institutions are most successful at recruiting minorities and to examine the impact of internal resources devoted to minority recruitment and external pressures directed toward influencing minority recruitment.

We have collected information on total and minority enrollments in medical and law schools in 1987. We use this as our post-*Bakke* data point since that is where the time-series ends. Since minority enrollment data for law schools are available only for all three classes together rather than just the freshman class, we analyze the entire minority enrollment for both medical and law schools.

We use 1977 black and Hispanic enrollment as our pre-*Bakke* comparison for medical schools. Data from 1977 are not available for law schools, and hence we analyze the minority enrollment in 1979. Unfortunately, the 1979 freshmen enrollment is post-*Bakke* and might have been affected by it. However, the remainder of the students still in law school in 1979 would have been enrolled before *Bakke*.

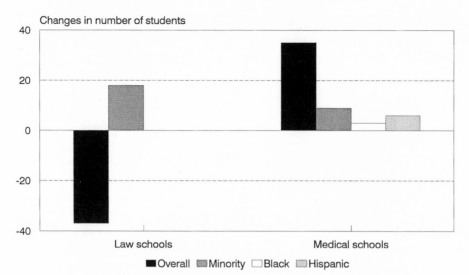

Fig. 5.5. Mean institutional changes in enrollment. Change is from 1977–87 for medical schools, 1979–87 for law schools. (Data for medical schools from Association of American Medical Schools, Medical School Admission Requirements; data for law schools from Law School Admission Council, the Official Guide to U.S. Law Schools.)

Data from law schools have another limitation. We cannot obtain separate enrollment figures for blacks and Hispanics. Instead, we have "minority" enrollment, which includes both blacks and Hispanics.[5] While we would like to examine these groups separately, that is not possible from existing data.

We will explore differences among institutions in both current levels of black and Hispanic enrollments and changes in these levels since *Bakke.* Change is calculated by subtracting the proportion of minorities in 1977 or 1979 from the proportion in 1987. The result is the gain or loss in minority percentages.

Figures 5.5 and 5.6 present some basic descriptive data on these changes. Figure 5.5 shows the change in the raw numbers of students. We see that medical schools increased their overall enrollment by about 35 students, and about one-third of that increase was minority students. However, the percentage difference between blacks in medical school in 1987 and a decade earlier is only .18 percent.[6] And, as figure 5.6 shows, the number of medical schools experiencing a decrease in black enrollments is greater than those experiencing an increase.

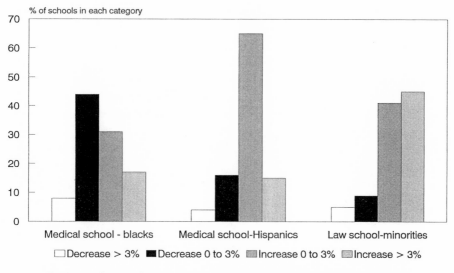

Fig. 5.6. Changes in percentage of minorities enrolled. (Data from *Lawyer's Almanac,* selected years, and AAMC, Medical School Admission Requirements, selected years.)

Gains in Hispanic enrollment are somewhat bigger, both in absolute numbers and in proportions (.75 percent). Figure 5.6 shows that many more schools increased their Hispanic enrollment than decreased it, though for most of these schools the gains were small.

The average law school shrank in size in this decade; many expanded in the 1970s to meet the enrollment boom and then decreased in size in the 1980s. Indeed, law schools decreased in average size by about the same amount that medical schools increased (fig. 5.5). Despite the overall decrease, law schools enrolled about twenty more minority students in 1987 than in 1979 (recall that we do not have data on individual minority groups), amounting to an increase in percentage of about 2.63 percent. Figure 5.6 illustrates that most law schools did increase the proportion of minorities enrolled during that decade.

Changes in Minority Enrollments

If *Bakke* had an effect on minority enrollments, we might expect that effect to be apparent in the distribution of minority gains and losses among different types of schools. For example, the rate of increase in minorities might slow more in southern than in northern schools. Traditions of segregation might temper enthusiasm for increasing black enrollments, and the decision could have signaled that it was all right to slow these efforts. We might also expect the effect to be less apparent in states with small minority populations. Absent a large statewide population of blacks or Hispanics, such schools had minimal minority enrollments before the decision and would no doubt continue to have minimal enrollments. We might also expect more effect in smaller schools than in larger ones. That is, lacking in some cases the resources or personnel for a big outreach effort, smaller schools might slacken their affirmative action recruiting pace more than larger ones. Finally, we might expect more effect on private schools than public ones. Public schools, especially those in states with significant minority populations, might feel pressure to continue efforts toward a more diverse student body. And these efforts might be greatest among the major state universities, where more public attention is focused. If these expectations hold true, we expect lower rates of gain in southern, smaller, private schools and in states with smaller minority populations. Table 5.5 illustrates these relationships.

Few of our expectations are met. In medical schools, no relationships between school and state characteristics and black enrollments are significant. Northern schools do have a larger increase between 1977 and 1987 than do southern schools, but the difference is minuscule. There is a difference between the smallest schools, where the proportion of black enrollment actually declined, and the largest, where it increased by over 1 percent, but the middle categories do not suggest a linear relationship.[7] The relationship is generally as we expected, but certainly not completely so. The same generalization can be made about the link between the proportion black and the increase in black enrollment. As expected, states with the smallest proportions of blacks[8] increased their black enrollments the least; indeed, they actually decreased. Gains were experienced by all other size categories of medical schools, though minimally in the "medium high" category. The largest gains were apparent, as expected, in the states with the largest percentage of blacks. However, this relationship is neither significant nor linear.

We did not expect a relationship between the proportion Hispanic in a state and black enrollment gains, and none was found. The last relationship, between the type of school and black enrollment gains, partly met our expectations, though again the relationship was not significant. Private schools actually decreased their black proportion, while public schools gained. Contrary to expectations, among the latter group, the major state universities increased their black enrollment less than did other state schools.

The same deviation from expectations is largely true of Hispanic enrollment gains. Larger schools did increase their Hispanic enrollment more than smaller ones, though the gain was not perfectly linear. The relationship with the state's Hispanic population was curvilinear and significant, with the most gains being in states with 3 to 5 percent Hispanic populations rather than those with the largest ones. The relationship with type of school only partially met our expectations, with the greatest gains in the major state universities but the smallest gains in the other state schools.

TABLE 5.5. Gains in Proportions of Minorities From Late 1970s to 1987 (% increase)

	Medical Schools		Law Schools
	Blacks	Hispanics	Minorities
Region			
South (26, 34)	.17	.41	2.02
North (86, 129)	.20	.86	2.79
Enrollment			
Low (31, 56)	−.19	.58	1.33
Medium low (27, 41)	.48	.45	2.85
Medium high (33, 42)	−.34	.74	3.74
High (21, 24)	1.22	1.42	3.33*
State's black population			
0 to 4.99% (25, 39)	−.39	.36	2.01
5 to 9.99% (21, 36)	.57	.64	3.02
10 to 19.99% (49, 66)	.11	1.17	3.19
20% and more (17, 22)	.80	.23	1.39
State's Hispanic population			
0 to 2.99% (61, 83)	.37	.50	1.80
3 to 4.99% (33, 49)	.43	1.50	3.66
5% and more (18, 31)	.23	.24*	3.23+
Type of school			
Private (49, 96)	−.12	.64	3.33
Major state university (49, 40)	.23	1.04	1.88
Other state school (20, 27)	.82	.33	1.24*

Note: Numbers in parentheses are *N*'s for medical and law school, respectively. Change in percent enrollment is calculated by subtracting the black, Hispanic, or minority proportion in 1977 (or 1979 for law schools) from that in 1987. The overall means are .19 for blacks in medical school, .75 for Hispanics in medical school, and 2.63 for all minorities in law schools.

*Indicates significance at .05; + significance at .10.

Minority enrollments in law school also showed few consistent patterns. Northern schools did gain more minority students than southern ones did, and larger schools more than smaller ones, though the relationship is somewhat curvilinear. The smallest increase in minority gains was in states with the largest black populations, a finding completely contradictory to our expectations, though in the first three size categories, the increases were as expected. States with Hispanic populations of more than 3 percent did increase their minority enrollment more than other states, but the states with the highest proportions of Hispanics increased less than those with 3 to 5 percent. And finally, the pattern among types of schools is not only contradictory to our expectations, since private schools have the largest gains, but contrary to the patterns displayed for blacks and Hispanics in medical school, too.

In sum, these patterns give only a few hints that our expectations about the impact of *Bakke* are correct. There is a link between increasing minority enrollment and enrollment size and to the state's minority population base, but the link is not a straightforward linear one. Likewise, there is a link between the school's size and its success in increasing its minority enrollment, but again not a perfectly linear relationship. Of course, the relationships could be influenced by other factors affecting enrollment gains.

Stability in Minority Enrollments

One likely possibility is that gains in minority enrollment in the decade after *Bakke,* instead of being primarily related to the decision, are related primarily to preexisting conditions in each school. That is, the schools most successful at recruiting minorities before *Bakke* continue to be successful. The biggest predictor of minority enrollment in 1987 might well be the minority enrollment a decade earlier. Such a finding would give support to the hypothesis that the major effort of the *Bakke* decision was to legitimize existing affirmative action practices rather than either stifle existing ones or mandate new ones.

Table 5.6 shows this assumption to be true. Institution by institution, minority enrollment in 1987 is very highly related to minority enrollment a decade earlier. This correlation is most true for blacks, where earlier enrollment explains over 93 percent of the variation in 1987 enrollment (shown in the table as R^2), almost as true for law schools, where the variation explained is 89 percent, and less true for Hispanics in medical school, where the explained variation is only 57 percent. A high proportion of variation explained means that those schools with high minority enrollments in 1987 also had them in 1977, and similarly for those with medium and low enrollments.

If *Bakke* had an effect on professional schools' treatment of minority applicants, one would expect this effect to vary greatly. Such variation would cause some schools with relatively high black or Hispanic enrollments to lag behind their peers a decade later. However, the strong relationship between previous and current minority enrollments suggests that the decision seemed to reinforce existing patterns of minority recruiting. Whatever factors promoted minority enrollment in 1977 did so in 1987. The possible exception is Hispanic medical school enrollment, where the variation explained in 1987 enrollment by 1977 enrollment, while substantial, is considerably less than in the other two cases. However, as we will see in the next table, there are other factors than *Bakke* that help explain changing Hispanic enrollments.

The huge impact of previous enrollment on 1987 enrollment provides a clue why the relationships between gains in proportions of minorities and characteristics of the state and school (as we saw in table 5.5) were inconsistent. Variations in enrollment gains in the post-*Bakke* de-

TABLE 5.6.   The Impact of Earlier Minority Enrollment on 1987
Minority Enrollment

	Medical Schools		Law Schools
	Blacks	Hispanics	Minorities
Percentage of group enrolled before *Bakke*	.93	.76	.84
(*t*)	(39.08)	(12.13)	(36.49)
Constant	.62	1.12	4.04
R^2	.93	.57	.89

Note: The dependent variable is the percentage of blacks, Hispanics, and minorities enrolled in 1987. The coefficients shown are unstandardized regression coefficients (*b* values). An example of the interpretation is as follows: for every percent of black enrollment before *Bakke,* in 1987 there was .93 percent black enrollment plus a constant of .62 percent. Thus, a medical school with a 10 percent black enrollment in 1977 can be predicted to have a 9.92 percent enrollment in 1987 (10 × .93 + .62). A law school with a 10 percent minority enrollment in 1977 can be predicted to have a 12.44 percent enrollment in 1987 (10 × .84 + 4.04).

$N = 112$ for medical schools and 164 for law schools.

cade have to be interpreted in light of enrollments before the decision. In table 5.7 we do so, looking at the effects of the variables we explored earlier, after taking into account the impact of earlier enrollments.[9] We also include as a predictor the change in overall enrollments. This factor does not relate to *Bakke* but only to the likely possibility that schools that grew in overall size may have been more likely to increase their minority enrollments.

The table indicates that none of these other factors affected black enrollment in medical schools. Although the 1977 enrollment remains an extremely strong predictor of 1987 enrollments, neither the proportion of blacks in the state population, enrollment, changing enrollment, nor the type of school are related to black enrollments in 1987. Indeed, adding these factors to the equation only increases the explained variation in enrollment by a nonsignificant 1 percent, from 93 percent to 94 percent.[10]

Hispanic enrollment continues to be strongly predicted by previous Hispanic enrollment (as we saw in table 5.6, it explains 57 percent of the variation), but the proportion Hispanic population in the state also is an

TABLE 5.7. Impact of Previous Minority Enrollment and Other Factors on 1987 Proportions of Minority Enrollment

	Medical Schools		Law Schools
	Blacks	Hispanics	Minorities
% of group enrolled before *Bakke*	.92	.35	.82
	(35.45)	(4.22)	(33.83)
% black in state's population	.03	−.01	.04
	(1.45)	(−1.31)	(1.77)
% Hispanic in state's population	−.00	.22	.15
	(−.01)	(5.90)	(3.24)
Number of students enrolled	.14	.12	.06
	(1.17)	(1.46)	(.57)
Change in number enrolled	−.32	−.11	−.35
	(−1.49)	(−.69)	(−1.98)
Major state university	.19	.01	−.47
	(.35)	(1.45)	(−.64)
Other state university	.92	.00	−.69
	(1.29)	(.06)	(−.82)
Constant	−.61	1.12	2.42
	(−.74)	(−.33)	(2.88)
R^2	.94	.70	.91

$N = 112$ for medical schools and 163 for law schools. Significant coefficients are in italic type.

important predictor of that enrollment. Hispanic medical enrollment grew by a larger proportion than did black enrollment, and it is clear that much of this growth took place in states with larger Hispanic populations. These states, such as Florida, Texas, and California, are also those where much of the increase in Hispanic population is occurring. The impact of the state's Hispanic population is largely responsible for the increase in the R^2 from .57, with only the 1977 enrollment figures as a predictor, to .70 in this equation.

Minority enrollment in law schools is somewhat affected by the black and Hispanic proportions in the state, though together the additional predictors increase the R^2 only from .89 (with only previous enrollment as a predictor) to .91. Still, beyond their effects on 1979 minority enrollment, the proportions of Hispanics in the state are significantly related to 1987 enrollment, too. Contrary to expectations, minority enrollment in 1987 is higher in those law schools that have decreased in overall enrollment, other things being equal. As with minority enrollments in medical school, there are no effects of overall enrollment and type of university.

In both medical and law schools, then, enrollment a decade after *Bakke* was very much related to enrollment before *Bakke*. Though some professional schools moved ahead faster than others in this decade, on the whole, schools that had larger proportions of minorities before the decision had them a decade later. But not all variation in 1987 minority enrollments was explained; we have seen that the Hispanic population of the state affected changes in Hispanic and, in law schools, overall minority enrollment.

The effects on minority enrollment we have examined thus far are effects of demographic and status factors that have nothing specifically to do with the schools' efforts to recruit minorities. Were gains in minority enrollments also affected either by the schools' having officials in charge of minority recruitment and retention or by the pressure from outside groups? It is to these questions we now turn.

Impact of Internal and External Affirmative Action Efforts

To examine these effects, we again look at 1987 minority enrollments. In our regression equations, we take into account those factors that had a significant impact on 1987 minority enrollments (table 5.7). Then we add to the equation the measures of internal and external affirmative action activities that we examined in chapters 3 and 4. We also add to the equation the perceptions of the admissions officers of the changing nature of the minority applicant pool. In table 5.8 we list only those variables that significantly predicted 1987 enrollments. Because our equations are based on variables derived from the questionnaire data, the number of cases is lower than in the earlier analyses, when all schools were examined. Since the sample size is fairly small, we use a more liberal, .10, test of statistical significance.

Almost all the variation among medical schools in their African American enrollment is predictable by these factors. As before, the proportion of blacks in the school in 1977 was by far the strongest predictor. However, perceptions of improvement in the quantity and quality of the black applicant pool also significantly predicted 1987 enrollment. This

TABLE 5.8.   The Impact of Internal and External Affirmative Action on Minority Enrollment, 1987

	Medical Schools		Law Schools
	Blacks	Hispanics	Minorities
Previous minority enrollment	.95	.31	.90
	(45.75)	(2.72)	(24.24)
Percent Hispanic	NA	.23	
		(3.63)	
Pressure from external groups		1.10	2.54
		(1.37)	(1.91)
Pressure from accreditation agencies		.86	
		(1.46)	
Pressure from federal government	.59		
	(1.46)		
Pressure from state government	−.62		
	(−1.77)		
Minority affairs person			−.57
			(−2.79)
Perceived change in quantity of black applicant pool	.80	NA	
	(3.83)		
Perceived change in quality of black applicant pool	.43	NA	
	(1.81)		
R^2	.98	.72	.94
N	55	55	74

Note: Only those coefficients significant at the .10 level are shown. Coefficients significant at the more traditional level of .05 are in italic type. Values are unstandardized regression coefficients with *t* values in parentheses. NA means that the variable was not significant in the equations of table 5.3 and hence was not entered into these equations. The percentage of the state's black population and the perceived changes in the quantity and quality of Hispanic applicants were not significant in any of these equations and are not shown.

provides an indicator of the validity of these perceptual variables. Because they predict 1987 enrollment after 1977 enrollment is controlled, they do appear to be measuring *changes* in the application pool.

Having a minority affairs officer does not predict changes in black enrollment at all. However, pressure from the federal government is positively, and pressure from the state government negatively, related to the 1987 enrollment. We have only the same interpretations to offer as before; perhaps state pressure comes as a result of poor performance but is not sufficient to promote better performance.

The variables explaining Hispanic enrollment are not as powerful predictors as those factors explaining black enrollment. The chief difference appears to be the lesser predictive power of the 1977 Hispanic enrollment, as we found in our larger sample of schools. It is, however, still a strong predictor. Also echoing earlier findings is the significant impact of the proportion Hispanic population on Hispanic enrollment. Of the other variables, only pressure from outside groups and from accreditation agencies are significantly related to Hispanic enrollment. Both are positively, but weakly, related. Government pressure has no predictive power, positive or negative. Neither do perceptions of the admissions officials about the applicant pool.

The pattern for minority enrollment in law schools combines some of the features we have just noted. As with black medical school enrollment, previous enrollment is a powerful predictor of 1987 minority enrollment in law schools. As with Hispanics in medical school, pressure from external groups is positively correlated with changes in minority enrollment. Contrary to patterns for either medical school group, however, having a person in charge of minority recruitment actually seems to be negatively related to 1987 law enrollment, other things being equal. This strange finding does not seem to be an artifact of interrelationships among the independent variables. The bivariate relationship between 1987 enrollment and the presence of such a minority officer was also negative, albeit not significantly so. The presence of that officer was unrelated to 1977 minority enrollment, so we cannot argue that those schools that did the most poorly in 1977 were the ones who hired such officers.

Interethnic Competition

Throughout most of the book, we have discussed *Bakke* and affirmative action efforts as if African Americans and Hispanics would be equally affected. But since Hispanic medical school enrollments have risen faster than black, it is possible that Hispanics have gained at the expense of blacks. Alternatively, schools that did increase their black enrollments could have done so at the expense of Hispanic enrollment. In other words, schools could improve their affirmative action record for one group by diminishing it for another.

There is certainly evidence for interethnic competition in socio-economic status and political power, though most of it is based on local studies. Some Hispanics believe they have not gained as much as blacks from affirmative action, especially since blacks appear to have gained more government jobs (G. Cohen 1982; Falcon 1988). Hispanics tend not to vote for black candidates in municipal elections (Hahn and Almy 1971; Mohl 1982); on the other hand, in some areas, blacks lag behind Hispanics in income gains (Warren, Stack, and Corbett 1986), and in others have not supported some issues important to Hispanics, such as bilingual education (Falcon 1988). An analysis of school board elections in major cities provides some evidence of negative relationships between black and Hispanic electoral and policy success (Meier and Stewart 1991).

However, a broader study of several kinds of black and Hispanic competition in forty-nine U.S. communities with at least 10 percent black and 10 percent Hispanic population indicated that black and Hispanic socioeconomic status was *positively* linked. Where blacks did better in income, education, and employment, so did Hispanics (McClain and Karnig 1990). Competition for political resources did seem to occur, though there were not strong negative effects between black and Hispanic control of councils and mayorships. Rather, both groups gained at the expense of whites.

We examined the relationship between enrollment growth of Hispanic and black students by determining if changes in the enrollment of one group would predict enrollment by the other group. If schools are increasing the enrollment of one group at the expense of another, the relationships should be negative. However, that is not what we found. Looking only at medical schools, since in our law data both groups are combined, the simple bivariate correlation between change in black enrollment and change in Hispanic enrollment is .33, indicating that schools gaining blacks also gained Hispanics.

In a more complex analysis of the sort we did in tables 5.7 and 5.8, we also found a positive relationship between changes in enrollments of the two groups (see table 5.9). That is, increases in the proportion of

TABLE 5.9.   The Relationship of Changes in Hispanic Enrollment to Changes in Black Enrollment (medical schools only)

	Black Enrollment	Hispanic Enrollment
Prior enrollment	.92	.41
Percent black in population	.03	−.02*
Percent Hispanic in population	−.02*	.21
Change in enrollment percent of other group	.38	.16
R^2	.94	.70

Note: $N = 112$. All coefficients significant at .05 except those *. Coefficients are unstandardized regression coefficients.

Hispanic enrollment were positively related to black enrollment in 1987 after controlling for black enrollment in 1977. And, increases in the proportion of black students were positively related to Hispanic enrollment in 1987 after controlling for earlier Hispanic enrollment. Thus, schools that improved their minority enrollment record for one group improved it for the other.

Conclusion

In this chapter, we have examined a variety of indicators measuring the performance of medical and law schools in increasing black and Hispanic enrollment. From these, we can draw several conclusions.

The overall growth in minority enrollments in the typical medical or law school between 1978, the time of *Bakke,* and 1987 was extremely small—less than 0.5 percent in the case of black medical students, nearly 1 percent for Hispanics, and close to 3 percent for both groups in law schools. Statis, rather than change, characterizes minority enrollments during this period. The growth in minority enrollments reached a plateau before the *Bakke* decision, and then rose and fell in a rather erratic fashion. It was not until the early 1980s that a clear decline set in, and that was generally reversed toward the middle of that decade. We concluded that these trends were probably more related to the economic climate of the times than to *Bakke.*

Our institutional analysis also supports the view that the decision largely served to institutionalize existing patterns and practices. The institutions that had larger minority enrollments in 1977 also had them in 1987. We assumed that if *Bakke* did have an impact in changing recruitment practices and targets, there would be more fluctuation in enrollment patterns across institutions. The fluctuations that did exist were largely explained by the minority population within the states. Especially in the case of Hispanics, a larger minority population in the state corresponded with greater growth in enrollments.

Few institutional characteristics explained growth in minority enrollments. Larger schools appeared to gain more minorities than other schools, but this relationship, not clear to begin with, disappeared when other factors were examined simultaneously. Having an official in charge of minority enrollments did not seem to have much of an impact on changing minority enrollment patterns. This lack of relationship may be due to the crudeness with which we measured this variable, however.

External pressures are somewhat related to enrollment changes. Hispanic and law enrollment seemed to be most sensitive to external group influences, including accreditation agencies in the case of Hispanic medical enrollment. Black enrollment in medical school was positively related to perceived federal pressure, though negatively related to perceived state pressure.

Finally, we examined the link between the officers' perceived changes in the minority applicant pool and 1987 enrollment. We found a substantial link between increased African American medical school enrollment and perceptions that the African American applicant pool was increasing in quality and quantity. However, this relationship did not prove helpful in explaining growth in Hispanic medical school enrollment or for minority law school enrollment.

Given the modest changes in minority enrollments in the decade after *Bakke* and our conclusion that, therefore, *Bakke* served to institutionalize rather than dramatically change affirmative action practices in place by the late 1970s, what relevance does the case have today? How have the effects of *Bakke*, the more current trends in minority enrollments, and recent changes in the judicial and political climate combined to shape the contemporary affirmative action debate? It is to these issues that we now turn.

CHAPTER 6

Minority Enrollment
and the Courts

Minority enrollment in medical and law school, which had been minuscule, began increasing substantially in the mid-1960s after years of
struggle for civil rights and after efforts by professional organizations
and schools to boost minority opportunities. Minority enrollment
peaked in the mid-1970s, before the *Bakke* decision in 1978. Yet its
proponents and opponents alike heralded the decision as one that would
determine the extent of minority enrollment in professional schools and
even the validity of affirmative action and the speed of civil rights progress for years. In particular, many commentators, referring to the "chilling effect of *Bakke,*" predicted that the ruling, by invalidating quotas,
would result in fewer applications by minority students, less pressure on
schools to admit them, and, consequently, smaller minority enrollments.

The Effects of *Bakke*

But *Bakke* did not have these effects. Based on this systematic study of
Bakke's impact, we conclude that its effect on boosting or curtailing
minority enrollment was far less than either supporters or opponents
initially predicted. Nonetheless, the decision was significant because it
legitimated and institutionalized the practice of affirmative action in admissions decisions. Although increasingly under challenge, it continues to
be the court decision underpinning affirmative action in higher education
admissions.

We are confident in our conclusions but realize there are limits to this
study. As with any examination of the impact of a court case, it is difficult
to separate the effect of the court ruling from the effects of other factors
occurring at the time. And the longer the time period examined, the more

difficult it is to separate these effects, because "the repercussions of all government actions ramify indefinitely and interrelate with other phenomena, both public and private, many of which simply cannot be quantified and indeed often cannot even be identified" (Choper 1984, 7).

Moreover, predicting individual behavior from aggregate characteristics is always risky. We have examined decisions made by a few thousand students and a few hundred schools in our aggregate analysis but have tried to predict their behavior with variables affecting millions. We have assumed that the few thousand applicants and enrollees have been affected by the changes in the entire black and Hispanic population. However, it is possible that a significant number of these students were not greatly affected by these changes; many of the applicants come from the solid middle and upper-middle class of the black or Hispanic community who, like their white, Anglo counterparts, were not seriously threatened by unemployment or recession or even negative political rhetoric about affirmative action.

Ideally, we would have conducted a before-and-after study of both individuals and institutions. It would be useful to have examined students' reasons for applying or not applying to professional schools to see if they differed before and after *Bakke,* and indeed to determine if students were even aware of *Bakke* and its predicted impact. Such a before-and-after design could have profitably been used to study the admissions process, too. The "before" portion could have assessed the existence of quotas or goals far more concretely than we were able to here.

Our study design falls far short of this ideal. Much time has passed since the decision. We have no "before" information from individuals and admissions committees except that based on recall. Most researchers, including us, lack the foresight to anticipate a decision such as this far enough in advance to get into the field and obtain all the data before the ruling alters the behavior of those affected (or before anticipation of the ruling alters the behavior, as perhaps occurred with *DeFunis* and similar cases attracting attention prior to *Bakke*). And so we must assemble the best evidence we can after the decision. We believe we have done so by tapping aggregate, institutional, and individual survey sources.[1]

Given this evidence, our conclusions are reasonably straightforward. Admissions officials said in response to our questionnaire that the impact on their decisions was "none" or "slight." Hardly any said it was "significant." Our analyses of aggregate applications, acceptances, and enrollments confirm these officials' impressions. The impact of *Bakke* was minimal in affecting the number of minority applicants or enrollees. The ruling apparently caused no decline in the quantity or quality of applications by minority students. Indeed, with the exception of the quantity of black male medical school applicants, the consensus of officials is that both the quality and the quantity of black and Hispanic applicants increased in the decade after *Bakke*. The ruling might have led to a small decrease in black enrollment in medical school for one year and a slower increase in Hispanic enrollment in medical school for two or three years. On the other hand, the ruling might have halted the decrease in the acceptance ratio for African Americans to medical school and, in the short run, for Latinos to medical school as well. But these results, even if caused by the ruling, were small.

The most significant finding about individual schools is that those with the most minorities the year before *Bakke* were the ones with the most minorities a decade after, and those with the least before were the ones with the least after. Thus, the factors that predicted minority enrollments before *Bakke*, such as the state's minority population, continued to account for them after. Patterns of institutional behavior tend to persist, and professional school enrollment before and after *Bakke* is certainly an example of that persistence.

Beyond this pattern, few systemic differences among schools emerged. Among medical schools, public schools increased their proportion of minority enrollment more than private schools. Yet the major state universities increased their proportion of Hispanic students the most, while other state universities increased their proportion of black students the most. Among law schools, private schools registered more gains than public schools.

Was the *Bakke* Case Typical?

Our conclusions reinforce those of some previous studies of the impact of court decisions. As we noted earlier, many studies of the implementation and effects of judicial decisions have found that impact is sometimes less than what would be expected simply from knowing the U.S. Supreme Court's decision or reading its opinion. Rulings do not always change behavior in the expected way, to the expected extent, or at all (Wasby 1970; 1993, 346–90; C. Johnson and Canon 1984; Rosenberg 1991).

For example, after the Supreme Court's *Miranda* decision (*Miranda v. Arizona*, 384 U.S. 436, [1966]), some police officers did not advise suspects of their rights to silence and an attorney before interrogating them. Other officers did advise suspects but found them more willing to confess than to exercise their rights (Wald et al. 1967; Medalie et al. 1968). Contrary to predictions, there was only a small decline in confessions (Seeburger and Wettick 1967). After the Court's school prayer decisions in 1962 and 1963 (*Engel v. Vitale,* 370 U.S. 421 [1962]; *Abington School District v. Schempp,* 374 U.S. 203 [1963]), public-school teachers reported less compliance with the ban on prayers by schools in the Midwest than those in the West and East, and much less compliance by those in the South than in other regions (Dolbeare and Hammond 1971).

The Supreme Court must rely upon others, sometimes called the "implementing population," to give a ruling any effect (C. Johnson and Canon 1984). This population includes individuals, normally authorities, who are charged with putting a ruling into effect and whose behavior can be sanctioned by the high court or lower courts. For the Miranda warnings, officials in police departments and officers in the field constituted the implementing population. For the school prayer restrictions, school board members, superintendents, principals, and teachers constituted this population. The reaction to the ruling by these implementers shapes the effect of the ruling. Often those in the implementing population hold opinions contrary to the justices'. Some law enforcement personnel did not want to start giving the Miranda warnings, nor did some educators want to stop offering school prayers.

For *Bakke,* admissions officials and others who affect admissions decisions formed the implementing population. Despite initial fears by civil rights organizations, hindsight indicates that most of these officials were at least somewhat committed to increasing minority enrollment. They believed they should make this effort, and they had established procedures to do so. To the extent that the Court's ruling made this goal more difficult to achieve, these officials might be less than enthusiastic to implement it. Nevertheless, they apparently did continue to implement it. Our findings that the schools with the best record of minority enrollment before *Bakke* were also the ones with the best record a decade after *Bakke* suggest the influence of the implementing population.

The Court must rely also upon others to communicate the rule to those who must implement it. The Court does not send word of a ruling to all parties whose behavior is affected by it. The litigants themselves receive word through their lawyers, but others are left to depend on more hit-or-miss methods. Most individuals and small organizations learn about developments through the media or by word of mouth (Milner 1971). Large organizations have legal staffs or law firms to keep them abreast of relevant judicial decisions. Thus, although few booksellers knew about obscenity rulings that in theory affected them, according to one survey (Levine 1969), the same could not be said about admissions officials and the *Bakke* ruling. As we have shown, there was ample communication, both before and after the ruling. Schools had a huge stake in this decision, and officials paid attention to the evaluations and predictions from their lawyers, the various professional associations to which the schools belonged, and the specialized publications to which they subscribed.

Yet the ruling itself was not clear. Ample communication of an ambiguous message still leaves an ambiguous message. Studies have shown that ambiguous rulings are less likely to change behavior (Canon 1977; Gruhl 1981b; Neubauer 1974; Rodgers and Bullock 1972; Romans 1974). There were three major opinions, but there was no majority opinion or even a plurality opinion. The controlling opinion was that of only one justice. This unusual situation indicated that the ruling was unstable and could change quickly. Further, this opinion pointed in two opposite directions. By invalidating quotas, it could be interpreted as weakening our societal commitment to civil rights progress, but by accepting the use of race as a positive factor, it could be interpreted as strengthening, or at least solidifying, this commitment. Both opponents and proponents of civil rights progress could take comfort or umbrage in the split ruling. But most significant, the ruling was ambiguous in its failure to sharply distinguish between quotas, on the one hand, and the use of race as a positive factor, or the use of "goals," "targets," or "numbers," on the other hand. And Powell's language granting schools leeway in making their admissions decisions signaled that not much in their procedures would have to change. At most, the remaining schools with obvious quotas would have to eliminate them.

These ambiguities might have been clarified by subsequent rulings, but the justices did not take any related cases. Although the Court did issue other affirmative action rulings, mostly in employment cases, it did not decide any other school admissions cases. When the Court issues a major ruling initiating doctrine in a new area, ordinarily it follows this ruling with others in the same area. In later cases it defines, articulates, and reinforces its new doctrine. This practice can increase the Court's impact (Gruhl 1981a), especially when the original ruling was ambiguous. Yet the Court has left its *Bakke* ruling as its last word on the subject of affirmative action in education (at least at the time of this writing, almost two decades later). Perhaps there were no more appropriate cases, for reasons that we will explore subsequently. Or perhaps the division among the justices discouraged them from trying to resolve this contentious issue any further. Possibly most of the justices were satisfied, if not with all aspects of the ruling, at least with their victory of either striking down quotas or upholding the use of race. Or conceivably most of the justices were satisfied with allowing schools latitude to establish their general admissions procedures and to make their specific decisions in individual cases.

For the most part, this study, unlike some studies of the impact of court decisions, cannot focus on noncompliance with or, more subtley, evasion of the decision in question. Because *Bakke* was not clear, it is virtually impossible to determine if schools refused to comply or tried to evade.

Not all rulings require people to change their behavior. Some simply allow officials or institutions to continue doing whatever they were doing. Others allow, but do not require, officials or institutions to begin doing something they were not doing. Such rulings are less likely to result in any apparent impact. Except for the admonition to abandon quotas, *Bakke* was such a ruling. A study especially relevant to *Bakke* assessed the impact of the Burger Court's obscenity doctrine established in *Miller v. California* (413 U.S. 15 [1973]). Although the ruling made it easier to prosecute individuals for producing and distributing pornography, the ruling did not require prosecutors to prosecute more, and prosecutors reported that they did not prosecute more (Project 1977). Many, in fact, said that they prosecuted fewer cases. Prosecutors said that they thought the ruling was somewhat ambiguous. Pornographers, in anticipation of prosecution, shielded their business in ways that made it difficult to trace and assess responsibility. Prosecutors also perceived that the public had become more tolerant of pornography and thus jurors had become less willing to convict. Thus, the Court's decision, which created the opportunity for change, did not result in change in the anticipated direction.

Whether a ruling has any effect also depends upon the "consumer population," those individuals who will gain benefits or suffer losses under the ruling. For the Miranda warnings, this population would include criminal defendants, who would get their rights read to them, and law enforcement officers, who would have this obligation imposed on their procedures. For the school prayer rulings, this population would include students, both those who opposed the prayers and those who appreciated them, and perhaps the teachers who also were exposed to them. For *Bakke,* those individuals affected were the potential and actual applicants to professional schools, both minorities and nonminorities. We found that the members of this population were relatively little affected, either in their rate of applying for professional school or in their opportunity to be admitted.

Finally, we can examine the impact of the decision on the "secondary population," everyone not directly affected. The media, of course, are a relevant part of the secondary population. The media clearly covered the *Bakke* decision. But except in a few cases, the coverage was superficial. An average reader could rightly have been puzzled as to what the decision meant. Very little information was provided to readers about the nature of affirmative action practices beyond those at Davis. It was well over a decade after *Bakke* that the media began to describe the way affirmative action practices work at a variety of institutions. In the few years following *Bakke,* the lack of intense media interest helped defuse the issue and contributed to the legitimization of affirmative action. The lack of media concern, coupled with the lack of further judicial scrutiny in the decade after *Bakke,* also allowed some institutions to drift back into near-quota systems in their affirmative action practices.

The lack of impact of the decision could have had positive or negative consequences for minorities, depending upon what schools were doing before *Bakke.* The decision had positive consequences for minorities in schools active in recruiting minorities before the decision. Those schools saw *Bakke* as a green light to continue this activity. However, the lack of impact would have negative consequences for minorities in those schools not interested in increasing minority enrollments, because nothing about the decision would cause those schools to accelerate their activity. But, in most cases, medical and law schools were interested in recruiting minorities. Officials said they did, and continued to, take race into account. In fact, they reported that they took it into account somewhat more after than before. By 1989, almost all law and medical schools gave extra consideration to blacks; almost all law schools gave special consideration to Hispanics and American Indians, too. Over two-thirds of all medical schools gave extra consideration to Hispanics and over three-fourths gave it to American Indians.

Thus, special recruitment and retention efforts were institutionalized. A faculty member at New York University law school stated that "minority applicants may be given enough of a preference based upon their race to ensure that the school's 'goal' of minority enrollment is met." Consequently, he insisted, "Virtually all universities and professional schools have maintained their program for minority admissions and have operated them to secure roughly the same percentage of minority students each year" (B. Schwartz 1988, 155). An admissions official responding to our survey was only slightly more circumspect: ". . . *Bakke* taught me that I should be careful not to think or express myself in terms of quotas. I think too that it vindicated what most law schools had been doing for a long time, i.e. bending over backwards to give minorities a chance. . . ."

Besides eliminating formal quotas, some schools implemented more detailed record keeping to protect them against charges of reverse discrimination. NYU law school, for example, began to keep records not only on the race of its new students, but also on their age, geographic region, and academic or employment background. The purpose was to enable the school to demonstrate diversity in various ways. Thus, one observer (Seligman 1978, 47) noted, "The case that many admissions officials feared would end special admissions may instead have shown universities how to insulate themselves from effective legal challenge." As Bakke's attorney predicted after his successful case, lawsuits against schools for reverse discrimination would be harder to win without the damaging evidence of formal quotas. This difficulty may account for the absence of similar court cases to clarify the doctrine until the 1990s.

With these findings in mind, we argue that rather than having no apparent, significant impact, *Bakke* appears to have had an important impact of solidifying the existing practice of affirmative action in admissions. While formal quotas disappeared, actions to maintain and increase minority enrollments became institutionalized. Admissions officials look differently at test scores and grade point averages of minority applicants compared with white, non-Hispanic applicants, and until the 1990s, this practice had been taken for granted, at least by most university officials. By legitimizing it, *Bakke* allowed the growth and further development of these race-conscious policies.

This result is not inconsequential. Legitimating executive and congressional policies is one of the most important functions of the courts. Although many people assume that *Marbury v. Madison* (1 Cranch 137

[1803]), which articulated the courts' authority to exercise judicial review, was the Supreme Court's most important ruling, some legal scholars insist that *McCulloch v. Maryland* (4 Wheat. 316 [1819]), which upheld the government's authority to create and operate a national bank, was actually more important. Robert McCloskey (1960, 66) wrote that *McCulloch* was "by almost any reckoning the greatest decision John Marshall ever handed down—the one most important to the future of America, most influential in the Court's own doctrinal history. . . ." *McCulloch* was important because the Court legitimated government action. In his analysis of the role of the Court, Robert Dahl (1972, 200–210) concluded that "the main contribution of the Court is to confer legitimacy on the fundamental policies" of the governing coalition. Otherwise, he said, the Court would interfere with the democratic process. It is not necessary for us to go this far to agree that legitimating governmental policy is an important function for the courts and to see that legitimating affirmative action was an important result of the *Bakke* case.

Affirmative Action and Minority Enrollment

Minority enrollment in professional schools obviously depends on previous minority enrollments at the undergraduate level. Though the enrollment of African Americans at that level dramatically increased in the late 1960s and early 1970s, by the mid-1970s, the spurt had slowed. After 1981, there was a downturn in black enrollment overall ("Trends" 1995; see also NSF 1990, 40; U.S. Department of Commerce 1991, table 1004). Hispanic enrollment, however, continued to increase; between 1976 and 1986, overall Hispanic college enrollment increased by over 60 percent ("Trends" 1995).

Black and Hispanic Enrollments in the Decade after *Bakke*

The number of minorities in medical and law schools showed little increase during the decade from 1976 to 1986. This stagnation is distressing, but it should not be startling. Minority enrollment in professional schools depends not only, or even primarily, upon affirmative action. Other factors in addition to public policy affect the socioeconomic behavior and status of any group. Research on the impact of affirmative action in employment has also found modest changes at best. Kellough and Kay (1986) discovered that authorization of goals and timetables in the federal bureaucracy in 1972 resulted in no major changes in the employment of blacks in the eight years after, compared with the ten years before the authorization; other studies also have found only modest gains (Dometrius and Sigelman 1984; Huron 1984; Welch, Karnig, and Eribes 1983; Badgett and Hartman 1996). The effects appear somewhat greater for blacks than for Hispanics (Rodgers and Springs 1996).

In higher education, the Reagan administration's negative stance on affirmative action, the downturn in the economy in the early 1980s, and the increased competitiveness for admission to law and medical schools might have had more effect on minority admissions than the Supreme Court did. Not surprisingly, several studies (Rice and Whitby 1986; Eisinger 1986) have concluded that major changes in the economy have as much effect on the employment of blacks as civil rights policies did. For example, though the Civil Rights Act of 1964 led to improvement in black employment relative to white employment until 1976, economic conditions, such as a shift from manufacturing to high-tech jobs, an increase in unemployment rates for jobs traditionally held by African Americans, and a decrease in hiring by governments all led to deterioration in black employment from 1977 to 1983, despite the Civil Rights Act.

Black and Hispanic income dropped during the 1980s and began to rebound only in the latter part of the decade (U.S. Department of Commerce 1994, table 714), before falling again in the early 1990s, along with that of other groups. To compound the problem, college costs soared and federal financial aid declined. Much of what remained was shifted from grants to loans. These economic slowdowns would appear to have had an effect on minority enrollment not just in professional schools, but also in the undergraduate institutions that launch students to professional schools. During the 1980s, blacks steadily increased their rate of high school graduation but not of college attendance.[2]

Demographic factors also contributed to the limited progress in black professional school enrollments. As we saw in chapter 2, the postwar baby boom boosted the number of applicants to the point where admission to professional schools became highly competitive for the first time. If the civil rights movement had been successful a decade earlier, before the baby boom generation descended on graduate and professional schools, the problem of competition and test scores would be of a much lesser magnitude.

Falling incomes and increasing competitiveness seemed to have hit young black men the hardest. The number of black men in college actually decreased by 7 percent between 1976 and 1986, compared to a growth of 17 percent for black women (see also Hill 1994). Perhaps the most disturbing findings in our study are those that reflect the slow progress of black men during the 1980s and early 1990s, findings that are echoed in almost every tally of black educational and economic progress.[3]

During the decade after *Bakke* and continuing into the 1990s, the test scores and grade point averages of minority students (except Asians in medical school) are well below those of white students. This difference has been documented in published reports concerning medical schools (S. Shea and Fullilove 1983; AAMC 1993), law schools (Law School Admission Council 1986), and undergraduate and other institutions (T. Cross 1994a, 1994b).[4] However, minority professional applicants improved their test scores relative to white applicants during at least part of this first post-*Bakke* decade. Evidence for this improvement comes from both the perceptions of admissions officials and analyses of test scores over time. One analysis of changing MCAT scores between 1977 and 1983 showed that not only had the average scores of black students improved, but they had improved more than those of white students (S. Shea and Fullilove 1985).

Booming African American and Hispanic Enrollments in the Late 1980s and 1990s

Bakke legitimized affirmative action in higher education during the 1980s and at least set the stage for dramatic growth in black and Hispanic enrollment in the early 1990s. The picture of stagnation in African American and Hispanic enrollment so clear in the mid-1980s has changed dramatically in the years since. Overall black college enrollment increased 30 percent between 1986 and 1994 (including an increase of 20 percent of black men). The number of degrees earned by African Americans increased at all levels, including a staggering 34 percent in bachelor's degrees and 40 percent in master's degrees ("Trends" 1995).

Hispanic educational gains have been even more dramatic, reflecting the growth in the Hispanic population. Overall Hispanic enrollments increased by over 50 percent during that time, as have the number of bachelor's degrees awarded. Increases in master's degrees have been nearly as high, and doctorates have increased by over one-third.

Progress in medical and law schools has been equally impressive (AAMC 1993; "Vital Signs" 1995; see figs. 6.1 and 6.2). Beginning in

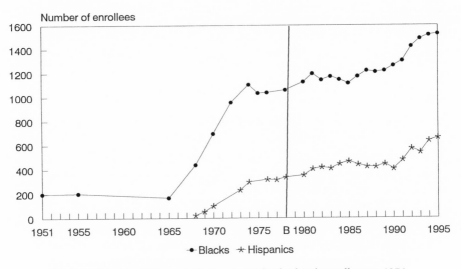

Fig. 6.1.   Black and Hispanic first-year medical school enrollment, 1951–95. "B" marks the date of the *Bakke* decision. (Data from Shea and Fullilove 1985; Medical School Admission Requirements, selected years.)

1988, the number of African Americans in first-year medical classes has increased each year, and in 1995, it was nearly 40 percent higher than in 1988. Mexican American and Puerto Rican first-year enrollment has increased by 43 percent during that time. Indeed, by the mid-1990s, white U.S. citizens were only a little more than two-thirds of total first-year enrollment in medical schools. African Americans, American Indians, Mexican Americans, and other Hispanics together accounted for 14.5 percent of the total. Asians accounted for 16.4 percent.[5] Similar trends occurred in law schools. The overall enrollment of African Americans and Hispanics there increased over 40 percent and almost 50 percent, respectively, between 1988 and 1995 (Mort and Moskowitz 1994).

These gains have been particularly dramatic in light of the falling real income of both groups in the early 1990s. The increases suggest that enrollment of African Americans and Hispanics achieved a momentum, at least in the short term, that defied the mild economic slump.

The Retreat from Affirmative Action

Although *Bakke* legitimized affirmative action in higher education for some years, in the 1990s support among governmental officials for affir-

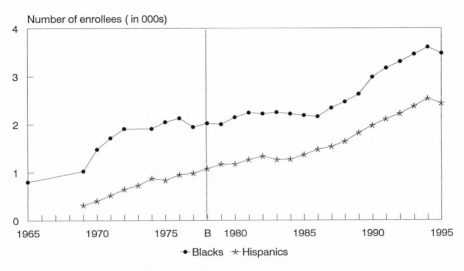

Fig. 6.2.   Black and Hispanic first-year law school enrollment. "B" marks the date of the Bakke decision. (Data from Shea and Fullilove 1985; *Lawyer's Almanac* 1986; American Bar Association Survey.)

mative action eroded significantly. By that time, most universities, along with other institutions, were examining their affirmative action practices.

The Courts

Although the Supreme Court showed signs of narrowing the scope of civil rights laws in the mid-1980s (*Grove City College v. Bell,* 465 U.S. 555 [1984]), it began to weaken its support for affirmative action practices in the late 1980s. In part, this weakening support occurred because Justice Powell, who retired in 1987, was replaced by Justice Kennedy, who was less supportive of affirmative action. Then Justice Brennan, who was a staunch supporter of affirmative action and a very effective coalition builder on the Court, retired in 1990. The Court's support of affirmative action was also weakened in 1991 by the retirement of Justice Marshall, also a staunch supporter of affirmative action, and by the appointment of Justice Thomas, a black justice opposed to affirmative action.

In a 1989 procedural case, the Court held that whites, or men, who did not challenge affirmative action agreements (consent decrees) when they were being formulated might be able to challenge them after they had been put into effect (*Martin v. Wilks*, 109 S.Ct. 2180 [1989]). This decision raised the specter that the Court might upend affirmative action programs that have long been considered settled. In a more substantive case that same year, the Court held that Richmond, Virginia, cannot set aside 30 percent of its construction funds for minority firms without establishing a record of past discrimination (*Richmond v. Croson*, 109 S.Ct. 706 [1989]). The ruling underscored the fact that the Court does not consider racial disparity itself to be evidence of past discrimination. The ruling did not necessarily doom set-asides. Many governments should have no trouble establishing a record of past discrimination, whether from their policies or from their passive participation in the policies of other segments of society (e.g., the local construction industry). The ruling, however, seems to have discouraged some governments from adopting set-asides (see Jaschik 1995a, 1995b). Together these two decisions sent a signal that the Court was now less sympathetic to affirmative action.[6]

Despite the signal sent in 1989, in the next term the Supreme Court said that the *Richmond* decision did not negate the earlier *Fullilove* decision on set-asides (see chap. 1), presumably because the *Fullilove* policy was established by Congress (*Metro Broadcasting v. FCC*, 110 S.Ct. 2997 [1990]). In this case, a five-justice majority upheld a policy that was established by another part of the federal government—the FCC—to increase the number of minority-owned television and radio stations. The majority justified the policy by saying it furthered the government's goal of promoting more diversity in broadcasting—a justification that hearkens back to Justice Powell's rationale for using race in admissions.

Yet, in 1995, the majority indicated that it probably would overrule the *Metro Broadcasting* ruling. In *Adarand Constructors Inc. v. Pena* (132 LEd2d 158 [1995]), which also involved a set-aside program (by the Department of Transportation for highway construction), the five-justice majority ruled that the "strict scrutiny" standard must be used for all racial classifications, even benign ones such as affirmative action programs. Therefore, the programs must demonstrate a "compelling government interest" and be "narrowly tailored." Although the case involved the Department of Transportation and its preferences for minority contractors, observers noted that this case would have significant impact on federal education programs. About forty such programs exist that involve racial preferences (Jaschik 1995a). Some award grants to minority students and faculty members (such as the Department of Education's fellowships for black graduate students), and others set aside portions of their grant budgets for historically black colleges and other schools that have large minority populations (such as the National Science Foundation's set-aside within its science-education budget). In 1995 and subsequent years, the Court also threw into question the practice of creating "minority-majority" voting districts (*Miller v. Johnson* 132 LEd2d 762 [1995]). While seemingly far removed from the question of criteria for admitting students to universities, the issue involved the extent to which race can be used as a positive factor in policy decisions. And there again, in a 5–4 vote, the Court held that race cannot be the compelling factor in creating voting districts, even if the objective is to create more proportional representation of the black population in Congress.

Some federal courts of appeals have been more aggressive than the Supreme Court. The court for the Fourth Circuit ruled that a University of Maryland scholarship program exclusively for blacks was unconstitutional because it was not narrowly tailored to remedy discrimination against them (*Kirwan v. Podberesky,* 38 F3d 147 [1995]). A Hispanic student who had earned a perfect 4.0 high school GPA and scored 1340 on his SATs had applied for one of the scholarships but was denied the opportunity to compete for them. The district court upheld the scholarship program as a remedy for past discriminatory practices at the school. (It was segregated until the 1954 *Brown* decision, and it resisted integration for another twenty years after that.) But the appeals court, saying that a history of discrimination by itself cannot justify race-conscious remedies, concluded that this program was not narrowly tailored to overcome the school's past discrimination because it was open to blacks from all states, not just from Maryland. The evidence showed that thirty-one of the seventy-six students who had received these awards were from other states. And forty-two were not financially needy (Jaschik 1995c). The school appealed, but the Supreme Court denied certiorari.

One law professor, commenting on the case, observed that there appears to be a sentiment among judges that schools and local governments have taken affirmative action too far. "*Bakke* set a 'yes, but . . . ' standard, [yet] schools have emphasized the 'yes,' not the 'but'" (Biskupic 1994).

The *Hopwood* case has brought issues of affirmative action in higher education into the public spotlight once again (*Hopwood v. University of Texas Board of Regents,* 861 F.Supp 551 W.D., Tex. [1994]). In the case sometimes called "The *Bakke* of the 90's" (Jaschik 1994a), a white woman, Cheryl Hopwood, and three white men sued the University of Texas Law School after being denied admission. They challenged the school's goal of 10 percent of the seats for Mexican Americans and 5 percent for African Americans, and also the school's procedures for evaluating the applications of minorities. The procedures used lower standards for GPAs and LSAT scores for the two minorities. The plaintiffs had substantially higher GPAs and test scores than the majority of black and Mexican American applicants who were admitted, and upon questioning at the trial, university officials indicated that the plaintiffs would "in all probability" have been admitted had they been black (Bernstein 1994a).

The federal district court upheld the numerical goal, noting that the percentages had varied during the past ten years, from 10 percent to 14 percent for Mexican Americans and from 3 percent to 9 percent for African Americans. Although the school argued that these procedures were "in the mainstream" of those used by "law schools and other schools throughout the country," and deans of the law schools at Stanford and the universities of Minnesota, Michigan, and North Carolina reportedly testified that they use similar procedures (Bernstein 1994a), the appeals court invalidated the procedures because they entailed separate screening of minorities from whites, as Powell's opinion in *Bakke* criticized. The university used a subcommittee of the full admission committee to screen minority applicants, while the full committee screened nonminority candidates. The subcommittee's decisions, though subject to review by the full committee, were virtually final. The district court's decision upheld the right of colleges to consider race and ethnicity but ruled out separate committees to evaluate white and minority applicants, as well as different minimum test scores and grade point averages.

Yet the court refused to order the admission of the challengers; it concluded that they did not prove they would have been admitted anyway. The plaintiffs were awarded $1 each and the right to reapply under the new procedures without a new application fee. In essence, the court reaffirmed the general principles of the *Bakke* case, and the university changed its practices.[7] As with the *Bakke* decision, both sides claimed victory. University of Texas officials claimed victory because the university was not ordered to admit the plaintiffs. The plaintiffs claimed victory because the law school was forced to change its admission practices.

But victory for University of Texas officials would be short lived. Hopwood appealed, and the appeals court for the Fifth Circuit overturned the district court and issued the most sweeping decision yet involving affirmative action in education (*Hopwood v. Texas*, 78 F3d 932 [1996] No. 94-50569). The three-judge panel ruled that the law school cannot use race or ethnicity as a factor in admissions. The court rejected all justifications the school put forth—to achieve a diverse student body, to combat a hostile environment at the school, to alleviate a poor reputation in the minority community, and to eliminate present effects of past discrimination by actors other than the law school itself. Apparently the only finding that could justify the use of race would be clear evidence of present effects of past discrimination by the law school itself. But the court couched this possibility in such restrictive language that such a finding would be nearly impossible to show to the judges' satisfaction. Though there had clearly been de jure discrimination before the 1960s, with the de jure discrimination of the university invalidated in *Sweatt v. Painter* in 1950 and the de jure segregation in public schools in the state invalidated in *Brown* in 1954, the court asserted that there was no discrimination since the 1960s.

The judges took aim at the *Bakke* decision directly. Referring to Justice Powell's "lonely opinion," they emphasized that there was no majority opinion and thus no binding precedent to justify race-conscious remedies as means to achieve diversity. Remarkably, they said that use of race in admissions promotes no more diversity than use of applicants' blood type would. To think otherwise, they argued, is to stereotype people. Essentially, then, they rejected the existence of any shared experience of persons due to their race. The judges did hold out the possibility that the school could use applicants' economic and social background as a factor. (And while they said schools could not use race as a proxy for class, they did not say schools could not use class as a proxy for race.)

The university appealed to the Supreme Court, and the Law School Admission Council prepared a friend-of-the-court brief, but the justices denied certiorari. As is their custom, they issued no opinion to explain why, but two justices did issue their own opinion. Although noting that the question of constitutionality of a public school's use of race or national origin is of great national importance, Justices Ginsburg and Souter said they considered the case moot because the law school discontinued separate admissions procedures for minority and nonminority applicants after the district court's decision (*Texas v. Hopwood*, 135 LEd2d 1095 No. 95-1773, July 1, 1996). Thus, the appellate judges, acting as conservative activists, made a more sweeping ruling than the facts of the case required. Ginsburg and Souter acknowledged that the use of race is an important national issue but said they would wait until this issue was squarely presented. Because other justices did not join or issue their own opinion, it is unclear if they agreed or if they perhaps simply hoped to postpone such a contentious and divisive matter.

As a result, the ruling applies only to the states in the Fifth Circuit—Texas, Louisiana, and Mississippi.[8] At the same time, however, some schools in these states are under orders from other federal courts to use race-conscious remedies in admissions and scholarship decisions to make amends for past discrimination. Although the Department of Education initially told these schools to continue affirmative action or risk losing federal funds, it reversed itself a month later and told them to comply with the appellate court ruling.

Ultimately the issue will have to be resolved by the Supreme Court. Its conservative membership and recent decisions on affirmative action and civil rights suggest that the Court might weaken, if not discard, Powell's opinion in *Bakke,* which heretofore has generally been accepted as the guiding hand of the law.

The President and Congress

During the 1980s, and until 1993, Congress was the protector of affirmative action and the executive its opponent. As we have seen, President Reagan was an outspoken opponent of affirmative action. President Bush was even more outspoken (Shull 1993, 4, 65). Bush also was more active in some other ways. In 1990 he used a congressional civil rights bill as a wedge issue against Democrats, calling it a "quota bill" and vetoing it. (After a similar bill passed by a wider margin the next year, he accepted it.) Bush, of course, appointed a vocal critic of affirmative action—Clarence Thomas—to the Supreme Court. His Justice Department joined suits against affirmative action, and the head of his Education Department's Office for Civil Rights announced that it was illegal for colleges to award any scholarships that were restricted to particular races or ethnic groups. After protests, the department issued a revised policy that differed little from the earlier pronouncement.

Near the end of Bush's term, just weeks before the presidential election, the Education Department charged that the law school of the University of California at Berkeley violated the law by using quotas, separate procedures to evaluate minority and nonminority candidates, and separate waiting lists for minority and nonminority candidates. The school denied that it used a quota; it insisted that it merely set a "target" of 23 percent to 27 percent minorities. The school announced that it would continue to set a "target" but that it might discontinue the second and third of these practices ("Back to *Bakke,*" 1992, 32).

The congressional majority, then Democratic, generally supported affirmative action. Although the subject of "quotas" raised hackles on both sides of the aisle, in 1990 the majority passed a civil rights bill intended to overturn portions of Supreme Court rulings and to shift the burden of proof from employees to employers in job discrimination cases (Idelson 1995). After Bush vetoed the bill, sponsors compromised on some provisions, and in 1991 a larger majority passed the bill.

After the presidential election in 1992 and the congressional elections in 1994, the tables were turned. Since then, the major attacks on affirmative action have been led by the Republican-controlled Congress, and the support has come from the Democratic executive. Though arguing that sometimes affirmative action has gone too far, and after ordering a full-fledged review of existing federal programs, in 1995 President Clinton made a forceful statement of support. Calling "hiring unqualified people" and "reverse discrimination" the negative outgrowth of affirmative action, he pledged to weed out these these parts and preserve the valuable parts. "Mend it; don't end it," he proclaimed.

The administration had the Commerce Department conduct an industry-by-industry review to determine the areas in which minority businesses have faced discrimination in receiving government contracts. The goal is to continue affirmative action in these areas but not in any areas in which minority businesses have competed successfully. Thus, the administration is seeking to provide a record of evidence of discrimination that the Supreme Court now demands for minority set-asides in awarding government contracts.

While President Clinton supports affirmative action, albeit a reformed affirmative action, the Republican majority is moving toward cutting it back substantially. Republican conservatives have traditionally opposed affirmative action; now even moderates are jumping on the the bandwagon. However, Republicans do not agree on how far the cutbacks should go. Primary targets are set-asides in contracting policies; however, court decisions limiting preferential treatment in university admissions and scholarships have also drawn positive responses from Republicans.

Many Democrats, responding to the views of constituents, especially working-class whites, are also beginning to have second thoughts about affirmative action. As one former supporter, Senator Joseph Lieberman (Conn.), commented, "That inconsistency [between group preferences and the ideal of individual opportunity] has become more and more evident over time and has become less and less tenable politically" (Idelson 1995).

Supporters, however, point out that serious discrimination continues to exist in many sectors of society, particularly against African Americans. In 1994, for example, the Equal Employment Opportunity Commission received 91,000 complaints of job discrimination (Idelson 1995). While not all were valid, undoubtedly many were. And other instances of discrimination are not challenged. Periodically, for example, experiments are conducted where blacks and whites with the same bank account or résumé are sent to apply for jobs, or loans, or housing, and whites consistently do better at winning the job, financing, or home (cf. Kinsley 1996). And of course, while blacks and women have advanced in many businesses and professions, including law and medicine, top jobs in every field are still held predominantly by white men.

Congress is considering two approaches. One would outlaw federal programs that create special preferences, such as scholarships and set-asides in federal contracting or grant awarding. This approach would make federal programs color-blind but would not forbid universities, businesses, and state and local governments from establishing affirmative action policies. The other, much more far-reaching, approach would be to forbid organizations from using race or ethnicity as part of their hiring procedure. This approach would affect all public and private organizations.

Some state officials and voters have tried to abolish affirmative action in their states. In at least a dozen states, opponents have mounted campaigns to amend their constitutions to prevent affirmative action, and in a number of other states, legislators have sponsored bills to do so. The most visible efforts have flared up in California. Two professors, prompted by a proposed legislative bill to establish quotas for admission to and graduation from state universities (which failed to pass), launched a petition for an initiative to prohibit the use of "race, sex, color, ethnicity, or national origin as a criterion for either discriminating against, or granting preferential treatment to, any individual or group in the operation of the state's system of public employment, public education, or public contracting." (The initiative allows private organizations to practice affirmative action.) In 1996 a majority of the state's voters adopted this legislation.

Other Institutions: Businesses and Universities

Businesses, especially large corporations, gradually came to support affirmative action and, to a significant extent, continue to do so. This support, one commentator notes, "is one of the better kept secrets of the debate" (Wolfe 1996, 107). They already were accustomed to counting things—for example, their revenues, expenditures, and taxes; the products they sold and the inventories they held; the size of their markets and the size of their competitors' markets—so it was not a huge change in habits to count their employees by race and sex as well. When President Reagan's Attorney General, Edwin Meese, tried to mobilize the Cabinet against racial preferences in contracting, he was stopped by Secretary of Labor William Brock who was more attuned to business thinking. Affirmative action has been endorsed by the National Association of Manufacturers and by the Equal Employment Advisory Council, which numbers most of the Fortune 300 companies, and by the heads of numerous individual corporations (Zelnick 1996). In 1996 the initiative designed to eliminate affirmative action in government and in universities in California was opposed by many executives and corporations there.

Businesses have found affirmative action advantageous for several reasons. It helps shield them from political pressure by supporters of the policy and also helps shield them from discrimination lawsuits by prospective employees who were not hired or disgruntled employees who were not promoted. At the same time, affirmative action leads companies to new pools of untapped talent and also enables them to reach untapped markets. With more minority and women workers, they are better positioned to sell to these groups. And affirmative action allows large companies to impose costs on smaller competitors. The expenses of implementing affirmative action can be absorbed more easily by companies with more size and resources.

Thus, even when the Reagan and Bush administrations reduced pressure to follow affirmative action, many large corporations continued to follow it (Bergmann 1996). Or perhaps we should say, they continued to diversify.

University officials generally continue to be strong supporters of affirmative action specifically and diversity more generally (see, for example, Lederman 1996). At most meetings of professional academics, including medical and law school faculty and administrators, the issue of minority admissions continues to be an important topic. Sessions devoted to improving recruitment of minorities and designing legal strategies to do so became increasingly common throughout the late 1980s and 1990s. Similarly, higher education journals devoted considerable inches of print to this topic.

University officials justify affirmative action largely on the basis of the need for a diverse student body. Critics from both Right and Left argue, however, that universities are often not honest about their policies and do not defend them openly. Said Dana Takagi, a supporter of affirmative action, "If there were no affirmative action, the top universities would be all white and Asian, and that's a moral problem for the United States. . . . universities should give honest answers about their admissions policies and acknowledge that different groups in American society have different levels of preparation" (Jaschik 1994a, A47).

Barry Gross, an affirmative action opponent, remarked that the University of Texas Law School practices discussed earlier were commonplace: "Everybody does it. It's ubiquitous. But they lie about it because they think they are lying for a higher cause" (Jaschik 1994a, A47). He went on to comment that "only nine Scalias" could cause universities to change their affirmative action practices.

Nonetheless, a number of universities have modified their affirmative action procedures in recent years (see Jaschik 1994a). In 1992, the University of California Law School agreed to end the practice of separate reviews and separate waiting lists for members of different ethnic groups after the U.S. Education Department charged it with bias. The University of Wisconsin Law School also ended its use of separate review committees for white and minority applications. The University of Michigan Law School terminated its practice of having minority students review minority applications, because no students reviewed white applications, and Stanford University's Law School ended its policy of having one person review all minority applications. But these procedures were all questionable after *Bakke,* and modifying or eliminating them does not necessarily affect the use of race as a positive factor in admissions.

Clearly the most publicized backing away from affirmative action was done by the regents of the University of California, many of whom were appointed by Governor Pete Wilson, who ran for the Republican nomination for president in 1996, partly on a platform to end affirmative action. Even before the initiative was passed in the state, the regents voted to end racial preferences in admission, employment, and other activities of the University of California system. (In an unusual twist, one of the leaders of the effort to remove these race-based practices was a black member of the Board of Regents, and one of the biggest supporters of the policy was the Asian American chancellor of the Berkeley campus [Applebome 1995, 1]). Under the new rules, the campuses must admit at least 50 percent and no more than 75 percent of their students strictly on academic marks. Various factors, including economic background, special skills, or location, can be used to admit the rest of the class, but race and ethnicity cannot be used. One of the opponents of affirmative action asked the university to develop new criteria to give special weight to those who have overcome a disadvantaged background (Sanchez 1995). It is not clear to what extent race and ethnicity might be included as a factor in determining whether someone is from a "disadvantaged background," but it appears that those from poor backgrounds, no matter what their race, would be given some preference.

University of California officials estimated that without affirmative action, black enrollment would drop about 50 percent from its current 3.9 percent of UC's enrollment; Hispanic enrollment would drop 5 to 15 percent from its 12 percent; and Asian American enrollment would increase from its 25 percent (Lively 1995a).[9] Indeed, there is now evidence that at many institutions, Asians must have higher academic achievements than whites to get admitted.[10] If the university takes into account economic background, as it probably would try to do, given administrators' support for affirmative action, this impact would be softened (Sanchez 1995).

Almost a year after the regents' vote, a newspaper investigation revealed that several regents who opposed affirmative action acted behind the scenes to get relatives, friends, and children of business partners accepted. One regent made thirty-two requests to UCLA alone ("UC Reports" 1996). These actions suggest that the underlying factor motivating these regents' decisions was not an absolute belief in a merit system as measured by test scores and grades.

The regents' rules went into effect for graduate programs for fall 1997. There was a dramatic drop in minority admissions to the law school at the University of California at Berkeley (Haworth 1997). The number of blacks admitted fell 81 percent from the previous year—just fourteen students rather than seventy-five. The number of Hispanics admitted fell 50 percent—thirty-nine students rather than seventy-eight. The number of Asians increased 18 percent, and the number of whites increased 15 percent (Locke 1997). The rules will go into effect for undergraduates in fall 1998. On the other hand, at the University of California overall, officials expect about the same number of black and Hispanic students in fall 1997 as the previous fall. Though the number of black students admitted decreased by 6 percent, and Hispanic admissions dropped .5 percent, the proportion of minority students accepted who planned to attend increased. At some campuses of the University of California system, the number of minorities in the class is actually expected to increase (Selingo 1997).

The Hopwood ruling also went into effect for fall 1997, and the law school at the University of Texas at Austin also saw a dramatic drop in minority admissions. With most students selected, the school projected an entering class with .7 percent black students and 2.3 percent Hispanic students, compared with 5.9 percent black students and 6.3 percent Hispanic students the previous year (Cose 1997). As elite institutions, the law schools at Berkeley and Austin might face more dramatic changes than less selective schools where standardized test scores are not considered as essential to distinguish between students with almost equally high grade point averages.

Worried that similar drops would occur for minorities applying to undergraduate schools, the Texas legislature passed a law in 1997 to circumvent the Hopwood ruling (Healy 1997). The law requires state universities to admit all applicants from Texas high schools who graduated in the top 10 percent of their class. Thus, the law essentially substitutes geography for race. After these slots are filled, the universities can use other race-neutral criteria to choose the remaining students. This creative approach, one commentator observed, "takes one of this country's worst social tragedies, its racially segregated neighborhoods, and uses it to create a college applicant pool that reflects the state's racial, ethnic, and economic diversity" (Page 1997). To some extent, this approach offsets the system of financing the lower grades. This system, which is based on local property taxes, results in more funding for schools in more well-to-do areas.

To interpret these mixed, but largely negative, signals, it will be important to examine the trends in minority applications as well as the decisions made by admissions officials. Many universities around the nation, not just those affected by specific court rulings or new laws, have reported declining numbers of minority applications to graduate and professional schools (Gose 1997). For example, applications to medical schools decreased by more than 8 percent between 1996 and 1997. Applications from African Americans decreased by about the same margin, 9 percent, while applications from Hispanics decreased by around 14 percent. The numbers admitted show a slightly different pattern. White students admitted decreased slightly more than 1 percent, black students more than 3 percent, and Hispanic students more than 11 percent. From these early returns, then, it appears that the major effects on minority admissions to medical schools were among Hispanics rather than African Americans. Indeed, during this same period, admissions officers increased the proportion of black applicants they accepted by more than 4 percent, compared to a 1 percent increase in the admission of Latino applicants (all data from the AAMC, October 1997).

These data suggest, then, that Hispanic applications and admissions, in particular, are being affected by factors in addition to overall trends, while black applications and admissions seem more similar to those of whites. Hispanic trends may be particularly unique because a large proportion of Hispanic students live in California and Texas, two of the states specifically covered by anti-affirmative action policies. This presumed effect is much greater than any effect we have been able to show of the *Bakke* decision and greater than the effects of other court decisions that have been examined. Nonetheless, media reports of these trends are often exaggerated by not reporting the context of a decreasing pool of white as well as minority candidates.

The Law School Admission Council, which administers the LSAT, continues to urge schools to use race in admissions decisions. "We may well have to overhaul the incredibly efficient process for law school admissions . . . in order to ensure that well-qualified minority students have access to a legal education" (Shelton 1996). The LSAC and the schools might have to devise new tests or different criteria to guarantee the admission of significant numbers of minority students. This seems to be a remarkable commitment from the organization that is responsible for, and benefits from, the current reliance upon the LSAT.

The Public

The diminished support for affirmative action in major institutions reflects public attitudes in some rough way, though it is not clear that public attitudes toward affirmative action have changed. It was certainly true that there has always been significant opposition to affirmative action among whites. Many white Americans are angry and fearful about race. In a recent year a random sample of Americans believed, on average, that about one-third of the U.S. population was African American and another 21 percent Hispanic. This exaggerated view of the size of these populations contributes substantially to this fear, and the sense that this large group is getting special preferences exacerbates the fear even more (see Gallup and Newport 1990).

Race has always divided Americans, and in recent years race issues have become intertwined with ideology and party. Race has split liberals and conservatives for decades, and Republicans and Democrats at least since the 1960s. Political scientists argue about exactly how much influence race has had on the changing alignments of the party system (see Huckfeldt and Kohfeld 1989; Carmines and Stimson 1989; Abramowitz 1994), but all agree that it is one of the defining elements of current American politics. The debates over civil rights of the 1950s and 1960s and the early debates over affirmative action pitted progressive Republicans and northern Democrats, on the one hand, against conservative Republicans and Southern Democrats, on the other. After the Voting Rights Act, Southern Democrats gradually became more liberal, responding to the new black electorate, and Republicans became more uniformly conservative, thus polarizing the debate over race along party as well as ideological lines. By the 1990s, opposition to affirmative action was led by conservative Republicans.

Affirmative action in universities was strongly opposed in the early 1990s by critics such as Dinesh D'Souza (1991) and the National Association of Scholars (1991). Their views were widely quoted and appeared in columns, editorial pages, and TV talk shows across the nation. Though many of D'Souza's arguments were dismissed (see, for example Menand 1991),[11] his critique of affirmative action as preferential treatment based on race resonated with many people inside and outside the academy and helped stimulate legal and political challenges. (In contrast, his more recent book appeared both more extreme and less well received (D'Souza 1995).)

Conservative interest groups are actively challenging affirmative action procedures that set different standards for whites and other groups. One representative of a conservative legal group noted that the practice of lower standards for minorities reflects "one of these open secrets that lots of law schools and virtually all colleges have admissions quotas, to the extent that they think they can get away with it."[12]

But while most conservatives have opposed affirmative action from the start (cf. Glazer 1975), liberals are split. Strong support exists for affirmative action among a minority of whites, particularly those in universities and civil rights advocacy groups. Negative court decisions have prompted some supporters to renew their vocal support of affirmative action policy (see Kinsley 1996; Michaelson 1996). But some liberals and those sympathetic to civil rights are joining the opposition. Liberals have heretofore felt constrained to criticize affirmative action because it seemed to put them in the same camp with those who have traditionally opposed equality and civil rights. But now that some prominent African Americans, such as Supreme Court justice Clarence Thomas, California Board of Regents member Ward Connerly, and Representative Gary Franks (R-Conn.), have publicly opposed affirmative action, opposition for liberals has become a bit easier.

Most surveys show that from 50 to 75 percent of the public (more among whites, less among blacks) openly oppose affirmative action (recent polls are reported in Morin 1995). Majority opposition is found not just among the older generations, but also among younger ones. Surveys have also shown considerable secret hostility toward affirmative action, mostly by liberals. One ingenious study asked people to tell them how many of a certain set of statements made them angry, but not to identify which ones made them angry (Gilens and Sniderman 1995). A control group was given statements not including anything about affirmative action (for example, "professional athletes earning large salaries" "requiring seat belts be used when driving," "corporations polluting the environment"); a treatment group was given the same statements plus one dealing with affirmative action (either "black leaders asking the government for affirmative action," or "awarding college scholarships on the basis of race"). By comparing the number of statements that made respondents in the control and treatment groups angry, the surveyors could estimate real feelings toward affirmative action. They found that for conservatives, the number feeling angry about affirmative action was about the same as the number who admitted they opposed affirmative action (55 percent compared to 51 percent). But for liberals, the number feeling angry about affirmative action was much greater than the number who indicated overtly that they did not support it (49 percent compared to 33 percent). To the extent that this survey is valid, the support for affirmative action among the liberal public is weaker than earlier estimated.[13]

Affirmative action seems to produce beliefs on the part of many whites that they are discriminated against. A 1991 study, in fact, showed that over 50 percent of white applicants to law school believed they were discriminated against because they were white (Daye 1991). And, based on LSAT scores alone, the perception has some basis for some students.[14] Yet, even if affirmative action did not exist, only a relatively few more whites would be able to enter law school; as we have seen, the number of minorities admitted is small, and the number admitted whose scores are below the average white is even smaller. (There are about 140,000 applicants to law school; half of them are turned down. The number of blacks and Hispanics in the first year of law school is less than 6,000, and a large proportion of them have test scores above many whites who are rejected.)

In other areas, too, some whites claim reverse discrimination. A 1995 poll, for example, showed that 13 percent of all whites believed they had been denied a job or promotion because of their race, and 10 percent of all men believed they had been denied a job or promotion because of their sex (Morin and Warden 1995).[15] In Detroit, a majority-black city, 9 percent of whites believed that "whites are discriminated against in getting a quality education," and a smaller percent felt that whites were discriminated against in other areas, such as obtaining housing, finding a job, getting equal wages, and getting promoted (Bledsoe et al. n.d.).

Although affirmative action has created resentment among many whites, one national study of its effects on white workers indicated that white workers in firms with affirmative action policies actually had more positive attitudes toward affirmative action and were more understanding about the need for race-conscious policies. Though the effects were small, they did not support the notion that affirmative action creates more resentment among workers (Taylor 1995; see also Hochschild 1995, 144).

Some blacks point out that affirmative action can be a burden for them. For example, many minority students feel that affirmative action singles them out and that other students automatically believe they are less qualified. Said one, "Students like me feel that they're here on their merits, and you wonder if you need to wear a shirt that tells everyone that" (Jaschik 1994b). However, there is no systematic evidence to show that affirmative action undermines the self-esteem of its recipients, and a majority of blacks continue to support most forms of affirmative action (see review in Crosby 1994; Hochschild 1995, 98–102; but see also Major, Feinstein, and Crocker 1994).

Rethinking Affirmative Action

Public opinion and the actions of elected leaders and the courts impel us to think more carefully about affirmative action. We have already examined some of the arguments used in this debate. But there are deeper changes occurring in American society that will force us to reconsider the nature of affirmative action, even in the absence of contemporary political currents. Moving in parallel with this debate is a major change in the face of America, or, more particularly, in the faces of Americans. These changes include the immigration of millions of nonwhites, the increasing intermarriage of whites and nonwhites, and, consequently, the increasing ambiguity of race and ethnicity in America. We are not so naive to argue that the United States has now become a true melting pot, but at a time when common wisdom indicates that the melting pot is only a myth, the melting is proceeding faster than at any time in the past.

Increasing Racial and Ethnic Pluralism

Increased immigration of nonwhites increases our racial and ethnic pluralism. New immigrant groups, particularly from Asia and Latin America, have joined the American population. Filipinos, Vietnamese, Cambodians, Koreans, Haitians, Cubans, and Central Americans from various nations have come by the thousands and tens of thousands. In the 1990 U.S. Census, Americans listed membership in nearly three hundred races and ethnic groups.

The presence of so many new nonwhite immigrants also changes the relationships among minorities. No longer are black Americans the dominant majority among U.S. minorities; in 1950, blacks made up 75 percent of all minorities, but by 1990 they accounted for less than half (O'Hare 1993). In another twenty years, Hispanics probably will be the largest minority.

Racial Ambiguity

Because of the increasing pluralism of the population and increasing intermarriage, racial ambiguity is increasing. The United States is becoming a multiracial society with a growing rate of intermarriage and mixed-race births. Race is no longer a polarity between black and white, with visible and invisible barriers between them. Race is now much more complex.

Between 1970 and 1994, the number of interracial married couples more than quadrupled (Younge 1996b). More then three million Americans are married to a person of another race (Fletcher 1997). A survey of Detroit area residents in the early 1990s found that 36 percent of blacks and 12 percent of whites claimed a relative of another race (Bledsoe et al. n.d.).[16] About 25 percent of marriages involving minorities other than blacks are interracial.

As a result of the increase in intermarriages there has been an increase in mixed-race births. Over 2 million children are in interracial families (Fletcher 1997). Currently about 3.5 percent of all births are of mixed races (and in another 15 percent the father's race is not reported; Haub 1993), but the proportion of mixed-race births is much higher among groups covered by affirmative action policies (Kalish 1992; Lott 1993; Spickard 1989; Wright 1994; Morganthau 1995). There are now 39 percent more Japanese-white births than there are births to two Japanese American parents (Kalish 1992). Interracial births between American Indians and non-Indians exceed single-race Indian births by 40 percent (Kalish 1992).

Hispanics are a growing proportion of the population, but they are not a single racial group. Most are white; some are black; many have Indian heritage. Nor are they a single ethnic group. Indeed, the 1990 U.S. Census reported seventy different categories of Hispanics. Over one-fourth of marriages involving Hispanics are to non-Hispanics (U.S. Department of Commerce 1994, table 62), indicating that the distinctiveness of this ambiguous category is eroding even further.

Black Americans have always been the most distinctive racial category, and, along with Native Americans, the race that has had the most distinctive history of oppression. Of course, historically, the black population is a result of a heavy intermixture of interracial births, though the proportion of blacks who have no white blood is impossible to assess.[17] Aside from historical racial intermixing, current intermarriage between blacks and whites is increasing at a rapid pace (Kalmijn 1993). Currently about 7 percent of marriages involving an African American are interracial. And, there is a growing popular literature and discussion on the topic of the mixed racial identity of those with black and white ancestry (see, e.g., Scales-Trent 1995; McBride 1996).

Thus, "race" is increasingly becoming a social category. For example, one study of infant deaths in the 1980s found that in many cases, infants had a different race on their death certificate than on their birth certificate (Wright 1994). As another example, between 1960 and 1990, the number of those who identify themselves as American Indians increased from 500,000 to nearly 2 million, a jump that is simply impossible through natural increases resulting from an excess of births over deaths (and by definition, Native Americans did not immigrate here since the 1960 census!—Kalish 1992). Clearly many who identified themselves as American Indians in 1990 had not done so in 1980. One national study found that 70 percent of those who identified themselves as Indians were seen as whites by interviewers (Wright 1994), and in the 1990 census, only 75 percent of those who identified themselves as American Indian by race reported having Indian ancestry (Wright 1994). This does not necessarily mean that most of those individuals were not Indian, only that the visual distinctiveness of the Indian population is minimal in many cases and being "Indian" is much more socially desirable than in the past.

Defining Race

The categorization of Americans by race and ethnicity is essential to the operation of affirmative action. The increasing ambiguity of racial and ethnic categories, resulting from the increased pluralization of the population and intermarriage, poses a challenge to those supporting the continuance of the policy. If a Hispanic woman marries a non-Hispanic man, should their children be covered by affirmative action? Their grandchildren? What is the rationale for coverage or noncoverage? The United States has long used the "one drop" categorization for blacks—if any ancestors were black, the person is black (unless the person defines himself or herself as white and is white enough to be considered white by others). Can that same logic be used in affirmative action?

What if the census returns to an interracial census category, as some now support?[18] How would those people be treated under affirmative action categories?[19] One study found that 49 percent of blacks and 36 percent of whites thought the U.S. Census should add a multiracial category, which presumably would include all those of mixed-race heritage, whether black and white, Asian and white, or another of the myriad possibilities. Already some states include the multiracial category on school forms (Younge 1996b). Nearly 50 percent of blacks and 47 percent of whites thought the census should stop collecting information on race entirely (Morganthau 1995, 65).[20]

And what do the existing categories mean now? "Hispanic" is neither a race nor an ethnicity, and different Hispanic groups stand in very different positions vis-à-vis their history of oppression in the United States. Are all entitled to affirmative action? Similar points can be made about Asians. Some, such as the Japanese, have ancestors who have suffered serious discrimination in this nation, particularly during World War II, while others are very recent immigrants.[21]

Reforming Affirmative Action

Answering these questions is not easy. Neither is raising them. It is difficult to discuss affirmative action in a dispassionate way because such a discussion has come to be associated with the sort of polarized politics now so common in Washington. And affirmative action is seen by some as a litmus test on race (or gender) issues. But there might be some common ground, even on affirmative action.

Affirmative Action for Women

Before discussing possible common ground, some discussion of affirmative action and gender is in order since changes in affirmative action will affect women. The focus of this book has been on race, but women too have benefited from affirmative action in higher education and employment. Women today are a majority of undergraduate students on American campuses, receiving 53 percent of the bachelor's degrees, compared to 43 percent in 1970. In medical and law schools, the increase has been even more dramatic. Women received 8 percent of the M.D.s and 5 percent of the law degrees in 1970; comparable figures today are 35 percent and 40 percent, respectively.

The growth of women in most other professions has also been astronomical, although women have not made significant progress in all areas of endeavor. Few women are engineers or police officers, for example. The so-called glass ceiling still persists in corporate America and in major institutions such as universities, government, and important foundations.

Dramatic societal changes in beliefs about women's roles brought about dramatic change in educational and employment patterns for women that occurred independent of government policies. But there is evidence that affirmative action was responsible for part of this growth, especially in the early stages of change. Recent effects have been less dramatic (Clayton and Crosby 1992; Leonard 1989; see review in Mattei, Winsky, and Sened 1996).

In higher education, affirmative action is probably not a major impetus for the advancement of women at this time. It has opened doors in the past, but now women are flooding through. In cases where they are not, it is either because their numbers in the pipeline remain small, such as in engineering and physics, to cite extreme examples, or in top management positions, where affirmative action is used to widen the pool of candidates but rarely to make the final choice. This is not to say that the status of women in universities is satisfactory. On the contrary, much remains to be done, but affirmative action as a specific technique probably plays a small part in continuing progress. Supporters of affirmative action might reasonably ask, however, whether gains would be sustained if affirmative action policies were to disappear.

Possible Areas of Agreement

Is there common ground between those who support and those who oppose affirmative action? Several possible areas seem worth exploring.

First, much of what the term *affirmative action* includes is not particularly controversial. Almost everyone believes that it is appropriate for universities and industries to look widely to fill their places with candidates from all races and ethnicities. Most people view as an improvement the broadened advertising and screening procedures put in place to comply with affirmative action.

There is also broad agreement that affirmative action should not cover those unqualified for jobs or admission. Hiring or admitting unqualified people was, of course, never supposed to be part of affirmative action. Affirmative action means giving an extra edge to *qualified* individuals from protected groups. While no doubt some unqualified people are hired in the name of affirmative action, no one has presented evidence that the number of such people is greater than the number of unqualified people who are hired though "old boy" networks or other traditional selection procedures.

However, implementing a policy that no one who is unqualified will be admitted to a medical or law school will not meet the objections of opponents of affirmative action in higher education admissions, especially in law and medical school, where there are many minority applicants who are highly qualified. Opponents of affirmative action in higher education usually do not argue that those being admitted are unqualified, but only that some are not as qualified or meritorious as some whites being turned away. Reaffirming that affirmative action does not protect the unqualified might, while worth doing, is not likely to reassure those suspicious of affirmative action initiatives.

Second, almost everyone can agree that businesses and universities should be diverse, reflecting in different ways the diversity of this nation. Promoting diversity, however, is not necessarily the same as favoring affirmative action. Energetic efforts to make sure every group has an opportunity to apply for admission and employment do not require special preferences for some groups. Affirmative action is neither a necessary nor a sufficient condition for diversity, and the diversity many institutions are striving for goes beyond affirmative action categories.

Third, there is agreement, given the existence of affirmative action, that it should be temporary. The notion of enshrining rights in law based on group membership does not sit well with American values. Pointing out that such rights were enshrined in law in the generations of slavery and Jim Crow is a useful antidote to the self-righteous opponents of affirmative action, perhaps, but two wrongs do not make a right. Affirmative action will never exist comfortably with the American creed (just as discrimination against blacks has not), and so must be seen as a temporary remedy. But how temporary is "temporary"? And what are the conditions under which affirmative action should be stopped? To abandon it now would be seen by many as giving up the fight for equality; yet to maintain affirmative action until every vestige of historical discrimination has been wiped out is unrealistic and flies in the face of deep public hostility to the policy.

Fourth, though the charge of reverse discrimination is frequently bandied about, repealing affirmative action would not make much of a dent in the numbers of those whites gaining access to competitive professional schools. As we have seen, while any white person is free to cry "reverse discrimination," only a few more would be admitted to professional schools without the existence of affirmative action programs. Of course, repealing affirmative action would remove one type of excuse for those rejected.

Fifth, most knowledgeable observers can agree that standardized test scores and GPAs were historically not the only criteria for admission to universities or for getting a job, and they should not be today. As we have shown earlier, the notion that high test scores and GPAs are essential to gaining entrance to medical or law school is a very recent idea, born of seeming necessity when the baby boom generation began hammering at the doors. And it is also true of admission to many selective undergraduate colleges and universities.

Supporters and opponents disagree vociferously on the extent to which standardized scores measure merit and thus the amount of weight they should be given in admissions decisions. Opponents of affirmative action appear to believe that quantitative measures are excellent indicators of merit (cf. Holmes 1995; Bolick 1988). They assume that such measures are valid indicators of success. They are undoubtedly right to a point: certainly a student who scores beneath a minimum level (however defined) would lack the necessary skills to complete a rigorous curriculum and learn the basics essential to practicing medicine or law.

Supporters of affirmative action argue that standardized tests and grade point averages are imperfect measures of the concept of "merit," and they are also certainly correct to a point. While extremely low scores suggest an incapacity to complete successfully the work required, variation among "good" scores, however defined, cannot predict with any certainty relative chances of success. A student with a 1000 SAT score and a 3.0 high school GPA might have as much academic aptitude as (or perhaps even more than) another student with a 1250 SAT and a 3.5 GPA if the former student attended a poor school, had parents who did not complete high school, and lived in a violent neighborhood with peer pressure to resist academic pursuits. Supporters argue that it is wrong to assume that the quality of an applicant has a perfect correlation with test scores. "Critics [of affirmative action] view these scores as talismanic," they charge (Stanfield 1995, 793).

Opponents of affirmative action charge reverse discrimination when an applicant who scores higher does not get the job or admission. Giving a job or a seat in medical school to a minority candidate who is less qualified than a white competitor is in American parlance "reverse discrimination," by definition, just as giving a seat to a white applicant who is less qualified than a minority one is "discrimination." However, the real victims of reverse discrimination (even if we accept that admission of an individual with lower test scores is an illustration of reverse discrimination), at least in admission to medical or law school, are far fewer than the complaints made about such discrimination.

Moreover, to base the charge of "less qualified" only on standardized test scores is not credible; such a narrow definition of "qualified" has not historically been the basis of admissions even to the most selective schools, let alone the less selective ones, and it still is not. Currently we find existing alongside the adoption of more rigorous test and grade standards, special provisions and exceptions that have little to do with either these standards or with race. Close kinship with alumni is one important factor in admission to many private schools and some public schools. For example, over a forty-year period, one-fifth of Harvard's students have had preferential treatment in admissions because their parents had attended; in the 1980s, Harvard's "legacies" were more than two times as likely to be admitted as blacks or Hispanics. Indeed, the U.S. Department of Education's Office of Civil Rights found that the number of Harvard's marginally qualified legacies was greater than the number of its black, Hispanic, and Native American students combined (Larew 1991; see also T. Cross and Slater 1994–95). In-state residence is another "nonmerit" factor that is important for public school admissions, while region of residence is sometimes important in private-school admissions. Most schools also give special preferences to athletes. Although most probably meet minimum requirements, presumably only a few athletes in revenue-generating sports at Division I schools would qualify for admission to selective schools using strict numerical criteria. Special skills in the arts, leadership ability, character in the face of adversity: these and other considerations also enter into admissions decisions in many schools.

Thus, almost everyone agrees that there needs to be flexibility in admissions requirements (and job requirements) beyond numerical scores,[22] but there is little meeting of the minds about the actual role that standardized tests and GPAs now play, let alone the role they should play.

Sixth, we need to think about affirmative action in light of its original intent. That intent best captures, in our view, the moral underpinnings for the policy. Affirmative action was initiated as a program to make up for the legacy of centuries of slavery and segregation of, and discrimination against, African Americans. It was to compensate victims of that oppression. Although most white Americans do not acknowledge the amount of racial discrimination blacks still face, there is at least some understanding of this historical oppression. But current affirmative action practices, at least in discussion, are much less focused. American Indians, Hispanics, and Asians of many language and ethnic groupings have also come under its umbrella. The major focus appears to have shifted from compensation for historical wrongs to promoting diversity (for a discussion of these different justifications see Rehfeld 1996). And diversity, though promoted by Justice Powell in *Bakke,* is not a value enshrined in American history or culture (Kahlenberg 1996; see discussion in Lederman 1996 and Skrentny 1996).

Thus, current affirmative action policies are an extremely unsophisticated and blunt instrument whose diverse beneficiaries are not easily understandable to a wider public. These policies benefit those who suffer from current discrimination, but they also benefit those who do not. Current policies benefit those whose ancestors were brought forcibly to this continent and who experienced systematic slavery, segregation, and discrimination (and in the case of Native Americans, "ethnic cleansing" would not be too strong a term), but they also benefit those whose ancestors or those who themselves came voluntarily in recent years. Current policies benefit those whose race, skin color, or language marks them as different from "white" Americans, but the policies also benefit those whose outward appearance suggests they *are* "white" Americans. A narrowly drawn affirmative action policy with specific, well defined targets, might win more public support.

For example, the high rate of intermarriage between white Americans and Native Americans means that any distinctive racial characteristics that marked American Indians for discrimination are receding, while the growth of those identifying themselves as Indians suggests that being Indian is perceived as a matter of choice for many people. These developments suggest that an affirmative action policy may increasingly be an unworkable policy for Indians, although it would be possible to visualize state policies targeted at helping those Indians still living in heavily Indian communities.

Finally, it is important to note that affirmative action alone can make only a little difference in improving equality of educational and employment opportunity. It is neither the key public policy that many supporters seem to believe nor a stumbling block to white achievement that critics charge it with being. Until now, its actual impact appears to be modest, its potential effects dwarfed by the fluctuation in economic conditions, the dramatic growth in higher education over the last four decades, the changing attitudes and educational opportunities opened by the Civil

Rights Act of 1964, and the increasing ethnic pluralism of American society.

Most studies of the effect of affirmative action have focused on employment. Affirmative action had some very modest effect on improving the job status of blacks (see summary in Welch et al. 1994), especially in the late 1970s and early 1980s. Middle-class blacks made significant gains in professional and management positions, particularly but not exclusively in government. Lower-middle-class and blue-collar blacks gained jobs in law enforcement, fire fighting, the construction trades, and the textile industry (Ezorsky 1991). But more recent studies suggest the effect in the 1980s was negligible ("Affirmative Action" 1991; "Analyzing Affirmative Action" 1995).

Our own findings indicate that, while *Bakke* legitimized affirmative action, there were no great surges in minority enrollment following the decision. Rather, minority enrollment grew in the late 1980s when the social and economic conditions became more favorable for increased numbers of students, minority and majority, to enter professional school. Moreover, there is a high correlation between success in minority recruitment before and after *Bakke*; the economic and social conditions that facilitated higher minority enrollment before the *Bakke* decision did so after it. Thus, it is quite likely that affirmative action is more a symbol than a major impetus to further change. One supporter, Jonathan S. Leonard, has argued that "to its critics [affirmative action] represents the decline of meritocracy, ethnic pork barrels writ large. To its proponents, it represents fairness and minority and female progress. In practice, it is neither a great angel or a great Satan. ("Analyzing Affirmative Action" 1995, A7).

Toward a New Affirmative Action Policy

We believe that criticisms of affirmative action will continue to resonate, despite the lack of evidence that discrimination against whites is a widespread problem and the continuing evidence that discrimination against blacks remains widespread, because affirmative action seems to conflict with the American value of individualism. Historically, the notion that people should be judged by their individual worth and not the color of their skin was ignored in practice but upheld in myth and rhetoric. Politicians and the public spoke it; newspapers, magazines, and books published it; and people came to believe it in a general, abstract way. Support for the idea underlay the ultimately successful attempt by civil rights activists to win support from whites for civil rights legislation. To the extent that affirmative action is seen as a program institutionalizing treatment of people according to their race, it conflicts with that value.

If this conflict with the American value of individualism is true, and if affirmative action has little specific effect at this time in American history, supporters of equality in our society need to rethink the best strategy for accelerating progress toward racial equality.[23] Perhaps a renewed commitment to enforcement of nondiscrimination laws, expansion of employment opportunities, and increase in financial aid for low-income students might be more effective than affirmative action itself. Affirmative action is unlikely ever to win the kind of support—even verbal support—that civil rights legislation has won. However, without some compensating policy initiatives indicating that, as a society, we are serious about overcoming racial discrimination, rolling back affirmative action would be perceived as a huge step backward in America's commitment to racial equality.

But if we choose to "mend it, not end it," how might that be done in ways that would increase public support for the policy? One possibility is to narrow the scope of federal affirmative action coverage to those groups that historically suffered substantial discrimination and continue to do so. There may already be a consensus that immigrants should not be covered by affirmative action. This is not to say that legal immigrants should not be treated equally in applying for admission to universities or for jobs. They should be. But they should not be given preferential treatment if we can agree that the ethical justification for affirmative action is the discriminatory treatment of groups for centuries. An immigrant who has recently come to this country voluntarily can hardly claim preferential treatment on the basis of historical discrimination in this country.

This narrowing might provide a foundation for greater support of affirmative action by whites, but it also might erode support among minorities other than African Americans. Political dynamics, for affirmative action as for other policies, drove the expansion of the programs to other groups partly as a way to build support for the policy. Would Hispanic groups accept a smaller scope for affirmative action? Indeed, would black groups be willing to sacrifice the potential alliance with Hispanic groups even if African Americans would likely benefit from a refocused affirmative action?

And, implementing these ideas would not solve the issues of coverage for those whose membership in a protected group is increasingly distant because of racial or ethnic intermarriage among one's ancestors. Trying to classify individuals on the basis of how many ancestors were black or Hispanic, for example, has uncomfortable echoes of racial classification policies used for malevolent ends.

A more sweeping proposal to reform affirmative action is to eliminate existing programs based on race and substitute new programs based on class (Kahlenberg 1996). The underlying assumption is that numerous minorities who are not disadvantaged are benefiting from affirmative action. For example, critics point to stories about set-asides for minority broadcasters that result in financial windfalls for a few wealthy minorities and some powerful corporations that bankroll them (Eastland 1996). But fine-tuning these programs, of course, could reduce or even eliminate such results. More commonly, critics point to middle-class minorities receiving preferential treatment over lower-class whites. We are unaware of any studies that attempt to separate middle-class minority beneficiaries from lower-class minority beneficiaries of affirmative action. The number of middle-class beneficiaries is probably not as large as critics assume, given the relative size of the black, Hispanic, and American Indian middle classes compared with these populations' lower classes. Regardless, it should be acknowledged that even middle-class African Americans, especially, face frequent affronts and at least some discrimination due to their race. Consequently, although they have more wealth than lower-class whites, it is not clear that they have a general advantage over lower-class whites in contemporary society.

The proposal to substitute new programs based on class also proceeds on the assumption that race is a treacherous foundation for any governmental policies. Indeed, it has been in the past, and even now it makes even supporters of affirmative action squirm. Although affirmative action is intended to be only a temporary measure to offset past discrimination, its predominantly racial basis sits uneasily alongside the ideal of a color-blind society that rewards individuals for their own performance. The proposal to substitute new programs based on class would have the advantage of eliminating this apparent contradiction for many people. (Although some well-off whites still would resent the poor who would benefit from the new programs, the racial symbolism might diminish and be less likely to inflame racial prejudice.) At the same time, the new programs might produce somewhat similar results. Because African Americans, Hispanics, and American Indians are disproportionately in the lower class, they would be expected to benefit disproportionately from such programs. And given the commitment of many schools to diversity, these groups likely would benefit from such programs.

Even so, lower-class whites who are more numerous than lower class blacks, would be expected to fill some significant number of seats. And lower class Asians also would compete for these seats. Moreover, schools would be under scrutiny, especially by the organizations fighting affirmative action now, and officials might feel less free to seek diversity than they did after *Bakke*. For these two reasons, programs based on class would result in fewer minorities than affirmative action programs have.[24]

Even if there were agreement to substitute class for race, such a policy would be difficult to operationalize and implement. Defining class, or even just measuring economic inequality, presents significant conceptual and practical problems (Malamud 1996). Whose economic position would be measured—that of the individual or that of the individual's family or household? The latter two are not the same. Further, would wealth be considered as well as income? For example, money from parents or other relatives to be used as a down payment on a house creates wealth for a family beyond whatever its income provides.

Would other indices of class, such as occupation or education, be incorporated? It is, of course, difficult to assess the status of some occupations or jobs within occupations. Education is usually measured by the number of years completed, but this ignores the type of school, much less the grades or honors received by a student or by a student's family. Would other, even softer, indices of class, such as consumption or consciousness be incorporated as well? The nature and extent of our consumption of society's goods reflects our class, as does our own consciousness of our position on the ladder. Yet these factors would be exceedingly difficult to measure. As one examination of this problem concluded, "Social scientists who specialize in the analysis of one specific element of economic inequality have great difficulty in reaching agreement on its proper definition and measurement. Working sophisticated versions of multiple elements into a legal definition of economic inequality would be beyond the technical capacity of most social scientists, let alone most governmental agencies (Malamud 1996, 70). Ultimately, it could be more problematic to measure class than it is to measure race, even as it is becoming more problematic to measure race due to increasing interracial births.

In the face of these difficulties, it is likely that an overly simplified index of class, based perhaps on income or on income in conjunction with occupation and the number of years of education, would be used. Such an index may well overstate the class of blacks, both those in the middle levels and those in the lower levels of society. For example, blacks tend to have less wealth than whites with the same income, and they tend to have lower positions than whites in the same job categories (Malamud 1996).

Is there any justification, then, for retaining affirmative action, beyond the desire for increasing racial diversity in our schools (a goal that would continue, albeit at a slower pace, with programs based on class)? That is, does affirmative action provide anything that class-based programs would not?

Perhaps the greatest benefit of affirmative action has been to combat current discrimination. Despite the judicial rulings and congressional laws, discrimination persists. Although affirmative action was designed to offset the effects of past discrimination, it has worked as a prod to discourage present discrimination (Bergmann 1996). This effect has been most noticeable in employment, but no doubt it has occurred in education as well. Proponents of class-based programs seem to assume that discrimination is an artifact of a bygone era. Were that true, class-based programs would be more appropriate.

But significant discrimination and unequal opportunities continue to exist; new public policies cannot be enacted in ignorance of that fact. Although affirmative action, in theory, was intended to be a temporary measure to allow special treatment of African Americans, Hispanics, and others until their educational backgrounds put them on a level playing field with whites, the irony—and tragedy—is that at the same time that we have begun to undo affirmative action programs, we have nearly completely abandoned our efforts to improve the quality of education and other public services that would help bring about that level playing field. Without improved quality in public education serving poor and working-class people, a real equality of opportunity cannot emerge. And it is especially ironic that those most opposed to affirmative action are also the most opposed to government action to solve the problems of our inner cities, so that the quality of education, family, and social life can support an environment where students can learn. The reluctance of policymakers to tackle seriously these problems is perhaps the best argument for the continuation of affirmative action in some form.

In short, we think there is ample historical justification for affirmative action for blacks at least. Their legacy of slavery, segregation, and discrimination is unique. We also think there is ample contemporary justification. Racial prejudice is still pervasive, and discrimination is still persistent. However, there are practical problems in determining individuals' race, and these are more troublesome every year. Moreover, there are political problems in maintaining affirmative action against white opposition, and these would be more difficult if the scope of affirmative action were shrunk to exclude most Hispanics and to exclude white women. As the number of potential beneficiaries shrinks, so does the number of potential supporters in the coalition. Perhaps the gains from affirmative action, which have been very real though not very large, do not justify more continued battles in the face of these political realities, especially if the alternative is class-based programs that would produce similar (though not equal) results and would defuse much (though not all) of the racial tension that affirmative action programs generate. Then the focus might shift from affirmative action benefits to more fundamental economic changes that conceivably could help a larger portion of the minority population. But we realize that it would not be easy for minority organizations that have fought for affirmative action to sacrifice it to the speculative possibility that they could somehow convince a society that has become jaded to government activism and unsympathetic to minority problems to undertake a new crusade.

In this debate over affirmative action, what role has the decision of the Supreme Court in the *Bakke* case served? It has legitimized a strategy that has some positive impact in the short run. It has enabled professional schools to continue practicing affirmative action and searching for minority students, and at the same time it has insulated most schools from legal challenges to their policies. And it has bought time for schools to recast their admissions procedures and articulate their diversity goals and to assess the results of enrolling some students who would not have been enrolled otherwise. Thus, it has helped some minority students get admitted who would not have gotten admitted if the Court had struck down the use of race as a criterion. In the future, the ruling's emphasis on diversity might help protect some aspects of affirmative action policies, but in the political climate of the late 1990s, the legitimization that *Bakke* provided affirmative action in higher education may be ending.

But even if the Supreme Court does reverse *Bakke*'s holding that race can be used as a positive factor, the debate will not end. The terms might change; the phrase *affirmative action* might not be used. But many institutions are committed to increasing their numbers of minorities and furthering their goal of diversity. As this study shows, and as other studies of other institutions show, patterns of behavior inside institutions tend to persist, even in the face of efforts outside them to force change. So the debate, in one guise or another, will continue.

Such a reversal will likely not, therefore, have the dramatic effects that both critics and supporters believe. As this study shows, the factors that produced large minority enrollments at some schools before *Bakke* also produced comparable enrollments after *Bakke*. These factors would remain and, presumably, would result in similar, if not quite as large, enrollments after a new ruling. If governments respond by discontinuing affirmative action based on race and by substituting programs based on class, which seems the most likely scenario, there might be very little change indeed, given the disproportionate concentration of African Americans, Hispanics, and American Indians in the lower class, and given the desire of schools to diversify. Just as schools blurred the distinction between quotas and affirmative action after *Bakke,* they might blur the distinction between affirmative action and class-based programs after a new ruling.

Appendixes

The Survey

The results of a survey questionnaire sent to every accredited law and medical school in existence in 1976 are the basis of part of our analysis. As explained in chapter 3, questionnaires, mailed in March 1989, were sent to the admissions officer at 164 law schools and 118 medical schools. Schools not in existence as of 1976 were excluded. Fifty-four percent of all law admissions offices ($N = 89$) and 59 percent of all medical school admissions offices ($N = 69$) returned their questionnaires, for an overall response rate of 56 percent ($N = 158$).

One part of the survey questioned the respondents about the pre--*Bakke* era and suggested that if the respondent was not familiar with admissions procedures, then he or she should send us the name of someone who was so we could contact that person. This procedure worked reasonably well, especially for medical officials. Sixty-eight percent of law respondents and 86 percent of the medical ones completed the entire questionnaire. Twenty respondents sent us names to contact; 60 percent of them responded to our mailing. We have, therefore, an N of 64 for law and 62 for medical schools on questions from this second part of the questionnaire. Many who did not provide names of possible contacts for this second part said they knew no one who was still at their institution who had been involved in admissions before *Bakke*.

The high response rate, in and of itself, does not guarantee representativeness. To assess how representative of the entire population of medical and law schools these institutions were, we collected information on some key characteristics of all medical and law schools and the states in which they are located: status as a private or public school, total enrollment, minority enrollment, the proportion of African American and Hispanic population in the state, and regional location. Table A.1 indicates that the medical and law schools of the admissions officers who returned our questionnaires are very similar to those who did not. Indeed, the only

TABLE A.1. Comparison of Schools That Did or Did Not Repsond

	Medical Schools		Law Schools	
	Response	No Response	Response	No Response
Total enrollment	515	563	696	687
Minority enrollment			79	78
Black	35	31	NA	NA
Hispanic	12	14	NA	NA
% South	26	22	25	16
% Private	33	53	53	65
State's % black population	12	15	14	11
State's % Hispanic population	5	6	6	6

Note: NA indicates that separate data for blacks and Hispanics are not available for law schools.

significant difference in the responding and nonresponding schools is that officials from private medical schools were more likely to return the questionnaires. Thus, while acknowledging that the characteristics we examined are only reflective of certain kinds of attributes of these schools, we can be somewhat confident that our sample is representative of the variety of law and medical schools across the country.

Schools Whose Surveys Were Completed

Medical Schools

Albert Einstein College
of Medicine
Baylor College of Medicine
Bowman Gray, Wake Forest
Brown University
Case Western Reserve University
Dartmouth Medical School
Duke University
East Carolina University
East Tennessee State University
Georgetown University
Harvard University
Howard University
Indiana University
Jefferson Medical College
Johns Hopkins University
Louisiana State University,
Shreveport
Loyola University
Mayo Medical School
Medical College of Ohio at
Toledo
Medical University of
South Carolina
Meharry Medical College
Morehouse School of Medicine

New York Medical College
New York University
Northwestern University
Rush University
Southern Illinois University
Stanford University
St. Louis University
SUNY-Stony Brook
Temple University
University of Alabama,
Birmingham
University of Alabama, Mobile
University of Arizona
University of Arkansas
University of California, Davis
University of California, Irvine
University of California,
Los Angeles
University of California, San
Diego
University of Colorado
University of Connecticut
University of Hawaii
University of Illinois
University of Kansas
University of Kentucky

University of Louisville
University of Maryland
University of Medicine and
  Dentistry, Newark, NJ
University of Medicine and
  Dentistry, Piscataway, NJ
University of Miami
University of Michigan
University of Minnesota
University of Minnesota,
  Duluth
University of Missouri
University of Missouri,
  Kansas City
University of Nebraska
University of North Dakota
University of Oklahoma

University of Pittsburgh
University of South Carolina
University of South Dakota
University of Southern California
University of South Florida
University of Tennessee
University of Texas, San Antonio
University of Utah
University of Vermont
University of Washington
University of Wisconsin
Vanderbilt University
Washington University
Wayne State University
West Virginia University
Wright State University
Yale University

Law Schools

Antioch School of Law
Arizona State University
Benjamin Cardozo School of Law
Boston University
California Western School of Law
Cleveland State University
College of William and Mary
Duke University
Emory University
Florida State University
Georgetown University
Gonzaga University
Hastings College of Law
Howard University
Indiana University, Indianapolis
John Marshall Law School
Loyola University
Loyola University (New Orleans)
Marquette University

New England School of Law
New York Law School
Northern Illinois University
Northern Kentucky University
Northwestern School of Law
Ohio State University
Rutgers University of Newark
Samford University
Seton Hall University
Southern Illinois University
Southern Methodist University
Southern University
South Texas College of Law
Southwestern University
Stanford Law School
Stetson University
St. Louis University
St. Mary's University
Suffolk University

Texas Southern University
Texas Tech University
Thomas M. Cooley Law School
Tulane University
Union University
University of Alabama
University of Arizona
University of Arkansas at
  Little Rock
University of Bridgeport
University of California,
  Berkeley
University of California,
  Los Angeles
University of Colorado
University of Dayton
University of Detroit
University of Hawaii at Manoa
University of Illinois
University of Iowa
University of Kansas
University of Kentucky
University of Michigan
University of Mississippi
University of Missouri
University of Missouri,
  Kansas City
University of Montana

University of Nebraska
University of North Carolina
University of North Dakota
University of Oklahoma
University of Oregon
University of Pennsylvania
University of Pittsburgh
University of Puget Sound
University of Richmond
University of San Francisco
University of South Carolina
University of South Dakota
University of Southern California
University of Tennessee
University of Texas
University of Utah
University of Virginia
University of Washington
University of Wisconsin
University of Wyoming
Vanderbilt University
Vermont Law School
Wake Forest University
Washburn University of Topeka
Washington and Lee University
Washington College of Law
Washington University
West Virginia University

Statistical Information
for Chapters 4 and 5

Included in our ITS regression were a trend variable (where, assuming 1968 is the first data point, $1968 = 1$, $1969 = 2$, ... $1986 = 19$), a before-and-after *Bakke* dummy variable, and a post-*Bakke* trend variable (where $1968 = 0$, $1969 = 0$ ... $1978 = 0$, $1979 = 1$ ... $1986 = 8$). The class of 1978 was considered pre-*Bakke*, the class of 1979 post-*Bakke*. That is because the *Bakke* decision was announced in April 1978, too late to affect applications and admission decisions for the class of 1978 but in plenty of time for 1979. The equation representing these terms is thus:

$$y = a + b_t x_t + b_d x_d + b_p x_p + e$$

where:

y is the dependent Hispanic or black enrollment variable;
a is the constant term;
b_t is the trend variable indicating the pre-*Bakke* slope;
b_d is the pre-post dummy variable indicating the change in the level of the time-series after *Bakke;*
and b_p is the postintervention trend variable, indicating the increment or decrement to the slope of the pre-*Bakke* time-series.

The interpretation of these coefficients is straightforward. The constant term indicates the level of the time-series prior to *Bakke*. When all of the other three terms are used, the trend variable, b_t, represents the preintervention slope.[1] This slope is the rate that black or Hispanic enrollment was growing or declining before the decision. The postintervention trend variable, b_p, is the change in the slope after the intervention.

Adding these two trend variables shows the rate at which black or Hispanic enrollment grew or declined after the decision. The dummy variable represents the short-term effect of the decision, any immediate jump or decline in enrollment.

Each equation was examined for first-, second-, and third-order autocorrelations.[2] To estimate and remove the effects of autocorrelation, we used the maximum likelihood algorithm found in the SAS mainframe software. This algorithm is considered superior to the alternatives in accurately estimating standard errors and dealing successfully with autocorrelations. The R^2 measure was used as our goodness-of-fit indicator.

Notes

Introduction

1. In fact, the author did not clearly report exactly when the questionnaires were sent. On page 150, he indicated that the "study was conducted during the 1979–80 academic year," but on page 139 he reported that one of the questions on the survey read, "Based on admissions for next year (1979–80), do you think . . . "

2. Most of Blackwell's data are collected from published sources, though he does devote one chapter to survey data that included information from thirty medical and fifteen law schools. We will refer to this study throughout our text, though its specific detail about medical and (especially) law schools is limited by his small sample. Some of the findings from chapters 4 and 5 of this book were previewed in Gruhl and Welch 1990.

3. In this book, we use "black" and "African American" interchangeably, acknowledging, however, that some hold strong views about the correctness of each. We also use "Hispanic" and "Latino" interchangeably, again acknowledging some strong but inconsistent views on these labels.

Chapter 1

1. In 1991 the Rehnquist Court indicated that it might restrict the authority of lower courts to mandate busing (*Board of Education of Oklahoma City v. Dowell*, 112 L. Ed.2d 715). The majority said busing was only intended to be temporary. It could be stopped if the school board had complied "in good faith" and if the vestiges of past discrimination had been eliminated "to the extent practical." Depending how these guidelines are interpreted, virtually all busing could be continued or virtually all could be stopped.

2. Jones (1993, 349–69) contends that its roots extend back to English courts of equity, which tried to make whole the victims of illegal actions.

3. Other drafters of the order included future Supreme Court justices Arthur Goldberg and Abe Fortas. The quote is by Hobart Taylor Jr., a young lawyer whom then Vice President Johnson asked to help draft the statement to ban discrimination in federal contracting.

4. That whites with lower scores than Bakke were admitted apparently was not made clear to the courts. The university presented the average of white applicants' scores rather than the individual scores or range of scores (Dreyfuss and Lawrence 1979, 21).

5. Yet from 1971 to 1974, 1 black and 6 Hispanics were admitted through the regular procedures, while 21 blacks, 30 Hispanics, and 12 Asians were admitted through the special program (438 U.S. 265, 265–66). It is not clear whether the 7 minority applicants admitted through the regular procedures were middle-class or poor. Regardless, this finding suggests that middle-class minorities might have had a viable chance. The United States Supreme Court would point to it as evidence that minorities had a shot at all 100 places, whereas whites did at only 84.

6. A white woman, who had immigrated from the Soviet Union seven years earlier and who had faced poverty in the United States, graduated from UCLA with an A– average but was denied admission to the medical school at Davis. She thought she should be eligible for the special admissions program, so she sued shortly after Bakke did ("Doctoral Program" 1977).

7. Bakke was admitted to Davis, completed his medical training, and did a residency at the Mayo Clinic in Rochester, Minnesota (Farrell 1983). Understandably, perhaps, he has consistently refused to talk to the press and in the mid-1990s was practicing medicine in Rochester (Lemann 1995).

8. For a good discussion of the infighting within the administration, see O'Neill 1985, 179–91.

9. For a thoughtful discussion of the causes and consequences of a radical "group rights" claim in the *Bakke* litigation, see O'Neill 1981.

10. For more discussion of equal protection tests, see Baer 1983, 105–30.

11. For persuasive arguments in support of quotas, see Fiscus 1992 and Livingston 1979.

12. The black sample in 1988 was very small.

Chapter 2

1. The Hispanic population is divided into groups of different cultural traditions. Members of the largest of these groups, Mexican Americans, live primarily in the Southwest, though many now live in the Midwest and other regions. Puerto Ricans, who compose the second largest group, live predominantly in the New York area, though a substantial number can be found in Chicago. Many Puerto Ricans see themselves as "temporary," and many frequently travel back and forth between Puerto Rico and the mainland. Cubans are a third group, living primarily in Florida, but with population clusters in New York and New Jersey. Cubans are more likely to be middle class than either of the other two groups. Hispanics of other origins, especially those from Central and Latin America and the Caribbean, make up an increasingly large number and a prominent portion of recent immigrants.

2. Increasing numbers of female-headed families, black and white, have

pulled themselves out of poverty in the last three decades. For example, 70 percent of black female-headed families were in poverty in 1960, but only 50 percent are now. In contrast, however, the poverty rates of two-parent black families plummeted from 51 percent in 1960 to 12 percent in 1987. The increasing impact of family disruption on black family income is not that black female-headed families are worse off than they used to be; it is, rather, that there are many more of them.

3.   Though homes do not represent liquid assets, they can be mortgaged to raise funds for college.

4.   There is an interesting gender difference here. More Hispanic men than black men attend college, but more black women do so than Hispanic women.

5.   In comparison, only 15 percent of these students received state aid, and 38 percent received aid from their institutions.

6.   And has decreased since, to 26 percent in 1990.

7.   About one-fourth of black and Hispanic students have fathers who graduated from college, compared to one-half of white students. The differences are somewhat less for mothers of these students; among freshmen college students in 1987, 34 percent of whites, 27 percent of blacks, and 21 percent of Hispanics had mothers with college degrees (National Science Foundation 1990, table 36).

8.   For blacks, whites, and Hispanics, the parental income profile of those not accepted was lower than of those accepted (AAMC 1993, table 9). Moreover, over one-third of black students, compared to only 13 percent of white students, appeared to be first-generation college students (AAMC 1993, table 8). We say "appeared to be" because mother's and father's education were listed separately, so it is impossible to tell whether either had gone to college.

9.   The table classifies as "underrepresented minorities" students including blacks, American Indians, Mexican Americans, and mainland Puerto Ricans. "Other" students include whites, Asians, commonwealth Puerto Ricans, and other Hispanics, such as Cubans.

Chapter 3

1.   Schools not in existence by 1976 were excluded from the survey on the grounds that they would not have had much opportunity to experience the impact, if any, of the 1978 *Bakke* decision. Multicampus universities with more than one medical (or law) school were treated as separate institutions unless their medical (or law) schools had a centralized admission process. Such was the case only for the University of Illinois and University of Oklahoma medical schools. No law schools had a combined admission process. In the survey return rates given in the text, campuses with combined admission process are treated as one institution. Otherwise, each medical school in a multicampus university is counted separately (as, for example, the University of California at Davis, Berkeley, and Los Angeles).

2.   In addition to the statistics listed in table A.1, we compared our list of

responding schools with a list of medical schools that graduated the most black doctors. Twelve of eighteen schools on that list responded (including historically black schools such as Howard, Meharry, and Morehouse, as well as predominantly white schools such as the University of Michigan, University of Illinois, Harvard, and Johns Hopkins, for example). It included seventeen of *U.S. News and World Report*'s 1995 list of the top twenty-five research-oriented medical schools and nine of their fourteen top primary-care medical schools.

Our list also included sixteen of the twenty-five law schools reputed to be the nation's best (in a 1995 *U.S News and World Report* study), and thirteen of the bottom twenty-five (see also Mort and Moskowitz 1994).

3. There was no meeting in 1978.

4. Moreover, there were other panels on minorities and legal education that focused on other concerns than admission but might have included references to admission.

5. UCLA, Colorado, Columbia, Detroit, Florida State, Georgetown, Harvard, Howard, Kentucky, Maryland, Michigan, New Mexico, Northwestern, Oregon, Pennsylvania, Santa Clara, Temple, Vanderbilt, Virginia, Washington (St. Louis), West Virginia, and Wisconsin.

6. The wordings of the questions were as follows: "Did your school have a quota, whether formally stated or not, of a certain percentage of minorities to admit before the *Bakke* case was decided in 1978?" "If your school did not have a quota, did it have a goal, or some target number, of minorities to admit before the *Bakke* case was decided in 1978?" "Do you believe that other medical (or law) schools had a quota, whether formally stated or not, of a certain percentage of minorities to admit before the *Bakke* case was decided in 1978?"

7. These proportions are very similar to those reported for black Americans by Wellington and Montero (1978) in their 1974 survey of medical schools, but lower for Native Americans, Asian Americans, and Hispanics (though of the same rank order, with blacks the most likely to receive preferential treatment, then Native Americans, then Hispanics, then Asian Americans). Differences could be in recall of our respondents and different samples, as well as changing practices.

8. A federal investigation supported charges that UCLA discriminates against Asian Americans in admission to at least one of its graduate programs, for example (*Chronicle of Higher Education,* 10 October 1990, 1). Another investigation found that Harvard had not discriminated against Asian Americans (*Chronicle of Higher Education,* 17 October 1990, 1).

Chapter 4

1. Published data on law school applications begin in 1980. See Law Services Report 1994.

2. See the discussion of this point in chapter 2.

3. These data, like those on acceptances and enrollments reported in the next chapter, are based on self-reports of ethnicity and race by individuals. These

data are collected and published by institution and aggregated in national reports. Their reliability depends on the accuracy of the information reported by individuals. While one might quibble with self-reports, in our society much ethnic identity and some racial identity is self-perception. Generally a dark skin denotes a societally defined as well as individually defined "black" racial identity, but light-skinned people of African descent along with light-skinned Hispanics may or may not choose to identify themselves as "black" or "Hispanic." For an examination of the ambiguity of Hispanic identification, see Tienda and Ortiz 1986. On the other hand, it is sometimes reported that a person who is defined by society as "white" and non-Hispanic will claim black or Hispanic identity in the hopes of receiving some benefit targeted for minorities. This phenomenon seems rare.

4. An earlier analysis of these data is found in Gruhl and Welch 1990.

5. Little information exists about the amount of private and public (other than federal) grants and loans for college students (Evangelauf 1987).

6. The Office of Civil Rights did not exist until the early 1970s, it since has been moved from one agency to another, and its functions have changed. Assessing changes in public opinion on affirmative action would be another way to examine changing "demand" for minority students. However, doing so is impossible given the lack of comparable over-time questions on the topic.

7. Large compared to its standard error. The t value is 1.11, as the appendix indicates.

8. Unlike other gender and ethnic categories, the proportion of black male high school graduates age fourteen to twenty-four enrolled in college fell between 1980 and 1988, from 27.0 percent to 25.1 percent. This finding contrasts with the case for young black women, who registered a slight increase (29.2 percent to 31.3 percent); white men, who registered a large increase (34.3 percent to 39.6 percent); Hispanic men, who registered a slight increase (31.2 percent to 32.2 percent); and Hispanic women, who also registered a slight increase (29.4 percent to 30.5 percent). The period of peak enrollment for both white and black men was in 1970, during the Vietnam War (U. S. Department of Commerce 1990, table 252). The proportion of black men enrolled did not increase after 1988 and now lags substantially behind black women, almost 40 percent of whom are enrolled (Slater 1994).

9. The exact wording of the questions was: "How would you judge the *quantity* of your applicants from these groups compared to a decade ago?" Immediately following was the question: "How would you judge the *quality* of your applicants from these groups compared to a decade ago?" Respondents could check "increased," "stayed same," or "decreased" to refer to each of six groups: black men, black women, Hispanic men, Hispanic women, white (non-Hispanic) men, and white (non-Hispanic) women.

10. Grace Saltzstein (1986) found that such organizational arrangements can be significant. The location of equal opportunity and affirmative action responsibility in one office rather than another affected the rate of employment of women in municipal government.

Chapter 5

1. These data, like those on applicants reported in the previous chapter, are based on self-reports of ethnicity and race by individuals.

2. Over 17 percent of Cuban Americans have college degrees, compared with only 7 percent of Mexican Americans and 10 percent of Puerto Ricans. "Other Hispanics" including those from Central and South America are also more likely to have college degrees than either Mexican Americans or Puerto Ricans (U.S. Department of Commerce 1990, table 45).

3. In contrast, by the late 1970s, the graduation rate for blacks was 75 percent for those admitted from 1978 through 1980, compared with 83 percent for Hispanics and 86 percent for nonminorities. For each level of LSAT scores, the graduation rate was almost identical for minorities and nonminorities. However, the average LSAT score of nonminority enrollees (602) was considerably greater than that for blacks (472) and Hispanics (515). See Law School Admission Council 1986.

4. Recall that black median income peaked in 1978, Hispanic in 1979.

5. The definition of *minority* is unstated in the data for individual institutions, but the aggregate national figures chart trends for blacks, Mexican Americans, mainland Puerto Ricans, and other Hispanics. From this, we assume that the term *minority* includes only blacks and Hispanics.

6. Note that the gain averaged across all schools will not be the same as the overall gain because each school is weighted the same in this institutional analysis. Schools that have only two hundred students have the same weight as those with one thousand. In an analysis aggregating enrollments over all these schools, the same proportion of minority students in each school would result in five times as many minority students in the larger school.

7. For this analysis, we have grouped medical schools into categories of "low," with enrollments of less than 400; "medium low," for schools with 400 to 535 students (535 is the mean size for medical schools), "medium high," for schools with enrollments from 536 through 699; and "high," for all schools with enrollments of 700 or more. Different enrollment cutoffs are used for law schools, where the average enrollment is 692. "Low" includes schools with enrollments of less than 500; "medium low" are those from 500 to 692; "medium high" are schools with enrollments from 693 to 1,099; and the "high" category includes schools with 1,100 or more students.

8. States are grouped in the following way: 0–4.99 percent, 5–9.99 percent, 10–19.99 percent, and 20 percent or greater. The proportion Hispanic categories are 0–2.99 percent, 3–4.99 percent, and 5 percent or greater. There is much less variability in statewide Hispanic than black population proportions. These cutoffs are derived from an inspection of the frequencies. We wanted to have categories with sufficient numbers but also be able to have a category containing states with significant numbers of minorities. This was difficult in the case of Hispanics.

9. Recall that multicollinearity between region and the proportion black impels us to delete region from the equations.

10. Note that this does not mean that the state's black population percentage is not related to 1987 enrollments. It is (the two are related at $r = .38$). But its effect is through its effect on the 1977 enrollment proportions.

Chapter 6

1. A weakness of our survey instrument was the limited amount of information we solicited on post-*Bakke* affirmative action efforts.

2. Moreover, those African Americans who attended four-year colleges had an attrition rate considerably higher than that of white students (Hall, Mays, and Allen 1984, 271).

3. *The Journal of Blacks in Higher Education* periodically reports on the gains black women are making relative to black men in educational accomplishment. For example, in 1992, black women were 61 percent of the black enrollment in colleges and universities, 63 percent of the bachelor's degree earners, 65 percent of the master's degree earners, 59 percent of the doctoral earners, and 53 percent of all the first professional degree earners, including 55 percent of all law degrees and 63 percent of all medical degrees ("Higher Education Gains," 1994–95; AAMC 1993).

4. This study showed that the average Law School Admission Test scores for nonminority enrollees was 602, compared with 472 for blacks, 499 for Puerto Ricans, 520 for Mexican Americans and other Hispanics, and 579 for Asian Americans. In 1991, when a Georgetown law student wrote an article in a student newspaper pointing out the lower scores of black students (based on his unauthorized scrutiny of student records), it created a national news story and started a new round of criticism of affirmative action.

5. The tiny residual are foreign students, one-fourth of whom are black.

6. These cases should have no impact on the analyses presented in earlier chapters because the decisions occurred at the end of the data series.

7. The university changed its practices before the final decision was rendered.

8. In another case affecting education, when a school board laid off a white rather than a black teacher with similar seniority and evaluations, the U.S. Court of Appeals for the Third Circuit stated that race cannot be used as a factor in such a decision (Haworth 1996).

9. Enrollment of these groups will probably not change much in the California state university system or the community college system after California voters enacted the civil rights initiative. The state system accepts all students who meet a minimum standard, and the community college system is an open enrollment system (Lively 1995a; 1995b). At the flagship campus, Berkeley, diversity is greater than in the system as a whole; 40 percent of Berkeley's undergrads were Asian, 32 percent were white, 14 percent were Latino, and 6 percent were black (the rest were unknown; Sanchez 1995).

10. At Harvard, for example, SAT scores of entering African Americans average 95 points less than whites, while Asians score 65 more. At eleven top

schools, blacks, on average, score 72 points less than average whites, Asians 48 more (T. Cross and Slater, 94–95, 89).

11.   D'Souza's much discussed book, *Illiberal Education* (1991), argued that affirmative action is responsible for many of American education's current ills, including intolerance of free speech and radical movements in literary theory.

12.   Michael S. Greve, executive director of the Center for Individual Rights, quoted in Jaschik 1994b.

13.   Similar experiments show that the hostility toward affirmative action is almost unanimous among southerners and substantial among northerners (see Kuklinski, Cobb, and Gilens 1996; see also Kuklinski et al. 1996).

14.   We have no current data for law school applicants, but, as we saw earlier, among 1992 medical school applicants, the mean MCAT scores and GPAs for whites who were rejected were higher than the mean for blacks who were accepted (AAMC 1993). Based on these criteria alone, approximately half the whites rejected could say that they were "discriminated against." However, given the disproportionate numbers of white and black applicants, and the fact that half the black applicants did much better than the mean rejected white applicant, only a small proportion of those whites rejected could have been accepted even if race were not a factor.

15.   Compared to 22 percent of women and 44 percent of blacks who answered similarly.

16.   Among whites, 4 percent claimed Asian relatives, 6 percent black relatives, and 3 percent American Indian relatives. Among blacks, 4 percent claimed Asian relatives, 30 percent claimed white relatives, and 18 percent claimed American Indian relatives. The latter figure is unexplainable, although of course historically there was some intermarriage among blacks and Indians in some regions of the South.

17.   Wright recounts the story from a meeting of the National Association of Black Journalists in which the audience members at one presentation were asked if they considered themselves black for political reasons. Almost everyone agreed. The speaker then asked how many thought they were of pure African descent. No one raised a hand.

18.   Multiracial categories have been used in some previous censuses. From 1850 to 1920, the category "mulatto" was included on the forms, and in 1870, "quadroon" and "octaroon" were added as further refinements (see Younge 1996a).

19.   The debate over this idea is heated. While many black activists oppose a multiracial category as undermining the perception of black demographic strength, others endorse it. Molefi Asante, the afrocentrist who is chair of the Department of African American Studies at Temple, argues, in fact, that "it could be very, very useful, because there is a need to clarify who is in and who is not . . . I think they should [also] identify those people who are in interracial marriages" (Wright 1994, 55). From the opposite perspective, Orlando Patterson, a Harvard sociologist, notes, "If your object is the eventual integration of the races, a mixed-race or middle group is something you'd want to see developing" (Morgenthau 1995, 65).

20.   Presumably there is some overlap between the two groups. A Census

Bureau trial run of the mixed race category showed that it was used most often by those who classified themselves as Native American or Asian American (Fletcher 1997).

21.   As further evidence of the social definition of race, in 1993 a white man, whose father's family had lived in Tanzania for three generations, applied to Georgetown Law School. Although he had checked "white" on his LSAT registration form, he had checked "black/African American" on his Georgetown application form (The question asked, "How would you describe yourself?"). After admission he informed the school he was white but said he considered himself African because he had some African heritage and cultural background. That is, he considered himself a white African American, saying he interpreted the "black/African American" option to mean black *or* African American. When Georgetown replied that it was investigating the situation, the student enrolled at another school instead, so the issue did not go to court (C. Shea 1994).

22.   As noted earlier, there is rather disturbing evidence now that Asians are held to higher standards than others at some universities (T. Cross and Slater 1994–95). If some opponents of affirmative action are motivated by racist considerations, certainly those individuals will be concerned to learn that college admissions based solely on test scores would result in a huge increase in Asian admissions to most of our most prestigious universities.

23.   Though Taylor (1995) shows that workers in firms with affirmative action policies seem more sensitive to racial issues rather than more negative toward blacks.

24.   Moreover, one rationale for affirmative action in professional schools is to increase service to minority communities by these professionals. Class-based affirmative action would not have these desired effects. For example, black physicians are more likely to serve the black community than are physicians whose parents were poor (see Cantor 1996).

Appendix C

1.   This may seem counterintuitive, since one normally thinks of this term as the overall slope, but a brief example will show that it is indeed the preintervention slope. In the standard equation, assume the year is a preintervention year, say 1977, with the trend line beginning in 1971. In this instance, $x_t = 7$ and $x_d = x_p = 0$. Thus, the x_d and x_p terms disappear from the equation, leaving $y = a + b_t x_t + e$. In years after *Bakke*, $x_d = 1$ and x_p assume positive values.

An alternative to this model is an ARIMA model (Box and Jenkins 1976; Box and Tiao 1975). However, ARIMA models are most appropriate when the number of cases in the series is at least thirty. Our series in this chapter and the next have only fifteen to twenty. The maximum likelihood algorithm for estimating autocorrelation used here (the SAS version) is, however, identical to the one used in ARIMA.

2.   Second- and even third-order autocorrelations are not uncommon with time-series this short. They indicate the presence of cycles in the data. In our analyses, no equation had to be corrected beyond the second order.

References

Abel, Richard. 1989. *American Lawyers*. New York: Oxford University Press.

Abraham, Henry J. 1993. *The Judicial Process*. 6th ed. New York: Oxford University Press.

Abramowitz, Alan. 1994. "Issue Evolution Reconsidered: Racial Attitudes and Partisanship in the U.S. Electorate." *American Journal of Political Science* 38 (January): 1–24.

"Affirmative Action's Effect Said Overstated." 1991. *Lincoln Journal-Star,* 29 August.

"The Age of Less." 1978. *Newsweek,* 10 July, 19–26.

Albritton, Robert. 1979. "Measuring Public Policy: Impacts of the Supplemental Social Security Program." *American Journal of Political Science* 23 (August): 559–78.

American Bar Association (ABA). 1987. *A Review of Legal Education in the United States*. Chicago: American Bar Association, Section of Legal Education and Admissions to the Bar.

American Council on Education (ACE). 1986. *Higher Education Almanac*. Washington, DC.

"Analyzing Affirmative Action." 1995. *Chronicle of Higher Education* 42 (November 17): 1–15.

Applebome, Peter. 1995. "Gains in Diversity Face Attack in California." *New York Times,* 4 June, 1.

Association of American Law Schools (AALS). Annual. *Annual Meeting Proceedings*. Newtown, PA: AALS.

Association of American Medical Colleges (AAMC). Annual. *Medical School Admission Requirements*. Washington, DC: AAMC.

———. 1969. "AAMC Proceedings for 1968: Meeting of the Group on Student Affairs." *Journal of Medical Education* 44 (May): 381–82.

———. 1978a. "AAMC Annual Report for 1978." *Journal of Medical Education* 53 (February): 184–85.

———. 1978b. "Program of the 1977 AAMC Annual Meeting." *Journal of Medical Education* 53 (March): 235.

———. 1979a. "National Policy: AAMC Annual Report for 1978." *Journal of Medical Education* 54 (February): 170–71.

———. 1979b. "The Councils: AAMC Annual Report for 1978." *Journal of Medical Education* 54 (February): 162–63.

———. 1993. *Minority Students in Medical Education: Facts and Figures VII.* Washington, DC: AAMC, Division of Minority Health Education and Prevention.

Astin, Alexander. 1982. *Minorities in Higher Education.* San Francisco: Jossey-Bass.

———. 1990. *The Black Undergraduate.* Los Angeles: UCLA Higher Education Research Institute.

Atesek, Frank J., and Irene L. Gomberg. 1978. *Special Programs for Female and Minority Graduate Students.* Higher Education Panel Report no. 41. Washington, DC: American Council on Education.

"Back to *Bakke*." 1992. *Time,* 12 October, 32.

Badgett, M., V. Lee, and Heidi Hartmann. 1995. "The Effectiveness of Equal Employment Opportunity Policies." In Margaret C. Simms, ed. *Economic Perspectives on Affirmative Action.* Washington, DC: Joint Center for Political and Economic Studies.

Baer, Judith. 1983. *Equality Under the Constitution: Reclaiming the Fourteenth Amendment.* Ithaca, NY: Cornell University Press.

Bakke and Beyond. 1978. Denver: Education Commission of the States and the Justice Program of the Aspen Institute.

"Bakke: Enduring Question." 1978. *National Review,* 24 July 24, 880–81.

"Bakke Wins, Quotas Lose." 1978. *Time,* 10 July, 16.

Beck, Paul, John Githens, Douglas Clinkscales, Don Yamamoto, Conrad Riley, and Harry Ward. 1978. *Journal of Medical Education* 53 (August): 651–57.

Bell, Derrick. 1978. "The High Price of Non-Representation." *Phi Beta Kappa Journal* (winter): 19.

Benedetto, Richard. 1995. "Affirmative Action Divides Blacks, Whites." *USA Today,* 25 July, 1.

Bennett, William, and Terry Eastland. 1978. "Why Bakke Won't End Reverse Discrimination." *Commentary* 46 (September): 34.

Bergmann, Barbara. 1996. *In Defense of Affirmative Action.* New York: New Republic/Basic Books.

Bernstein, Richard. 1994a. "Law School Calls Bias Ruling a Victory." *New York Times,* 21 August, 26.

———. 1994b. "UT Accused of Race Bias in Lawsuit." *Fort Worth Star-Telegram,* 13 July, A16.

Birkby, Robert. 1966. "The Supreme Court and the Bible Belt." *Midwest Journal of Political Science* 10 (August): 304–19.

Biskupic, Joan. 1994. "A Negative View on Affirmative Action." *Washington Post National Weekly Edition,* 7–13 November, 34.

Blackwell, James E. 1987. "The Access of Black Students to Medical and Law Schools." In *Mainstreaming Outsiders,* 2d ed., edited by James E. Blackwell. Dix Hills, NY: General Hall.

Bledsoe, Timothey, Michael Combs, Lee Sigelman, and Susan Welch. n.d. unpublished data.

Bolick, Clint. 1988. *Changing Course: Civil Rights at the Crossroads.* New Brunswick, NJ: Transaction Books.

Booker, John, and Jasper L. McPhail. 1979. "American Indians in U.S. Medical Education: Trends and Prospects." *Journal of Medical Education* 54 (August): 651–52.

Bowman, Angella. 1990. "The *Bakke* Decision and Its Effects on Black Admissions to Medical Schools." University of Nebraska, typescript.

Box, G. E. P., and G. M. Jenkins. 1976. *Time Series Analysis: Forecasting and Control.* Rev. ed. San Francisco: Holden-Day.

Box, G. E. P., and G .C. Tiao. 1975. "Intervention Analysis with Applications to Economic and Environmental Problems." *Journal of the American Statistical Association* 70:70–92.

Cain, Bruce. 1990. "Voting Rights and Democratic Theory: Toward a Color-Blind Society?" Paper presented at the Conference of the Twenty-Fifth Anniversary of the Voting Rights Act of 1965, at Brookings Institution, Washington, D.C. Cited in Stephen Wasby, preface to *The Constitutional Logic of Affirmative Action,* by Ronald J. Fiscus (Durham, NC: Duke University Press, 1992).

Calkins, Virginia, and Lee Willoughby. 1981. "Impact of an Innovative Selection Procedure on Medical School Admissions." In *Black Students in Higher Education,* edited by Gail Thomas. Westport, CT: Greenwood Press.

Campbell, Donald T., and H. Laurence Ross. 1968. "The Connecticut Crackdown on Speeding: Time Series Data in Quasi-Experimental Analysis." *Law and Society Review* 3 (August): 33–53.

Canon, Bradley. 1977. "Testing the Effectiveness of Civil Liberties Policies at the State and Federal Levels: The Case of the Exclusionary Rule." *American Politics Quarterly* 5 (January): 51–82.

Cantor, Joel C. 1996. Study reported in *Chronicle of Higher Education Academe Today.* Www.chronicle . . . /newstday.htmttart-20, 30 July.

Caporaso, James, and A. L. Pelowski. 1971. "Economic and Political Integration in Europe: A Time Series Quasi-Experimental Analysis." *American Political Science Review* 65:418–33.

Carmines, Edward, and James Stimson. 1989. *Issue Evolution, Race, and the Transformation of American Politics.* Princeton: Princeton University Press.

Carter, Stephen L. 1991. *Reflections of an Affirmative Action Baby.* New York: Basic Books.

Chapa, Jorge. 1990. "The Myth of Hispanic Progress." *Journal of Hispanic Policy* 4:3–18.

Choper, Jesse. 1984. "Consequences of Supreme Court Decisions Upholding Individual Constitutional Rights." *Michigan Law Review* 83 (October): 4–212.

"Civil Rights." 1965. *CQ Almanac.* Washington, DC: CQ Press, 358–72.

Clark, Ramsey. 1978. "The Bakke Decision." *Nation,* 8–15 July, 37–38.

Clayton, Susan, and Faye J. Crosby. 1992. *Justice, Gender, and Affirmative Action.* Ann Arbor: University of Michigan Press.

Cohen, Gaynor. 1982. "Alliance and Conflict among Mexican Americans." *Ethnic and Racial Studies* 5:175–95.

Cohen, Richard, and John Kaplan. 1976. *Bill of Rights*. Mineola, NY: Foundation.

Cole, Richard. 1995. "Med Schools Cited for Dominant Racial Bias." *Collegian*, 13 June, 4.

Combs, Michael W., and John Gruhl, eds. *Affirmative Action: Theory, Analysis, and Prospects*. Jefferson, NC: McFarland.

Cooper, John A. D. 1978. "The *Bakke* Decision." *Journal of Medical Education* 53 (September): 776–77.

Cose, Ellis. 1997. "The Color Bind." *Newsweek* (May 12): 58–60.

Coughlin, Ellen. 1995. "The Great Divide: Public Views, Private Thoughts." *Chronicle of Higher Education* 42 (November 17): A6.

Crawford, N. C. Jr. 1966. "Effects of Offers of Financial Assistance in the College-Going Decisions of Talented Students with Limited Financial Means." ERIC Cited in Faye Whitaker Moulton, "The Enrollment of Black and Low Income Students in Postsecondary Education: The Effects of Student Financial Aid." Master's thesis, University of Nebraska, 1988.

Crosby, Faye. 1994. "Understanding Affirmative Action." *Basic and Applied Social Psychology* 13 (1–2): 13–41.

Cross, Patricia, and Helen Astin. 1981. "Factors Affecting Black Students' Persistence in College." In *Black Students in Higher Education*, edited by Gail Thomas. Westport, CT: Greenwood Press.

Cross, Theodore. 1994a. "Suppose There Was No Affirmative Action at the Most Prestigious Colleges and Graduate Schools." *Journal of Blacks in Higher Education* (spring): 44–51.

Cross, Theodore. 1994b. "What If There Was [*sic*] No Affirmative Action in College Admissions?" *Journal of Blacks in Higher Education* (autumn): 52–55.

Cross, Theodore, and Robert Bruce Slater. 1994–95. "Alumni Children Admissions Preferences at Risk: The Strange Irony of How the Academic Achievements of Asians May Rescue Affirmative Action for Blacks." *Journal of Blacks in Higher Education* (winter): 87–90.

Crowley, Anne, Sylvia Etzel, and Edward Petersen. 1987. "Undergraduate Medical Education." *JAMA* 258 (August 28): 1013–20.

Dahl, Robert. 1957. "Decision-Making in a Democracy: The Supreme Court as National Policy Maker." *Journal of Public Law* 6 (fall): 279–95.

———. 1972. *Democracy in the United States*. Chicago: Rand McNally.

Daye, Charles E. 1991. "Of New and Old: Have We Oversold Affirmative Action?" *Law Services Report* 91-5 (October, November, December): 2.

"Doctored Program." 1977. *Time,* 10 October: 89.

Dolbeare, Kenneth, and Phillip Hammond. 1971. *The School Prayer Decisions*. Chicago: University of Chicago Press.

Dometrius, Nelson, and Lee Sigelman. 1984. "Assessing Progress toward Affirmative Action Goals in State and Local Government." *Public Administration Review* 44 (May–June): 241–47.

Dreyfuss, Joel, and Charles Lawrence III. 1979. *The Bakke Case*. New York: Harcourt Brace Jovanovich.

D'Souza, Dinesh. 1991. *Illiberal Education: The Politics of Race and Sex on Campus.* New York: Free Press.

D'Souza, Dinesh. 1995. *The End of Racism.* New York: Free Press.

Dugan, Mary Kay. 1996. "Affirmative Action: Does It Exist in Graduate Business Schools?" *Selections,* Graduate Management Admissions Council (winter): 11. Quoted in "What If There Was [*sic*] No Affirmative Action at the Nation's Leading Business Schools?" *Journal of Blacks in Higher Education* (summer 1996): 50.

Dworkin, Ronald. 1977. "Why Bakke Has No Case." *New York Review of Books* 10 (July): 11.

Eastland, Terry. 1996. *Ending Affirmative Action: The Case for Colorblind Justice.* New York: Basic Books.

Edwards, Harry T. 1994. "Personal Reflections on 30 Years of Legal Education for Minorities." *Law Quadrangle Notes.* 37 (Summer): 38–43.

Eisinger, Peter K. 1986. "The Impact of Economic Transformation on Black Municipal Employment." In *Affirmative Action: Theory, Analysis, and Prospects,* edited by Michael W. Combs and John Gruhl. Jefferson, NC: McFarland.

Evangelauf, Jean. 1987. "Students' Borrowing Quintuples in Decade, Raising the Specter of a 'Debtor Generation.'" *Chronicle of Higher Education* 34 (January 7): 1.

Evans, Franklin R. 1977. "Applications and Admissions to ABA Accredited Law Schools: An Analysis of National Data for the Class Entering in the Fall of 1976." In *Reports of LSCA Sponsored Research,* vol. 3. Princeton, NJ: Law School Admissions Council.

Ezorsky, Gertrude. 1991. *Racism and Justice: The Case for Affirmative Action.* Ithaca, NY: Cornell University Press.

Falcon, Angelo. 1988. "Black and Latino Politics in New York City." In *Latinos in the Political System,* edited by F. Chris Garcia. Notre Dame, IN: Notre Dame University Press.

Farley, Reynolds. 1984. *Blacks and Whites: Narrowing the Gap?* Cambridge: Harvard University Press.

Farley, Reynolds, and Walter Allen. 1987. *The Color Line and the Quality of Life in America.* New York: Russell Sage.

Farrell, Charles S. 1983. "Five Years Later, Allan Bakke Is a Doctor, but Effects of His Suit are Still Debated." *Chronicle of Higher Education* 30 (June 22): 11–12.

Fields, Charles, and Morris LeMay. 1973. "Student Financial Aid: Effects on Educational Decisions and Academic Achievement." *Journal of College Student Personnel* 14 (September): 425–29.

Fields, Cheryl. 1978. "In *Bakke's* Victory No Death Knell for Affirmative Action." *Chronicle of Higher Education* 16 (July 3): 1.

Fife, Jonathan D. 1975. *Applying the Goals of Student Financial Aid.* Washington, DC: American Association for Higher Education.

Fisher, Ada M. 1981. "Black Medical Students: Too Few for So Large a Task." In *Black Students in Higher Education,* edited by Gail Thomas. Westport, CT: Greenwood Press.

Fiscus, Ronald J. 1992. *The Constitutional Logic of Affirmative Action.* Durham, NC: Duke University Press.

Fitt, Alfred B. 1978. "Legal Implications for the College Admissions Process." In *Bakke and Beyond.* Denver: Education Commission of the States and the Justice Program of the Aspen Institute.

Fletcher, Michael. 1997. "More Than a Black-or-White Issue." *Washington Post National Weekly Edition* (May 26): 34.

Fosburgh, Lacey. 1975. "Coast Suit May Be Test Case for University Special Admissions Program." *New York Times,* 16 January.

Gallup, George, and Frank Newport. 1990. "Americans Ignorant of Basic Census Facts." *Gallup Poll Monthly* no. 294 (March).

Garand, James, and Donald Gross. 1984. "Changes in Vote Margins for Congressional Candidates: A Specification of Historical Trends." *American Political Science Review* 78 (March): 17–30.

Garfield, Leslie Yolof. 1996. "Squaring Affirmative Action Admissions Policies with Federal Judicial Guidelines: A Model for the 21st Century." *Journal of College and University Law* 22:895–934.

Gilens, Martin, and Paul Sniderman. 1995. "Affirmative Action and the Politics of Realignment." Paper presented at the annual meeting of the Midwest Political Science Association, April, Chicago. April 6–8.

Glazer, Nathan. 1975. *Affirmative Discrimination: Ethnic Inequality and Public Policy.* New York: Basic Books.

———. 1978. "Why Bakke Won't End Reverse Discrimination." *Commentary* 66 (September): 38, 41.

Gose, Ben. 1994. "Old 'Quota' under Attack." *Chronicle of Higher Education* 41 (June 29): A29–30.

Gose, Ben. 1997. "Elite Private Colleges See a Drop in Applications." *Chronicle of Higher Education* (March 7): A35.

Greene, Kathanne. 1989. *Affirmative Action and Principles of Justice.* New York: Greenwood Press.

Gruhl, John. 1981a. "Anticipatory Compliance with Supreme Court Rulings." *Polity* 15 (winter): 296–313.

———. 1981b. "State Supreme Courts and the United States Supreme Court's Post-Miranda Rulings." *Journal of Criminal Law and Criminology* 72 (fall): 886–913.

Gruhl, John, and Susan Welch. 1990. "Impact of the *Bakke* Decision on Minority Enrollments in Medical and Law Schools." *Social Science Quarterly* 71 (September): 458–73.

Guernsey, Lisa. 1996. "Study Finds Race-Based Medical-School Admissions Key to Minority Care." *Chronicle of Higher Education* (July 30): 3.

Hahn, Harlan, and Timothy Almy. 1971. "Ethnic Politics and Racial Issues: Voting in Los Angeles." *Western Political Quarterly* 24:719–30.

Hall, Marcia, Arlene F. Mays, and Walter Allen. 1984. "Dreams Deferred: Black Student Career Goals and Fields of Study in Graduate/Professional Schools." *Phylon* 45(4): 271–83.

Haltom, William. [1985?]. "Before and After *Bakke*: Editorialists and Judicial Mediation." Typescript.

Harrison, Bennett, and Barry Bluestone. 1988. *The Great U-Turn.* New York: Basic Books.

Haub, Carl. 1993. "Births per U.S. Woman?" *Population Today* 21 (September): 6–9.

Haworth, Karla. 1996. "Federal-Court Ruling in J. J. Deals Another Blow to Affirmative Action in Education." *Chronicle of Higher Education* 43 (September 6): A57.

Haworth, Karla. 1997. "Number of Minority Students Applying to U. of Cal. Plunges." *Chronicle of Higher Education* 43 (February 14): A32.

Healy, Patrick. 1995. "Opponents of Racial Preferences Buoyed by Decision in California." *Chronicle of Higher Education* 42 (August 4): A20.

Healy, Patrick. 1997. "Texas Lawmakers Take an Activist Role on Issues Affecting Higher Education." *Chronicle of Higher Education* 44 (June 13): A28–29.

Hibbs, Douglas. 1974. "Problems of Statistical Estimation and Causal Inference in Dynamic Time Series Models." In *Sociological Methodology 1973/1974,* edited by Herbert Costner. San Francisco: Jossey-Bass.

"Higher Education Gains by Black Women Are Across the Board." 1994–95. *Journal of Blacks in Higher Education* (winter): 49.

Hill, Retha. 1994. "Giving Up and Getting Out." *Washington Post National Weekly Edition,* 26 March–3 April, 31.

Hochschild, Jennifer. 1995. *Facing Up to the American Dream.* Princeton: Princeton University Press.

Holloway, Charles M. 1978. *The Bakke Decision: Retrospect and Prospect— Summary Report on Six Seminars Held by the College Board in July and August 1978.* New York: College Entrance Examination Board.

Holmes, Steven. 1995. "A Rage for Merit, Whatever That Is." *New York Times,* 30 July, 6.

Huckfeldt, Robert, and Carol W. Kohfeld. 1989. *Race and the Decline of Class in American Politics.* Urbana: University of Illinois Press.

Huron, Douglas. 1984. "It's Fashionable to Denigrate Hiring Quotas—But It's Wrong." *Washington Post National Weekly Edition,* 27 August, 23.

Idelson, Holly. 1995. "Pressure Builds for Retreat on Affirmative Action." *CQ* 53 (June 3): 1578–82.

Jackson, Gregory, and George Weathersby. 1975. "Individual Demand for Higher Education: A Review and Analysis of Recent Empirical Studies." *Journal of Higher Education* (November): 623–52.

Jacobson, Cardell. 1983. "Black Support for Affirmative Action Programs." *Phylon* 44 (4): 299–311.

Jarecky, R. K. 1969. "Medical School Efforts to Increase Minority Representation in Medicine." *Journal of Medical Education* 44:912–18.

Jaschik, Scott. 1995a. "Affirmative Action under Fire." *Chronicle of Higher Education* 42 (March 10): A22–23.

———. 1995b. "A Valuable Tool or Bias in Reverse?" *Chronicle of Higher Education* 42 (April 28): A14–15.

———. 1995c. "Blow to Affirmative Action." *Chronicle of Higher Education* 42 (June 23): A21–22.

———. 1995d. "'No' on Black Scholarships." *Chronicle of Higher Education* 42 (June 2): A25.

———. 1990. "Student-Aid Changes Affect Blacks More, A UCLA Study Finds." *Chronicle of Higher Education* 37 (September 5): A21.

———. 1994a. "Court Backs Use of Race in Admission." *Chronicle of Higher Education* (September 7): A40.

———. 1994b. "Suit Against U. of Texas Challenges Law School's Affirmative-Action Effort." 41 *Chronicle of Higher Education* (February 9): A32.

Jeffries, John C. 1994. *Justice Lewis F. Powell, Jr.* New York: Scribner's Sons.

Johnson, Charles, and Bradley Canon. 1984. *Judicial Policies.* Washington, DC: CQ Press.

Johnson, Davis. 1964. "The Study of Applicants." *Journal of Medical Education* 39 (October): 899.

———. 1969. "Conference on Increasing Representation in Medical Schools of Afro-Americans, Mexican Americans, and American Indians." *Journal of Medical Education* 44 (August): 710–11.

Johnson, Lyndon B. 1971. *The Vantage Point: Perspectives on the Presidency, 1963–1969.* New York: Holt, Rinehart and Winston.

Johnson, Richard. 1967. *The Dynamics of Compliance.* Evanston, IL: Northwestern University Press.

Jolly, Paul, Leon Taskel, and Robert Beran. 1987. "U.S. Medical School Finances." *Journal of the American Medical Association (JAMA)* 258 (August 28): 1022–30.

Jones, James E. Jr. 1993. "The Rise and Fall of Affirmative Action." In *Race in America,* edited by Herbert Hill and James E. Jones. Madison: University of Wisconsin Press.

Kahlenberg, Richard D. 1996. *The Remedy: Class, Race, and Affirmative Action.* New York: New Republic/Basic Books.

Kalish, Susan. 1992. "Interracial Baby Boomlet in Progress?" *Population Today* 20 (December): 1–2.

Kalmijn, Matthijs. 1993. "Trends in Black/White Intermarriage." *Social Forces* 72 (September): 119–46.

Kellough, James E., and Susan Ann Kay. 1986. "Affirmative Action in the Federal Bureaucracy: An Impact Assessment." *Review of Public Personnel Administration* 6 (spring): 1–13.

Kinsley, Michael. 1996. "The Spoils of Victimhood." *New Yorker,* 27 March, 62–69.

Klein, Joe. 1995. "The End of Affirmative Action." *Newsweek,* 13 February, 36–37.

Klitgaard, Robert. 1985. *Choosing Elites.* New York: Basic Books.

Kluger, Richard. 1976. *Simple Justice.* New York: Alfred A. Knopf.

Koziara, Karen Shallcross. 1987. "Women and Work: The Evolving Policy." In *Working Women: Past, Present, Future,* edited by Karen Shallcross Koziara, Michael H. Moskow, and Lucretia Dewey Tanner. Washington, DC: Bureau of National Affairs.

Kuklinski, James H., Michael D. Cobb, and Martin Gilens. 1996. "Racial Attitudes and the 'New South.'" Urbana: University of Illinois, working paper.

Kuklinski, James H., Paul M. Sniderman, Kathleen Knight, Thomas Piazza, Philip E. Tetlock, Gordon R. Lawrence, and Barbara Mellers. 1997. "Racial Prejudice and Attitudes toward Affirmative Action." *American Journal of Political Science* 41 (April): 402–19.

Kuran, Timur. 1995. *The Social Consequences of Preference Falsification.* Cambridge: Harvard University Press.

"Landmark Bakke Ruling." 1978. *Newsweek,* 10 July, 31.

Lane, H. W. 1971. "Where Do Black Students Go to College and Why?" *Journal of National Association of College Admission Counselors* 16 (September): 22–24.

Larew, John. 1991. "Why Are Droves of Unqualified, Unprepared Kids Getting Into Our Top Colleges?" *Washington Monthly* 23 (June): 10–14.

Laubach, John. 1969. *School Prayers: Congress, the Courts, and the Public.* Washington, DC: Public Affairs Press.

Law School Admission Council. 1981. *The Challenge of Minority Enrollment.* Minority Enrollment Task Force of the Law School Admission Council.

———. 1986. *Law School Admission and Graduation: Minority Student Experiences and Success Rates.* Prepared for the Affirmative Action Committee of the Section of Legal Education and Admissions to the Bar of the American Bar Association.

———. 1987. *Analyses of Minority Law School Applicants 1980–1981 to 1985–86.* Chicago: Affirmative Action Committee, American Bar Association.

Law Services Report. 1994. "Welcome to Affirmative Action Revisited." *Law Services Report* 92 (March, April, May): 4.

Lawyer's Almanac. Annual. Clifton, NY: Harcourt, Brace Jovanovich.

Lederman, Douglas. 1995. "The Special Preferences Are Not Limited to Blacks." *Chronicle of Higher Education* 42 (April 28): A16–18.

———. 1996. "Split on Racial Preferences." *Chronicle of Higher Education* 43 (April 5): A23.

Lemann, Nicholas. 1995. "Taking Affirmative Action Apart." *New York Times Magazine,* 11 June, 36–54.

Leonard, Jonathan S. 1989. "Women and Affirmative Action." *Journal of Economic Perspectives* 3:61–75.

Levine, James P. 1969. "Constitutional Law and Obscene Literature: An Investigation of Bookseller Censorship Practices." In *The Impact of Supreme Court Decisions,* edited by Theodore L. Becker and Malcolm Feeley. New York: Oxford University Press.

Levy, Frank. 1988. *Dollars and Dreams.* New York: W. W. Norton.

Lewis-Beck, Michael. 1979. "Some Economic Effects of Revolution: Models, Measurement and Cuban Evidence." *American Journal of Sociology* 86:1130–33.

———. 1981. "Can We Assess the Effects of Revolution? A Third Look at the Cuban Evidence." *American Journal of Sociology* 86:1130–33.

———. 1986. "Interrupted Time Series." In *New Tools for Social Scientists,* edited by William D. Berry and Michael S. Lewis-Beck. Beverly Hills, CA: Sage.

Lewis-Beck, Michael, and John Alford. 1980. "Can Government Regulate Safety? The Coal Mine Example." *American Political Science Review* 74 (September): 745–56.

Lively, Kit. 1995a. "A Jolt from Sacramento." *Chronicle of Higher Education* 42 (June 9): A25.

———. 1995b. "At Berkeley, Regents' Vote Stirs Anger below the Surface." *Chronicle of Higher Education* 42 (August 4): A19.

Livingston, John C. 1979. *Fair Game? Equality and Affirmative Action.* San Francisco: W. H. Freeman.

Lloyd, Sterling, Davis Johnson, and Marion Mann. 1978. "Survey of Graduates of a Traditionally Black College of Medicine." *Journal of Medical Education* 53 (August): 640–50.

Locke, Michelle. 1997. "Without Affirmative Action, College Sees Blacks Admitted Plunge 81%." *Lincoln Journal-Star/AP* (May 15, 1997): A2.

Lott, Juanita. 1993. "Do United States Racial/Ethnic Categories Still Fit?" *Population Today* 21 (January): 6.

Lynch, Frederick R. 1985. "Affirmative Action, the Media, and the Public." *American Behavioral Scientist* 28 (July–August): 807–27.

Major, Brenda, Jeffrey Feinstein, and Jennifer Crocker. 1994. "Attributional Ambiguity of Affirmative Action." *Basic and Applied Social Psychology* 13 (1–2): 113–41.

Malamud, Deborah C. 1996. "Class-based Affirmative Action: Look Carefully Before You Leap." *University of Michigan Law Quadrangle Notes* (fall/winter): 61–72.

Mallson, Dale, Davis G. Johnson, and William Sedlacek. 1968. "The Study of Applicants, 1966–1967." *Journal of Medical Education* 43 (January): 1–13.

Mathews, Jay. 1995. "Putting Affirmative Action under the Microscope." *Washington Post National Weekly Edition,* 10–16 July, 22.

Mattei, Laura, R. Winsky, and Itai Sened. 1996. "Equal Opportunity and Gender: Assessing Affirmative Action as Public Policy." Paper presented at the annual meeting of the Midwest Political Science Association, Chicago, April 18–20.

McAdam, Doug. 1982. *Political Process and the Development of Black Insurgency 1930–1970.* Chicago: University of Chicago Press.

McBride, James. 1996. *The Color of Water.* New York: Riverhead Books.

McClain, Paula, and Albert K. Karnig. 1990. "Black and Hispanic Socioeconomic and Political Competition." *American Political Science Review* 84 (June): 535–48.

McCloskey, Robert G. 1960. *The American Supreme Court.* Chicago: University of Chicago Press.

McCormack, Wayne, ed. 1978. *The Bakke Decision: Implications for Higher Education Admissions—A Report of the ACE-AALS Committee on Bakke.* Washington, DC: American Council on Education and Association of American Law Schools.

McCrone, Donald, and Richard Hardy. 1978. "Civil Rights Policies and the

Achievement of Racial Income Equality." *American Journal of Political Science* 22 (February): 1–17.

Medalie, Richard, Leonard Zeitz, and Paul Alexander. 1968. "Custodial Police Interrogation in Our Nation's Capital: An Attempt to Implement Miranda." *Michigan Law Review* 66 (May): 1347–1421.

"Medical School Enrollment, 1971–72 through 1975–76." 1976. *Journal of Medical Education* 51 (February): 144–46.

Meier, Kenneth J. 1985. *Regulation: Politics, Bureaucracy, and Economics.* New York: St. Martin's Press.

Meier, Kenneth, and Joseph Stewart. 1991. *The Politics of Hispanic Education.* Albany: SUNY Press.

Melton, Marli Schenck. 1968. "Health Manpower and Negro Health: The Negro Physician." *Journal of Medical Education* 43 (July): 798–813.

Menand, Louis. 1991. "Illiberalisms." *New Yorker,* 20 May, 101–107.

Michaelson, Martin. 1996. "Affirmative Action: Few Easy Answers." *Priorities* 7 (Summer): 1–15 (a newsletter of the Association of Governing Boards).

Middleton, Lorenzo. 1978. "Those Vanishing Quotas." *Chronicle of Higher Education* 25 (July 10): 8.

Milner, Neal. 1971. *The Supreme Court and Local Law Enforcement: The Impact of Miranda.* Beverly Hills, CA: Sage.

Mohl, Raymond. 1982. "Race, Ethnicity, and Urban Politics in the Miami Metropolitan Area." *Florida Environmental and Urban Issues* 3:1–6.

Morganthau, Tom. 1995. "What Color Is Black?" *Newsweek,* 13 February, 63–68.

Morin, Richard. 1995. "No Place for Calm and Quiet Opinions." *Washington Post National Weekly Edition,* 24–30 April, 34.

Morin, Richard, and Sharon Warden. 1995. "Poll Says Americans Angry about Affirmative Action." *Washington Post,* 24 March, 1.

Morris, Aldo. 1984. *The Origins of the Civil Rights Movement.* New York: Free Press.

Mort, Leigh Ann, and Milton Moskowitz. 1994. "The Best Law Schools for Blacks." *Journal of Blacks in Higher Education* (summer): 57–63.

Moskowitz, Milton. 1994. "The Black Medical Schools Remain the Prime Training Ground for Black Doctors." *Journal of Blacks in Higher Education* (autumn): 69–76.

Moulton, Faye Whitaker. 1988. "The Enrollment of Black and Low Income Students in Postsecondary Education: The Effects of Student Financial Aid." Master's thesis, University of Nebraska.

Muir, William. 1967. *Prayer in the Public Schools: Law and Attitude Change.* Chicago: University of Chicago Press.

Murphy, Walter F., and C. Herman Pritchett. 1979. *Courts, Judges, and Politics.* 3d ed. New York: Random House.

Murrell, Audrey, Beth L. Dietz-Uhler, John Dovidio, Samuel Gaertner, and Cheryl Drout. 1994. "Aversive Racism and Resistance to Affirmative Action: Perceptions of Justice Are Not Necessarily Color Blind." *Basic and Applied Social Psychology* 13 (1–2): 71–86.

"The Nation." 1996. *Chronicle of Higher Education* 43 (September 2): 6–14.

National Association for the Advancement of Colored People (NAACP). 1979. "NAACP Statement on Implications of the Bakke Decision." *Crisis* 86 (February): 42.

National Association of Scholars. 1991. "The Wrong Way to Reduce Campus Tensions." *Chronicle of Higher Education* 38 (April 24): A15.

National Science Foundation (NSF). 1990. *Women and Minorities in Science and Engineering.* Washington, DC: National Science Foundation.

"Negro Students and Graduates." 1939. *JAMA* 113:771.

Neubauer, David. 1974. *Criminal Justice in Middle America.* Morristown, NJ: General Learning Press.

O'Hare, William P. 1993. "Diversity Trend: More Minorities Looking Less Alike." *Population Today* 21 (April): 1–2.

Oliver, Melvin, and Thomas Shapiro. 1989. "Race and Wealth." *Review of Black Political Economy* 17 (spring): 5–26.

O'Neill, Timothy. 1981. "The Language of Equality in a Constitutional Order." *American Political Science Review* 75:626–35.

———. 1985. *Bakke and the Politics of Equality.* Middletown, CT: Wesleyan University Press.

Orfield, Gerry. 1978. *Must We Bus?* Washington, DC: Brookings Institution.

Ostrom, Charles W. 1978. *Time Series Analysis: Regression Techniques.* University Paper series, Quantitative Applications in the Social Sciences. Beverly Hills, CA: Sage.

Page, Clarence. 1997. "Anti-quota Crusades To Bear Useful Fruit on College Campuses." *Lincoln Journal-Star/Chicago Tribune* (June 5): B4.

Peltason, Jack. 1961. *Fifty-eight Lonely Men: Southern Federal Judges and School Desegregation.* New York: Harcourt Brace and World.

Perry, Charles. 1982. "Government Regulation of Coal Mine Safety." *American Politics Quarterly* 10 (July): 303–14.

Plant, Jeremy, and Frank J. Thompson. 1986. "Deregulation, the Bureaucracy, and Employment Discrimination: The Case of the EEOC." In *Affirmative Action: Theory, Analysis, and Prospects,* edited by Michael W. Combs and John Gruhl. Jefferson, NC: McFarland.

Prelaw Adviser. 1987. "Number of Minority Applicants Up." *Prelaw Adviser Bulletin* (November–December): 8.

Preston, Michael B. 1986. "Affirmative Action Policy: Can It Survive the Reaganites?" In *Affirmative Action: Theory, Analysis, and Prospects,* edited by Michael W. Combs and John Gruhl. Jefferson, NC: McFarland.

Prieto, Dario. 1978. "Minorities in Medical Schools, 1968–78." *Journal of Medical Education* 53 (August): 694–95.

"The Progress of African Americans in Medical School Education." 1994. *Journal of Blacks in Higher Education* (spring): 38–39.

Project. 1977. "An Empirical Inquiry into the Effects of *Miller v. California* on the Control of Obscenity." *New York University Law Review* 52 (October): 810–939.

Raup, Ruth, and Elizabeth A. Williams. 1964. "Negro Students in Medical

Schools in the United States." *Journal of Medical Education* 39 (May): 4444–50.

Rehfeld, Andrew. 1996. "Public Debate and the Justifications for Affirmative Action." Paper presented at the annual meeting of the Midwest Political Science Association, Chicago, April 18–20.

Rice, Tom W., and Kenneth Whitby. 1986. "Racial Inequality in Unemployment: The Effectiveness of the Civil Rights Act of 1964." In *Affirmative Action,* edited by Michael Combs and John Gruhl. Jefferson, NC: McFarland.

Rich, Spencer. 1987. "College is a Loaning Experience." *Washington Post National Weekly Edition,* 12 January, 33.

Rich, Spencer. 1991. "Gap Found in Wealth Among Races." *Washington Post* (January 11): A3.

Roberts, Paul Craig. 1995. *The New Color Line.* New York: Regnery.

Rodgers, Harrell, and Charles Bullock. 1972. *Law and Social Change.* New York: McGraw-Hill.

Rodgers, William, and William E. Spriggs. 1996. "The Effect of Federal Contractor Status on Racial Differences in Establishment-Level Employment Shares: 1979–1992." *American Economic Association Papers and Proceedings* 86:290–93.

Romans, Neil T. 1974. "The Role of State Supreme Courts in Judicial Policy Making: Escobedo, Miranda, and the Use of Judicial Impact Analysis." *Western Political Quarterly* 27:38–59.

Rosenberg, Gerald N. 1991. *The Hollow Hope: Can Courts Bring About Social Change?* Chicago: University of Chicago Press.

Roybal, Edward R. 1979. "Minorities in Medicine: The Next Decade." *Journal of Medical Education* 54 (August): 652–54.

Ruhe, C. H. William. 1978. "Recent Events of Special Interest to Medical Education." *JAMA* 240 (December 22–29): 2810–11.

Saltzstein, Grace Hall. 1986. "Affirmative Action, Organizational Constraints, and Employment Change." In *Affirmative Action: Theory, Analysis, and Prospects,* edited by Michael W. Combs and John Gruhl. Jefferson, NC: McFarland.

Samuelson, Robert J. 1995. "End Affirmative Action." *Washington Post National Weekly Edition,* 6–12 March, 5.

Sanchez, Rene. 1995. "The End of Affirmative Action as California Knows It." *Washington Post National Weekly Edition,* 31 July–6 August, 32.

Scales-Trent, Judy. 1995. *Notes of a White Black Woman.* University Park: Penn State Press.

Schwartz, Bernard. 1988. *Behind Bakke.* New York: New York University Press.

Schwartz, John. 1987. "Why the Decline?" *Newsweek on Campus,* February, 16–18.

Seeburger, Richard, and Stanton Wettick Jr. 1967. "Miranda in Pittsburgh: A Statistical Study." *University of Pittsburgh Law Review* 29 (October): 1–26.

Seligman, Joel. 1978. "Special Admissions Are Still Special." *Student Lawyer* 7 (December): 24.

Selingo, Jeffrey. 1997. "U. Of California Regent Says Law Dean Sought to Discourage Minority Students." *Chronicle of Higher Education* (July 14): A.

Sewell, William, and Vimal Shah. 1968. "Social Class, Parental Encouragement, and Educational Aspirations." *American Journal of Sociology* 73 (March): 559–72.

Shea, Christopher. 1994. "Application from 'White African American' Causes Coast to Coast Stir." *Chronicle of Higher Education* 41 (July 20): A28.

———. 1995. "Under UCLA's Elaborate System Race Makes a Big Difference." *Chronicle of Higher Education* 42 (April 28): A12–14.

Shea, Steven, and Mindy Thompson Fullilove. 1985. "Entry of Black and Other Minority Students into U.S. Medical Schools." *New England Journal of Medicine* 313 (October 10): 933–40.

Shelton, Philip D. 1996. "Heat in St. Pete." *Law Service Report*. Newtown, PA: Law School Admission Council (May–June): 2.

Shull, Steven. 1993. *A Kinder, Gentler Racism? The Reagan-Bush Civil Rights Legacy*. Armonk, NY: M. E. Sharpe.

Sigelman, Lee, and Susan Welch. 1991. *Black Attitudes on Race and Inequality: A Dream Deferred*. Cambridge: Cambridge University Press.

Simmons, Ron. 1982. *Affirmative Action: Conflict and Change in Higher Education after Bakke*. Cambridge, MA: Schenkman.

Sindler, Allan P. 1978. *Bakke, DeFunis, and Minority Admissions*. New York: Longman.

———. 1983. *Equal Opportunity: On the Policy and Politics of Compensatory Minority Preferences*. Washington, DC: American Enterprise Institute for Public Policy Research.

Skrentny, John David. 1996. *The Ironies of Affirmative Action*. Chicago: University of Chicago Press.

Slater, Robert Bruce. 1994. "The Growing Gender Gap in Black Higher Education." *Journal of Blacks in Higher Education* (spring): 52.

Slotnick, Elliot. 1991. "Television News and the Supreme Court: 'Game Day' Coverage of the *Bakke* Case." Paper presented at the annual convention of the Midwest Political Science Association, April 18–20, Chicago.

Smith, James P., and Finis Welch. 1987. "Race and Poverty: A Forty-Year Record." *American Economic Review* 77:152–58.

Smith, Ralph. 1981. "Black Law Students and the Law School Experience: Issues of Access and Survival." In *Black Students in Higher Education*, edited by Gail Thomas. Westport, CT: Greenwood Press.

Sniderman, Paul, and Thomas Piazza. 1993. *The Scar of Race*. Cambridge, MA: Harvard University Press.

Spearman, Leonard. 1981. "Federal Roles and Responsibilities Relative to Higher Education of Blacks Since 1967." *Journal of Negro Education* 50 (summer): 285–98.

Speich, Don. 1978. "How Special Admissions Are Working." *Los Angeles Times*, 15 January, 1.

Spickard, Paul. 1989. *Mixed Blood: Intermarriage and Ethnic Identity in Twentieth Century America*. Madison: University of Wisconsin Press.

Spickard, Paul, and Rowena Fong. 1995. "Pacific Islander Americans and Multi-ethnicity: A Vision of America's Future?" *Social Forces* 73 (June): 1365–83.

Spinner, Jeff. 1994. *The Boundaries of Citizenship: Race, Ethnicity, and Nationality in the Liberal State.* Baltimore: Johns Hopkins Press.

Stanfield, Rochelle. 1995. "The Wedge Issue." *National Journal* 27 (April 1): 790–93.

"Students." 1976. *Journal of Medical Education* 51 (March): 264–65.

"Students: 86 Pct. of Students Attend College in Home States, U.S. Study Finds." 1987. *Chronicle of Higher Education* 34 (January 21): 31.

Taylor, Marylee. C. 1994. "Impact of Affirmative Action on Beneficiary Groups: Evidence from the 1990 General Social Survey." *Basic and Applied Social Psychology* 15 (1–2): 143–78.

———. 1995. "White Backlash to Workplace Affirmative Action: Peril or Myth?" *Social Forces* 73 (June): 1385–1414.

Thomas, Gail. 1981a. "The Effects of Standardized Achievement Test Performance and Family Status on Black and White College Access." In *Black Students in Higher Education,* edited by Gail Thomas. Westport, CT: Greenwood Press.

Thomas, Gail, ed. 1981b. *Black Students in Higher Education.* Westport, CT: Greenwood Press.

Tienda, Marta, and Vilma Ortiz. 1986. "Hispanieity and the 1980 Census," *Social Science Quarterly* 67 (March): 3–20.

Tillery, Dale, and Ted Kildegaard. 1973. *Educational Goals, Attitudes, and Behavior: A Comparative Study of High School Seniors.* Cambridge, MA: Ballinger.

Tollett, Kenneth S. 1978. "A Historical Perspective: What Led to Bakke." In *Bakke and Beyond.* Denver: Education Commission of the States and the Justice Program of the Aspen Institute.

"Trends Affecting Affirmative Action." 1995. *Chronicle of Higher Education* 42 (April 28): A22.

Tufte, Edward R. 1974. *Data Analysis for Politics and Policy.* New York: Prentice Hall.

Turner, Marlene E., and Anthony R. Pratkanis. 1994. "Affirmative Action: Insights from Social Psychological and Organizational Research." *Basic and Applied Social Psychology* 13 (1–2): 1–11.

"Undergraduate Medical Education." 1975. *Journal of the American Medical Association* 234 (December 29): 1333–1351.

"UC Reports Aided Own, Paper Says." 1996. *San Diego Tribune,* 17 March, A-3.

U.S. Bureau of Labor Statistics. Monthly. *Employment and Earnings.* Washington DC: U.S. Government Printing Office.

U.S. Department of Commerce. Annual. *Statistical Abstract of the United States.* Washington, DC: U.S. Government Printing Office.

U.S. Department of Education. Annual. *Digest of Educational Statistics.* Washington, DC: U.S. Government Printing Office.

"Vital Signs: Statistics That Measure the State of Racial Inequality." 1995. *Journal of Blacks in Higher Education* (spring): 53–54.

Vobejda, Barbara. 1989. "Class, Color, and College." *Washington Post National Weekly Edition,* 13 June, 7.

Wald, Michael, Richard Ayres, David Hess, Mark Schantz, and Charles Whitebread. 1967. "Interrogations in New Haven: The Impact of Miranda." *Yale University Law Journal* 76 (July): 1521–1648.

Warren, Christopher, John Stack Jr., and John Corbett. 1986. "Minority Mobilization in an International City: Rivalry and Conflict." *PS* 19:626–34.

Wasby, Stephen L. 1970. *The Impact of the United States Supreme Court.* Homewood, IL: Dorsey.

———. 1993. *The Supreme Court.* 4th ed. Chicago: Nelson-Hall.

Welch, Susan, John Gruhl, Michael Steinman, and John Comer, and Susan Regolon 1994. *American Government.* St. Paul, MN: West Publishing.

Welch, Susan, Albert Karnig, and Richard Eribes. 1983. "Changes in Hispanic Local Employment in the Southwest." *Western Political Quarterly.* December: 660–73.

Wellington, John S,. and Pilar Montero. 1978. "Equal Educational Opportunity Programs in American Medical Schools." *Journal of Medical Education* 53 (August): 633–39.

Wightman, Linda F., and David G. Muller 1990. "An Analysis of Differential Validity and Differential Prediction for Black, Mexican American, Hispanic, and White Law School Students." *Law School Admission Council Research Report 90-03* (June): 1–29.

Will, George. 1994. "The Road to Color-Blind Policy." *Centre Daily Times,* 3 November, 4a.

Wilson, William J. 1978. *The Declining Significance of Race.* New York: McGraw Hill.

———. 1987. *The Truly Disadvantaged.* Chicago: University of Chicago Press.

———. 1996. *When Work Disappears.* New York: Knopf.

Wolfe, Alan. 1996. "Affirmative Action, Inc." *New Yorker* (25 November): 106–15.

"Women Enrollment and Its Minority Component in U.S. Medical Schools." 1976. *Journal of Medical Education* 51 (August): 691–93.

Wood, B. Dan. 1991. "Does Politics Make a Difference at the EEOC." *American Journal of Political Science* 34 (May): 503–30.

Wright, Lawrence. 1994. "One Drop of Blood." *New Yorker,* 25 July, 44–55.

Younge, Gary. 1996a. "Multiracial Citizens Divided on Idea of Separate Census Classification." *Washington Post,* 19 July, A3.

———. 1996b. "What Am I?" *Washington Post National Weekly Edition,* 29 July–4 August, 30–31.

Zelnick, Bob. 1996. *Backfire.* New York: Regnery.

Subject and Author Index

AALS, 57, 62, 64, 65
AAMC, 50, 53, 54–56, 58, 64–67, 72, 82, 86, 87, 98, 143
Abramowitz, Alan, 158
Accreditation agencies, pressure for affirmative action, 81–82
Admissions and nonmerit factors, 168; policies before *Bakke,* 70–72
Admissions, medical school: of blacks 114–19; of Hispanics 114–19; ratio of minorities to others, 116–19
Admissions officers, 3, 5; awareness of *Bakke,* 67–69; history of, 12–36, 54–59; opinion on impact of *Bakke,* 134–35; opinion toward *Bakke,* 72–75, 82; perception of attrition rates, 119; perceptions of applicant pool, 92–105, 128; sources of news on *Bakke,* 68; survey of, 61
Affirmative action, 1–5, 12–36; and applications to professional schools, 85–106; California policies, 152–53; common ground, 165–70; compelling government interest rationale, 24; compensation rationale, 27; criticisms of, 166–70; diversity rationale, 27, 56, 149; discrimination rationale, 22–23, 33, 34, 49; eliminating unqualified candidates, 165–66; and employment, 32, 141–42; and firing decisions, 34; goals and quotas, 13–15, 21, 26, 28, 33–36, 55, 58, 63, 70–

73, 82, 151–52; and partisan politics, 151–52; reasons for, 168–69; retreat from, 144–55; "set-asides," 146–47; targets of, 55–56; University of California, 18, 19, 25 (*see also* University of California at Davis); and women, 34, 164–65
Affirmative action officers, 78
Affirmative action offices, 97–104; and minority enrollment change, 127–29
African American candidates, 4; female applicants, 92–95; male applicants, 91–95; socioeconomic status, 37. *See also* Black Americans
Alabama, 9, 34
Albritton, Robert, 86
Aleuts, 27
Alford, John, 86
Almy, Timothy, 30
American Bar Association, 57, 81
American Council on Education, 62
American Indians as targets of affirmative action, 56, 139. *See also* Indians
Amsterdam News, 30
Anti-Defamation League, 30
Applebome, Peter, 155
Applicants: African Americans, 87–106; demand for, 87; Hispanic, 87–106; law school, 86, 94–98, 103–5; to medical schools, 85–94, 98–103; supply of, 87

Applications, influences on, 85–88

Asian Americans, 164; and admissions decisions, 76–77; at Berkeley, 155; bias against, 155; enrollments of, 156; as targets of affirmative action, 56

Association of American Law Schools. *See* AALS

Association of American Medical Colleges. *See* AAMC

Astin, Alexander, 46, 48–50

Atesek, Frank J., 2

Attrition rates, 119

Badgett, M., 142

Bakke, Allan, 17–21, 31

Bakke (Regents of the University of California v. Bakke), 1–5, 14, 16, 17–36, 52, 53, 56, 59, 169, 170; and admissions decisions, 107–32; ambiguity of, 138; and applications to professional schools, 85–106; awareness of decision, 67–68; as compromise decision, 28–29; enrollment impact, 133–35; impact of, 74–76, 82, 136–41; legitimizing function of, 78, 82, 133, 140–41, 143; media coverage of, 61, 62, 139; as precedent, 146–48; projected impact of, 30–31; reaction to, 31–32, 62–67, 72–75; similarity with other high court decisions in terms of impact, 135–41; support by AAMC, 66–67

Bell, Derrick, 20

Bennett, William, 31

Beran, Paul, 92

Bergmann, Barbara, 153

Bernstein, Richard, 148

Birkby, Robert, 3

Biskupic, Joan, 147

Black Americans: and admissions decisions, 76–77; applicants to law school, 94–96, 103–5; applicants to medical school, 93–95, 98–103

Black enrollments, 102–37; at Berkeley, 135; institutional stability in, 124–27; in law schools, 57–59, 111–13; of males, 142–43; in medical schools, 54–57, 109–11; undergraduate, 141–42. *See also* Minority enrollments

Blackmun, Justice Harry, 22, 24, 28

Black state population, effect on applicants, 97–104

Blackwell, James, 2

Bledsoe, Timothy, 160, 162

Bluestone, Barry, 42

Boalt Hall. *See* University of California Law School

Bolick, Clint, 167

Brennan, Justice William, 14, 17, 22, 23, 24, 25, 27, 28, 62, 63, 145

Brock, William, 153

Bullock, Charles, 3, 138

Burger, Chief Justice Warren, 10, 11, 17, 22, 33

Bush, George, 150, 153; politics of affirmative action, 35

Businesses and affirmative action, 153

Busing as remedy for school segregation, 10, 11

Cain, Bruce, 17

California: affirmative action policies, 152–53; Supreme Court, 20, 21

Calkins, Virginia, 72

Campbell, Donald, 86

Canon, Bradley, 2, 3, 135, 136, 138

Caporaso, James, 86

Carmines, Edward, 158

Carter administration, 21, 29

Carter, Stephen, 30

CBS-*New York Times* poll, 32

Chapa, Jorge, 47

Charlotte (North Carolina), 10

Chinese language instruction,16

Choper, Jesse, 134

Chronicle of Higher Education, 21, 62

Civil Rights Act of 1964, 10, 13, 22,

51–52, 54, 86; effect on employment of blacks, 142
Civil Rights Act of 1968, 10
Civil rights groups, 20, 21, 30, 31, 32, 98–104, 138. *See also* MALDEF; NAACP
Civil rights legislation, 150
Clark, Kenneth, 30
Clayton, Susan, 165
Cleveland (Ohio), 34
Clinton, William, 151
Cohen, Gaynor, 130
Cohen, Richard, 10
College attendance. *See* Enrollments
College Board, 62
Columbia University, 26
Combs, Michael, 160, 162
"Compelling governmental interest," 146
Competition between black and Hispanic enrollment gains, 129–31
Congress and affirmative action, 150–53
Congressional Black Caucus, 30
Connerly, Ward, 159
Conservatives, 158–59
Cooper, John A. D., 66, 71, 82
Corbett, Christopher, 130
Cose, Ellis, 156
Council on Legal Educational Opportunity, 57
Crawford, N. C., 48
Crocker, Jennifer, 161
Crosby, Faye, 161, 165
Cross, Patricia, 50
Cross, Theodore, 143, 168
Crowley, Anne, 86

Dahl, Robert, 141
Davis. *See* University of California at Davis
Daye, Charles, 160
DeFunis, Marco, 14–17. See also *De-Funis* in Index of Court Opinions
Democrats and affirmative action, 152

Demographic factors: and employment of blacks and Hispanics, 142; enrollment trends, 142
Department of Commerce, 40, 44, 46, 47, 151
Department of Education, 150, 154
Department of Justice, 150
Department of Labor, 13; Bureau of Labor Statistics, 40
Department of Transportation, 146
Desegregation, 7–12
Detroit, 160
District of Columbia, 8, 9, 12
Diversity as rationale for affirmative action. *See* Affirmative action, diversity rationale
Dolbeare, Kenneth, 3, 136
Dometrius, Nelson, 142
Douglas, Justice William, 14
Downstate Medical Center (NY), 16
Dreyfuss, Joel, 18, 19, 29, 30, 52, 53, 55
D'Souza, Dinesh, 158
Dworkin, Ronald, 21

Eastland, Terry, 31
Education, ethnic differences in levels of secondary, 44
EEOC (Equal Employment Opportunity Commission), 13, 35, 152
Eisenhower, Dwight, 9
Eisinger, Peter, 142
Enrollments: blacks in 1990s, 143–44; factors predicting, 37; Hispanics in 1990s, 143–44
Enrollment size and minority enrollment changes, 121–24
Equal Employment Advisory Council, 153
Equal Employment Opportunity Commission. *See* EEOC
Equal Employment Opportunity offices, 102
Equal protection. *See* Fourteenth Amendment
Eribes, Richard, 142

Etzel, Sylvia, 86
Evans, Franklin, 58
Ezorsky, Gertrude, 33, 170

Falcon, Angelo, 130
Family composition: black, 40–43,
    Hispanic, 40–43
Farley, Reyolds, 40
Farrell, Charles, 31
FCC, 146
Feinstein, Brenda, 161
Fields, Cheryl, 30, 48
Fife, Jonathan, 38
Fifth Circuit Court of Appeals, 147–
    50
Financial aid, 5, 46–50, 86, 90, 109,
    118, 142
Firing decisions and affirmative ac-
    tion, 33–34
Fiscus, Ronald, 23
Fisher, Ada, 115
Fitt, Alfred, 62
Fletcher, Michael, 162
Fortune 300, 153
Fosburgh, Lacey, 21
Fourteenth Amendment, 7, 19, 20
Frankfurter, Justice Felix, 28
Franks, Gary, 159
Freedmen's Bureau Act, 12
Freedom of choice (school desegrega-
    tion plans), 9
Fullilove, Mindy T., 2, 54, 116, 143

Gallup, George, 158
Garand, James, 86
Garfield, Leslie, 58
Geography as criteria for admission,
    156
Georgetown College, 14
Gilens, Martin, 159
Ginsburg, Justice Ruth Bader, 149–
    50
Glass ceiling (for women), 164–65
Glazer, Nathan, 31, 159
Goals. *See* Affirmative action, goals
    and quotas

Gomberg, Irene, 2
Gose, Ben, 156
Government pressure: for affirmative
    action, 80–81; on application pro-
    cess, 97–104
Grandfather clause, 8
Gross, Donald, 86
Gross, Barry, 154
Gruhl, John, 138
Guernsey, Lisa, 24

Hahn, Harlan, 130
Haltom, William, 29
Hammond, Phillip, 3, 136
Hardy, Richard, 86
Harlan, Justice John, 7
Harris polls, 31–32
Harrison, Bennett, 42
Hartman, Heidi, 142
Harvard University, 57, 168; affirma-
    tive action plan, 24, 26–28, 31,
    62–63, 64
Hasidic Jews, 16
Haworth, Karla, 155
Healy, Patrick, 156
Hill, Retha, 143
Hispanic applicants, 93–95; and ad-
    missions decisions, 76–77; to law
    school, 94–96, 103–5; to medical
    school, 56, 93–95, 98–103
Hispanic candidates, 4
Hispanic enrollments, 107–32; at
    Berkeley, 155; institutional stability
    in, 124–27; in law schools, 58,
    111–13; in medical schools 109–
    11; undergraduate, 141. *See also*
    Minority enrollments
Hispanic income, 39–43
Hispanic socioeconomic status, 37
Hispanic state population, effect on
    applicants, 97–104
Hochschild, Jennifer, 160, 161
Holloway, Charles, 62, 63, 64
Holmes, Steven, 167
Hooks, Benjamin, 43
Hopwood, Cheryl, 148

Hopwood. See Index of Court
  Opinions
Housing discrimination, 10
Howard University, 13, 54, 65
Huckfeldt, Robert, 158
Huron, Douglas, 142

Idelson, Holly, 152
Ideology and race, 158–59
Immigration and affirmative action,
  161–64
Impact of judicial decisions, 2, 135–
  41; impact of ambiguity, 137–38.
  See also Supreme Court
Income: black, 38–43; black and His-
  panic, 142, 144; white, 39–43
Indians, 163; and admissions deci-
  sions, 76–77; and affirmative ac-
  tion, 169
Institutional differences in minority
  recruitment, 119–27
Intermarriage, 161–64, 169
Interrupted time series, 86

Jackson, Gregory, 48
Jackson, Jesse, 30
Jackson (Michigan), 34
Jacobson, Cardell, 31
Japanese Americans, 164
Jarecky, R. K., 56
Jaschik, Scott, 146, 147, 154, 160
Jews, Hasidic, 16
Jim Crow laws, 7, 8, 166
Johnson, Charles, 2, 3, 135, 136
Johnson, Davis, 65
Johnson, Lyndon B., 13
Johnson, Richard, 3
Jolly, Paul, 92
Jones, James, 12
*Journal of the American Medical
  Associaton (JAMA),*
  67
Journal of Medical Education, 65, 66

Kahlenberg, Richard, 169
Kalish, Susan, 162, 163

Kalmijn, Matthijs, 162
Kaplan, John, 10
Karnig, Albert, 130, 142
Kay, Susan Ann, 141
Kellough, James, 141
Kennedy, John, 9, 12
Kennedy, Justice Anthony, 145
Kildegard, Ted, 48
Kinsley, Michael, 152, 159
Klitgaard, Robert, 58
Kluger, Richard, 8
Kohfeld, Carol, 158

Lane, H. W., 48
Larew, John, 168
Laubauch, John, 3
Law school admission: efforts to
  recruit minorities, 53, 57–59;
  standards for, 52–53
Law School Admission Council, 57,
  58, 81, 93, 143, 149, 156
Law School Admission Test. *See*
  LSAT
Law Services Report, 94
Law schools, history of black enroll-
  ments, 57–59
Lawrence, Charles, 18, 19, 29, 30,
  52, 53, 55
Lederman, Douglas, 169
Lemann, Nicholas, 13
LeMay, Morris, 48
Leonard, Jonathan, 165, 170
Levine, James, 137
Levy, Frank, 42
Lewis-Beck, Michael, 86
Liberals, 158–59
Lieberman, Joseph, 152
Little Rock (Arkansas), 9
Lively, Kit, 155
Livingston, John C., 28
Lloyd, Sterling, 65
Locke, Michelle, 156
Lott, Juanita, 162
LSAT (Law School Admission Test),
  14, 52, 57, 58, 64, 148, 160
Lynch, Frederick, 29

Major, Brenda, 161
MALDEF (Mexican American Legal Defense and Education Fund), 21, 30
Mann, Marion, 65
Marriages between those of different races and ethnicities, 161–64
Marshall, Chief Justice John, 141
Marshall, Justice Thurgood, 9, 14, 22–24, 26, 145
Mattei, Laura, 165
MCAT (Medical College Admission Test), 18, 53, 58–59, 143
McBride, James, 163
McClain, Paula, 130
McCloskey, Robert, 29, 141
McCormack, Wayne, 62, 63, 64
McCrone, Donald, 86
Medalie, Richard, 3, 136
Media coverage of *Bakke,* 29–32
Median income as predictor of admissions, 118–19
Medical College Admission Test. *See* MCAT
Medical school admission, efforts to recruit minorities, 53–57
Medical schools: admission standards for, 52–53; history of black enrollments, 54–56
Meese, Edwin, 153
Meharry Medical College, 54
Meier, Kenneth, 54, 130
Memphis (Tennessee), 33–34
Menand, Louis, 158
Mexican American Legal Defense and Educational Fund. *See* MALDEF
Michaelson, Martin, 159
Middleton, Lorenzo, 71
Milner, Neal, 137
Minority candidates, 4, 5. *See also* African American candidates; Hispanic candidates
Minority contractors, 146
Minority enrollments, institutional stability in, 124–27, 135

Minority affairs officers. *See* Affirmative action officers
Minority populations and minority enrollment changes, 121–29
Minority recruitment, 78–80; impact of external factors on, 127–31; institutional differences in, 119–27; offices, 97–104
Minority recruitment officials and minority enrollment change, 127–29
Minority-majority districts, 147
Miranda rights, 135–36
Mississippi, 9
Mohl, Raymond, 130
Montero, Pilar, 55, 56, 65, 79
Morganthau, Tom, 162, 164
Morin, Richard, 159, 160
Mort, Leigh Ann, 144
Moskowitz, Milton, 144
Moulton, Faye, 40, 48–49, 118
Muir, William, 3
Muller, David G., 58
Multiracial classifications, 163–64
Murphy, Walter, 1

NAACP (National Association for the Advancement of Colored People), 8–10, 20, 30, 43
Nashville (Tennessee), 54
National Association for the Advancement of Colored People. *See* NAACP
National Association of Manufacturers, 153
National Association of Scholars, 158
National bank, 141
National Bar Association, 57
National Review, 30
National Science Foundation, 49, 141, 147
Native Americans. *See* Indians
Neubauer, David, 3, 138
New York City, 34
New York Times, 21, 29, 61
New York University, 16, 72, 140
Newport, 158

Nixon, Richard, 10, 13, administration of, 91
Non-merit factors and admission, 168
Nongovernmental pressure for affirmative action, 81
Norton, Eleanor Holmes, 30
NSF. *See* National Science Foundation

Obscenity rulings, 137, 138
Office of Civil Rights, 87, 150
Office of Education, 13
O'Hare, William, 161
Oliver, Melvin, 43
O'Neill, Timothy, 2, 17, 18, 20–22, 26
Orfield, Gary, 12

Page, Clarence, 156
Partisan identification and race, 158
Pell Grants, 47. *See also* Financial aid
Pelowski, A. L., 86
Peltason, Jack, 10
Perry, Charles, 86
Petersen, Edward, 86
Philadelphia Plan, 13
Piazza, Thomas, 32
Pluralism of racial groups, 161–64
Polls. *See* CBS-*New York Times* poll; Harris polls; Public opinion
Powell, Justice Lewis, 1, 22, 24–29, 31, 33, 34, 62, 63, 138, 145, 146, 149, 150, 169
Preferential treatment. *See* Affirmative action
Prelaw Adviser, 94
Presidents and affirmative action, 150–53
Prieto, Dario, 56, 65–66
Princeton University, 26
Pritchett, C. Herman, 1
Public opinion and affirmative action, 32, 35–36, 159; and *Bakke* case, 31–32

Quotas. *See* Affirmative action, goals and quotas
Quotas before *Bakke,* 70–72

Race and admissions decisions, 76–77, 147–50; ambiguity in, 161–64; and partisanship, 158; and redistricting, 147; and scholarships, 147; as a social category, 163; and standardized tests, 58–59
Race-conscious policies, 7, 22–23. *See also* Affirmative action
Racial classifications, strict scrutiny standard, 146
Reagan, Ronald, 150, 153; administration of, 87–88, 90, 109, 142; era of, 42; policies toward affirmative action, 35–36
Reapportionment and minorities, 17
Reconstruction, 12
Region and minority enrollment changes, 121–24
Rehfield, Andrew, 169
Rehnquist, Chief Justice William, 17, 22, 33, 34
Republicans and affirmative action, 151
Retention rates, 107–8
Reverse discrimination, 13, 160, 166–67
Rice, Tom, 86, 142
Rich, Spencer, 42, 43
Richmond (Virginia), 27, 146
Rodgers, Harrell, 3, 138
Rodgers, William, 142
Romans, Neil, 138
Rosenberg, Gerald, 2, 3, 135
Ross, H. Laurence, 86
Ruhe, E. H., 67

Sanchez, Rene, 155
Santa Clara County (California), 34
SAT scores, 167
Scales-Trent, Judy, 163
Scalia, Justice Anthony, 154
School prayers, 136, 139

School segregation, 8–12
Schwartz, Bernard, 1, 24, 28, 29, 72, 140
Seeburger, Richard, 136
Segregation: de facto, 10, 11; de jure, 9–11
Seligman, Joel, 57, 140
Selingo, Jeffrey, 156
Sened, Itai, 165
Seniority and affirmative action, 33–34
Separate-but-equal, 7, 8, 9
Set-asides, 151–52; for minorities, 32–33
Sewell, William, 48
Shah, Vimal, 48
Shapiro, Thomas, 43
Shea, Steven, 2, 54, 116, 143
Shelton, Philip, 156
Shull, Steven, 150
Sigelman, Lee, 31–32, 36, 38, 142, 160, 162
Simmons, Ron, 2
Sindler, Allan, 11, 13, 14, 15, 28, 30, 31
Skrentny, John David, 169
Slater, Robert Bruce, 168
Slotnik, Elliot, 31
Smith, James, 38–40
Smith, Ralph, 115, 119
Sniderman, Paul, 32, 159
Social Security, 86
Souter, Justice David, 149–50
Southern Illinois University, 97
Spearman, Leonard, 48
Speich, Don, 53, 54, 57, 115
Spickard, Paul, 162
Springs, William, 142
Stack, John, 130
Standardized test scores, 143; use in admissions 58–59, 167–68. *See also* LSAT; MCAT; SAT
Stanfield, Rochelle, 167
Stanford University, 19, 26, 148, 154; Medical School, 55
State characteristics and minority enrollment changes, 121–27

Stevens, Justice John Paul, 22, 62, 63
Stewart, Joseph, 130
Stewart, Justice Potter, 22
Stimson, James, 158
Supreme Court, 1–2, 7, 8–12, 32–35; and affirmative action after *Bakke,* 144–50; and *Bakke* case, 20–36; and *Hopwood* case, 149; impact of decisions, 135–41

Takagi, Dana, 154
Taskel, Leon, 92
Taylor, Marylee, 160
Test scores. *See* Standardized test scores
Texas legislature, 156
Thomas, Clarence, vii, 150, 159
Thomas, Gail, 50
Tillery, Dale, 48
Topeka (Kansas), 9

UCLA. *See* University of California at Los Angeles
Unemployment: black, 40; Hispanic, 40
United States Congress. *See* Congress
United States Supreme Court. *See* Supreme Court
Universities and affirmative action, 154–55
University of Arkansas, 16
University of California, 1, 52, 154; Asian American enrollment at, 155; at Berkeley, 150–51, 154–55; at Berkeley Law School, 55; black enrollment at, 155; at Davis, 17–20, 25, 27, 33, 62; Hispanic enrollment at, 155; at Irvine, 55; at Los Angeles, 55, 57, 155; Regents of, 155–56; at San Diego, 55; at San Francisco, 55
University of Maryland, 147
University of Michigan, 97, 148, 154
University of Minnesota, 148
University of Missouri-Kansas City, 72

University of North Carolina, 148
University of Oklahoma, 8
University of Pennsylvania, 26
University of Southern California, 55
University of Texas, 8, 148, 154, 156
University of Washington, 14, 55
University of Wisconsin, 154

Vobedja, Barbara, 42
Voting Rights Act of 1965, 16–17, 158

Wald, Michael, 136
Wall Street Journal, 29
Warden, Sharon, 160
Warren, Christopher, 130
Warren, Chief Justice Earl, 9, 10
Wasby, Stephen, 2, 135
Washington D.C., 54
Wayne State University, 97
Wealth, differences among black, Hispanic, and white groups, 43

Weathersby, George, 48
Weber, Brian, 33
Welch, Finis, 38–40
Welch, Susan, 31–32, 36, 38, 142, 160, 162, 170
Wellington, John, 55, 56, 65, 79
Wettick, Stanton, 136
Whitby, Kenneth, 86, 142
White applicants, 93–95
Wightman, Linda, 58
Willoughby, Lee, 72
Wilson, Pete, 154
Winsky, R. 165
Wolfe, Alan, 153
Women and affirmative action, 164–65. *See also* Affirmative action and women
Wood, B. Dan, 35, 88
Wright, Lawrence, 162, 163

Younge, Gary, 162, 164

Zelnick, Bob, 153

Index of Court Opinions

Abington School District v. Schempp, 136

Adarand Constructors Inc. v. Pena, 146–47

Alevy v. Downstate Medical Center, 16

Anderson v. San Francisco Unified School District, 14

Bakke. See Subject Index

Beer v. United States, 17

Brown v. Board of Education, 1, 2, 9–10, 27, 147

Buchanan v. Warley, 8

Columbus Board of Education v. Penick, 11

Cumming v. Richmond County Board of Education, 7

Dayton Board of Education v. Brink-man, 11

DeFunis v. Odegaard, 2, 14–17, 64, 72, 134

Engel v. Vitale, 136

Firefighters Local Union v. Stotts, 33–34

Flanagan v. Georgetown College, 14

Fullilove v. Klutznicek, 33, 146

Gilmore v. Montgomery, 9

Green v. New Kent County School Board, 9

Griffin v. Prince Edward County School Board, 9

Grove City College v. Bell, 145

Guinn v. United States, 8

Hopwood v. University of Texas Board of Regents, 146–50

International Association of Fire-fighters v. Cleveland, 34

Johnson v. Transportation Agency, 34

Kaiser Aluminum and Chemical, 32–34

Keyes v. School District 1, Denver, 11

Kirwan v. Podberesky, 147

Lau v. Nichols, 16, 24

Marbury v. Madison, 140

Martin v. Wilks, 146

McCulloch v. Maryland, 141

McLaurin v. Oklahoma State Re-gents, 8

McLeod v. Dilworth, 28

Metro Broadcasting v. FCC, 146

Miller v. California, 138

Miller v. Johnson, 147

Milliken v. Bradley, 11

Miranda v. Arizona, 135

Missouri ex rel. Gaines v. Canada, 8

Norwood v. Harrison, 9